"How could a good God allow so much suffering?"

"Why should I believe heaven and hell exist?"

"Why do you condemn homosexuals?"

THE QUESTIONS CHRISTIANS HOPE NO ONE WILL ASK

(with answers)

Questions from a Recent National Survey

"Why trust the Bible? It's full of myths."

"Why are Christians so judgmental?"

MARK MIT

Tyndale House Publishers, Inc.

Visit Tyndale's exciting Web site at www.tyndale.com.

TYNDALE and Tyndale's quill logo are registered trademarks of Tyndale House Publishers, Inc.

The Questions Christians Hope No One Will Ask (With Answers)

Copyright © 2010 by Mark Mittelberg. All rights reserved.

Cover photo of notes copyright © by Sergey Galushko/iStockphoto. All rights reserved.

Author photo copyright © by Gary Payne. All rights reserved.

Cover designed by Tobias' Outerwear for Books

Published in association with the literary agency of Alive Communications, Inc., 7680 Goddard Street, Suite 200, Colorado Springs, CO 80920, www.alivecommunications.com.

Unless otherwise indicated, all Scripture quotations are taken from the *Holy Bible*, New Living Translation, second edition, copyright © 1996, 2004, 2007 by Tyndale House Foundation. (Some quotations may be from the NLT, first edition, copyright © 1996.) Used by permission of Tyndale House Publishers, Inc., Carol Stream, Illinois 60188. All rights reserved.

Scripture quotations marked NIV are taken from the Holy Bible, *New International Version,*® *NIV.*® Copyright © 1973, 1978, 1984 by Biblica, Inc.™ Used by permission of Zondervan. All rights reserved worldwide. www.zondervan.com.

Scripture quotations marked NASB are taken from the New American Standard Bible,® copyright © 1960, 1962, 1963, 1968, 1971, 1972, 1973, 1975, 1977, 1995 by The Lockman Foundation. Used by permission.

Scripture quotations marked KJV are taken from the *Holy Bible*, King James Version.

Library of Congress Cataloging-in-Publication Data

Mittelberg, Mark.
    The questions Christians hope no one will ask : (with answers) / Mark Mittelberg.
        p. cm.
    Includes bibliographical references (p.   ).
    ISBN 978-1-4143-1591-1 (sc)
    1. Apologetics. I. Title.
    BT1103.M58193 2010
    239'.7—dc22   2010031769

Printed in the United States of America

16   15   14   13   12   11
7   6   5   4   3   2

To Emma Jean and Matthew,
who have grown up in a world that seems
to have more questions than answers,
but who have learned to seek and
to follow the Truth

CONTENTS

FOREWORD

Have you ever experienced "spiritual vertigo"—a queasy sense of disorientation, confusion, and even panic that can overtake us when a critic challenges the core of our faith in a way that we cannot answer?

I first experienced that phenomenon when I was a young Christian and volunteered at our church to respond to questions submitted on cards at our weekend services. One Sunday I got an inquiry from a twelve-year-old girl who said she just wanted to know more about Jesus.

When I called her, she invited Leslie and me to her home to talk with her and her father about Christ. "Aw, isn't that cute?" I said to Leslie as I hung up the phone. "This is gonna be fun!"

But as her father ushered us into their apartment, I glanced at the coffee table and saw stacks of heavyweight books. It turns out her dad is a scientist who had spent years studying scholarly articles and weighty tomes attacking the foundations of Christianity.

Over a dinner of pizza and soft drinks, he peppered me for hours with tough objections to the reliability of the

New Testament and the divinity of Jesus. While I was able to answer some of his questions, he kept raising issues that I had never even considered. Before long my head was starting to spin—and I began to experience spiritual vertigo.

Here's my prediction: if you've never felt this sort of divine disequilibrium, the chances are you will—and soon, because challenges to the Christian faith are coming fast and furious in best-selling books, popular magazines, college classrooms, television documentaries, and on the Internet. Your family members, friends, neighbors, and colleagues may be influenced by what these skeptics are saying—and they may very well come to you with their doubts and concerns.

Fortunately, there *is* an antidote for spiritual vertigo. In fact, you're holding it in your hands! Mark Mittelberg's excellent new book, *The Questions Christians Hope No One Will Ask*, will equip you to define and defend your faith in the face of a variety of intimidating objections. Reading Mark's insightful and practical guide will heighten your sense of confidence and, as a friend of mine likes to say, "load your lips" with answers to the tricky questions that many Christians fear they'll be asked.

When 1 Peter 3:15 tells us to "always be ready" to defend our faith—well, here is the kind of preparation that all of us need. Mark's topics include such foundational issues as the existence of God, science versus Christianity, and the reliability of the Bible, but they also cover touchy social topics such as abortion and homosexuality. Mark's analysis is always cogent, his answers are always thorough and accurate, and his heart is always inclined toward people sincerely seeking the truth about God.

For more than twenty-three years, Mark and I have been ministry associates and close friends. We've stood together in front of thousands of people, including skeptics, to answer any and all questions. We've staged debates between atheists and Christians. We've trained people on how to share Christ with others and deal with the common objections they're likely to hear. Some say we're "joined at the brain." If that's true, then I'm the one who has benefited more!

Through it all, I've consistently been impressed by Mark's theological acumen, his gift for articulating clear and compelling answers to the toughest of questions, and his authenticity and personal integrity. You won't find a better teacher to help train you to confidently yet humbly engage in conversations with spiritual seekers.

What happened with the scientist who plunged me into spiritual vertigo so many years ago? "You've raised a lot of good issues," I said at the conclusion of the evening. "But I suspect that after two thousand years, you haven't come up with the objection that's finally going to topple Christianity. Let me investigate as honestly as I can and get back to you."

And sure enough, as I probed the thorny issues he had raised that night, I was able to find satisfying answers to each and every one of them. But frankly, that process would have been a whole lot easier if I had had the benefit of this invaluable new resource by Mark Mittelberg!

—Lee Strobel, author
The Case for Christ and *The Case for the Real Jesus*

ACKNOWLEDGMENTS

Deep thanks to the friends and family who helped and supported me through the writing of this book:

Heidi, Emma Jean, and Matthew, for your faithful encouragement and persistent prayers—not to mention coffee, energy drinks, and snacks at all hours of the day and night. I can't imagine a better "family group" than you guys!

Lee Strobel, for your friendship and ministry partnership now and over the years, including the endless flow of ideas, enthusiasm, advice, and editorial input—as well as conversational excursions into the worlds of cars, kids, and the latest NBA contest. Borrowing from the movie theme, "I ain't never had a friend like you!"

Brad Mitchell, for your steadfast prayers, encouragement, and friendship through all of life's ups and downs. I appreciate you immensely.

Several brilliant ministry colleagues: Gretchen Passantino Coburn, Chad Meister, Robert Bowman, Judson Poling, and Garry Poole—whose research and input brought significant shape to these chapters. Thanks also, Chad, for the extra editorial feedback; you are wise beyond your years.

My publishing partners at Tyndale—especially Jon Farrar, Ron Beers, and Cara Peterson—for your creative direction, support, and patience throughout the writing of this book.

My literary agent at Alive Communications, Lee Hough, for your help in making this happen and for the encouragement along the way.

All the others who prayed for me and the writing process, especially my parents, Orland and Ginny Mittelberg; Heidi's parents, Hillis and Jean Hugelen; and many other friends, including Carla and the "Wonderful Wilsons," Kevin and Sherry Harney, Nancy Grisham, and Sam Wall. Your "spiritual air support" sustained me in ways I barely understand—but certainly do appreciate.

INTRODUCTION

WHY THE QUESTIONS MATTER SO MUCH

"I used to be a Christian."

The opening words from the young man on the other end of the telephone line certainly caught my attention.

"What do you mean, you used to be a Christian?" I asked.

As the story unfolded, first on the phone and later when he and his friend met with me in my office, I learned what had happened. These sharp high school students had been asking a variety of spiritual questions at their church youth group meetings, but they had not received helpful answers.

The first time they raised their objections was during a Bible class, but their teacher shut them down. "Those are things that people of faith must accept by faith," he insisted. "You just need to believe and then you'll know that they're true."

To these guys—and I'll have to admit to me, too—that sounded like an admission that there are no good reasons to believe in Christianity.

Later that summer they had gone to their church's youth camp and again asked their questions, but to a different set of leaders. This time they were told, "You mustn't raise these issues here—you'll only confuse the other campers!"

So they held in their questions while their doubts grew and festered, increasingly poisoning what faith they had. Eventually, they abandoned their belief in God altogether. What's more, they turned a weekly Bible study that had been meeting in a home into what they called a Skeptics Group—a place they now invited their friends from school to come to and hear the evidence against the Bible and Christianity.

"So what made you come and tell me all this?" I asked.

"A friend of ours challenged us to slow down and test our thinking one more time. He gave us your name and said you might be able to help."

Spiritual questions. When answered, they can bring truth and light, and they can help open a person's way to spiritual life. Jesus said, "You will know the truth, and the truth will set you free" (John 8:32). For us as Christians, our friends' questions can turn into exciting opportunities to share God's truth.

When left unanswered, those same questions can lead to doubt, frustration, and ultimately spiritual alienation from God. In a radio interview I once heard, the late apologist Walter Martin declared, "When we fail to answer someone's questions and objections, we become just one more excuse for them to disbelieve."

Once we understand what's at stake, it's clear that helping our friends find answers to their spiritual questions is one of the most important tasks we could possibly engage in. The writers of Scripture certainly thought so.

As the apostle Paul challenged us, "Live wisely among

those who are not believers, and make the most of every opportunity. Let your conversation be gracious and attractive so that you will have the right response for everyone" (Col. 4:5-6).

The apostle Peter echoed those thoughts: "If someone asks about your Christian hope, always be ready to explain it. But do this in a gentle and respectful way" (1 Pet. 3:15-16).

The Bible is clear, and the crisis in our culture is great: people—of all ages, but especially younger folks—need help sorting out what to believe, and we who are followers of Christ are called to respond to their questions and to point them to the truth of Jesus.

But let's be honest. Many of us are not ready. When someone looks us in the eye and sincerely asks a challenging spiritual question—such as "Why do you believe the Bible?" or "How can you trust that God is good when he lets so many awful things happen?" or "Why should I join a church that is full of hypocrites?" or "Why are Christians antigay?"—most of us don't know how to respond.

This problem was underscored when Tyndale House Publishers and I, through the Barna Group, ran a national survey of one thousand self-proclaimed Christians. We asked each person what faith questions they would feel most uncomfortable being asked by a friend or colleague. We then compiled their responses into a list—and the top ten questions formed the outline of this book (with two similar questions combined in chapter 8).

THREE VITAL ELEMENTS

Considering these ten areas of greatest concern, what can we do to make sure we "have the right response for everyone," as Paul challenges us in Colossians 4:6? Let me suggest three things: preparation, prayer, and proximity.

Preparation

The verse I quoted earlier said to "always be ready to explain" your Christian faith (1 Pet. 3:15). How? My friend Rickey Bolden, who played professional football in the NFL for six seasons, shared a phrase with me that one of his coaches used to drill into him and his teammates: "Proper preparation prevents poor performance." It's true, isn't it? And on the flip side of the coin, proper preparation provides us with poise and confidence.

Have you ever had to give a lesson or present a talk that you knew you hadn't adequately prepared for? If so, you remember the nervousness and second-guessing that goes with standing in front of a group—even if it's a handful of Cub Scouts—to speak on something you're not ready to talk about.

But turn that around. Have you given a similar presentation when you had done everything necessary to be really ready? What a great feeling it was to stand up and confidently present that information!

The difference? Proper preparation. And there's no substitute for reading and reflecting on some key spiritual questions before you get into conversations about them. That's what this book is designed to help you do. So let me urge you to read each chapter slowly and thoroughly. Mark it up; jot down questions to explore further; fold over the corners of pages that address issues you think your friends might ask about. (Or if you're reading electronically, use the bookmarks and note-taking features.) Make the most relevant information easy to come back to. This will help you remember the most important ideas for the people you talk to—and it will make the book more useful as a reference tool when you need to look up information later.

Go over and over what you are learning. Prayerfully think of your friends as you read through the "Tips for Talking about This Issue" sections. Also, consider reading this book with some other Christians in a small group or a class at your church, and then together discuss the questions at the end of each chapter. As you do these things, your knowledge, confidence, and overall sense of readiness will grow, making you an increasingly effective conduit of God's truth and grace.

One more point about preparation. As James 1:19 reminds us, "Understand this, my dear brothers and sisters: You must all be quick to listen, slow to speak, and slow to get angry." It will be tempting, especially as you study and get increasingly ready to answer hard questions, to talk more and more but listen less and less. You must discipline yourself to do the opposite. Before your friends will pay a lot of attention to what you have to say, they'll want to see that you care enough to really listen to them. This needs to be conversation, not oration; dialogue, not monologue; discussion, not instruction. What's more, talking less and listening more will enhance your ability to understand your friends' concerns and to formulate responses that are genuinely helpful and wise.

Prayer

It's important to remember that when we seek to answer our friends' questions, we are engaged in more than just the presentation of information. According to the Bible, we're also in a spiritual struggle. Paul says, "We use God's mighty weapons, not worldly weapons, to knock down the strongholds of human reasoning and to destroy false arguments. We destroy every proud obstacle that keeps people from knowing God. We capture their rebellious thoughts and teach them to obey Christ" (2 Cor. 10:4-5). Elsewhere, the Bible explains that we're in hand-to-hand combat with spiritual forces that go beyond the ordinary human realm (see Eph. 6:10-18), and it tells us that people's eyes are blinded to the truth (see Acts 26:17-18).

Therefore, this isn't a battle that we should try to fight—or expect to win—in our own strength alone. Rather, we need to go to God in prayer and ask him to work through us, giving us the knowledge and wisdom we need. We should also pray for the people we're talking to (before, during, and after actual conversations), asking that their eyes would be opened, their minds made receptive, their hearts humbled, and their spirits made sensitive to what the Holy Spirit is saying—even as we seek to give answers and present God's truth.

Korean church leader Billy Kim summed it up well when he said, "Prayer is my first advice. Prayer is my second suggestion. And prayer is my third suggestion. . . . If I had to do it all over, I would do more praying and less preaching."[1]

Proximity

Finally, we need proximity with the people we want to talk to. It's not enough to just prepare and pray, as important as those elements are. We've also got to get close to the people who need the answers—friends, family members, and acquaintances who, whether they realize it or not, are starving for God's truth and desperate for his grace.

God didn't just love the world—he came to it in the person of Jesus (see John 3:16). Jesus didn't just pray for this world—he went into the towns and villages to "seek and save those who are lost" (Luke 19:10). Paul didn't just talk about communicating the gospel—he went to great efforts to "find common ground with everyone, doing everything . . . to spread the Good News and share in its blessings" (1 Cor. 9:22-23).

Likewise, we can't sit and wait for people with spiritual questions to come seek us out. In the Great Commission, Jesus tells us to go into our world to tell people about him (which will naturally include answering their spiritual questions) and to encourage them to become his followers (see Matt. 28:19-20).

OUR PURPOSE

We've discussed the importance of preparation, prayer, and proximity. Now a word about *purpose*: our aim should not be to address every fine point or nuance about every issue or to try to exhaustively satisfy our friends' curiosity regarding each question. Rather, as the verse puts it, our goal should be to "destroy every proud obstacle *that keeps people from knowing God*" (2 Cor. 10:5, emphasis mine).

So don't elevate every issue or make your friends feel that they must agree with you on every subpoint before becoming a Christian. Doing so could inadvertently add new and dangerous obstacles to their spiritual journey. Instead, give just enough information to help them move past their spiritual barriers and toward faith in Christ. Then, after they are committed followers of his, they can go back and study every subject to their hearts' content—now with the help of the Holy Spirit illuminating their search as children of God.

OUR MOTIVATION

Finally, our purpose must be motivated by love. Our goal cannot be merely to win the argument, but rather—with the help of the Holy Spirit—to win the person to Christ. This is the purpose that will shape how we'll address each of the questions in the chapters that follow because ultimately it will be the care and concern that we show, even more than the words we say, that will draw our friends to God.

Let me end by coming back to the story we started with. As you prepare to answer the people with questions in your own life, I hope you are encouraged and helped to see how God wants to use you.

"I'm really glad you're here," I said to my two new high-school-aged buddies as they entered my office. "And I'm willing to do whatever it takes to help you get answers to your objections."

With that, we launched into a three-hour conversation. By the end I could tell that their doubts were starting to dissolve.

"Before we go," my friend asked, "I was wondering if you'd be willing to come to our next Skeptics Group to explain some of this information to our friends."

"Yes!" I said, probably sounding a bit more enthusiastic than I should have. "And would it be okay if I bring a friend with me?"

"Of course!" he answered.

The following week Lee Strobel and I went to his house and talked with a living room full of skeptical students. We had a great time sharing our spiritual stories and addressing their many questions. By the end of the evening—and by God's grace—the original student who called me had recommitted his life to Christ, and within two weeks the friend he had brought to my office realized he had never really trusted in Christ, so he put his faith in him as well.

Thankfully, they immediately turned their Skeptics Group back into a bona fide Bible study—and started reaching out to their friends at school with the truth that they had discovered.

—Mark Mittelberg
June 2010

CHAPTER 1:

"What makes you so sure that God exists at all—especially when you can't see, hear, or touch him?"

This was it—the day I was finally going to pop the question.

After years of friendship and many hours hanging out together, I knew my feelings for Heidi had grown beyond merely "being in like"—the truth is, I was really in love with her!

Was Heidi in love with me—enough to be willing to become my wife? That's what I was about to find out. I felt fairly confident, but as any guy in my shoes knows, until you actually hear her say "yes," you live with a certain amount of trepidation and doubt.

When the moment came, I worked up the nerve and blurted out the question. Heidi's reply? After a brief hesitation—one that felt like a million years—she agreed to marry me! I don't want to imply that I was excited, but the fact that I shouted, "She said YES!" over and over probably gives away my true feelings.

Was our love real? It certainly seemed to be on that day. As it did on the day of our wedding. And when each of our kids was born. And when Heidi brought me freshly brewed coffee this morning. After more than twenty-five years of marriage, I think we've made a pretty strong case: our love for each other is genuine.

Love is not a physical entity, and yet it's very real. In fact, for those who are in love, it can be more real than the world around them! But in order to *know* if there is true love in a particular situation, sometimes we need evidence. And being the skeptic that I am, I needed fairly strong evidence.

In my relationship with Heidi, evidence of her love emerged along the way—she wrote me notes that reflected her affection; she spent hours with me on the phone; she seemed to enjoy being around me; she even gave me loving looks sometimes. Then there was the big day when she agreed to marry me. While each one of these actions pointed to her love for me, taken together they provided overwhelming confirmation. I could put it like this: *the cumulative evidence was more than enough to believe that Heidi's love for me was the real deal.*

But can I prove it to you? Can I show you our love for each other in a tangible way—one that you can see, hear, or touch? No, the love itself is invisible. It's one of those things that you have to detect through its effects. Much like air: You can't see it (unless you're in downtown Los Angeles), but you can breathe it, experience it, and move in it. Or like gravity—it's not visible, but you'd better not try to ignore it!

THE INVISIBLE GOD

One of the most important issues that surfaced in the survey we talked about in the introduction—in fact, tied for first place as the question respondents most hoped nobody would ask them—was this: how can you know there's a God? He's not tangible; you can't weigh him, measure him, touch him, or see him with the naked eye—or detect him with radar, for that matter! His presence doesn't register with any of our senses, and yet you believe in him. Why?

It's a challenging question that's obviously central to all we believe as followers of Christ. So how can we respond?

First, we can point out to our friend, as I did above, that there are plenty of important things we believe in without seeing, hearing, or touching them. Love, as I've explained, is a profound reality, and most of us believe in love. But love itself is not a material thing. It's not something we can see, hear, or touch directly.

The Christian understanding is that God is not a material thing either. This is clear in John 4:24, in which Jesus tells us "God is Spirit." Unlike my friends, my dog Charlie, my iPod, or my mountain bike—all of which I can see, hear, and touch because they are physical, material things—God is a spiritual being or reality, and spiritual realities are not the kinds of things that can be seen with physical eyes or heard with physical ears or touched with physical hands. So I guess we shouldn't really be surprised that we can't experience God in the same way we can experience those other things.

A PERSONAL RESPONSE

But that's not to say we don't experience God in other ways. If you are one of his true followers, you have experienced him on a personal level, and I trust you sense his presence and work in your life on at least a periodic basis. I know that years ago in my own life I felt God's touch on me in numerous ways, leading up to the point at which I put my trust in

Christ. Some of those "touches" were wake-up calls in which he showed me the dead-end path my life was on, convicted me of sins, and revealed that I was made for much greater purposes than I was experiencing at the time.

Then, when I finally gave in to what I'm confident was the Holy Spirit drawing me to trust and follow Christ, I sensed his forgiveness and his acceptance as God's newly adopted son. That squared with what I later read in Romans 8:15-16, where Paul says, "You received God's Spirit when he adopted you as his own children. Now we call him, 'Abba, Father.' For his Spirit joins with our spirit to affirm that we are God's children."

And since that time I often know, in hard-to-explain and internal ways, that God is prompting me to speak to a person, send an encouraging note, challenge a wayward brother in the faith, or pray for someone in need. And occasionally I sense him guiding me in bigger life decisions regarding my work, ministry involvements, moves to new locales, and so forth. These leadings don't come every day, but there's a marked pattern of them in my life—they've had a huge influence in my overall direction and impact.

I share some of these details to show that one of the ways I know God is real and active in our world is that he's real and active in my life, and I'm guessing you'd say the same thing if you're a committed Christian. If so, then that's a natural part of our answer to people who ask us this question about God's existence. We know he exists because he's our friend! He has forgiven us and turned our lives around, and he speaks to us, guides us, redirects us, and rebukes us when we need it (see Heb. 12:5-12)—always acting out of love for us and what's best for our lives. So one point we can make is our humble acknowledgment of his presence and activity in our daily experience.

Our testimony alone can have a powerful influence on others, especially those who know us well and are therefore inclined to trust what we say. It can also influence those who have seen clear evidence of God's work in us—they can't see him, but they can see what he's done in our lives.

Experience is hard to argue with. That's why the apostle Paul often appealed to it, as did other biblical writers. He said to his skeptical listeners in Acts 26:12-16, for example, "One day I was on such a mission to Damascus. . . . A light from heaven brighter than the sun shone down on me. . . . I heard a voice saying to me in Aramaic, 'Saul, Saul, why are you persecuting me? . . . I am Jesus, the one you are persecuting. Now get to your feet! For I have appeared to you to appoint you as my servant and witness.'" Paul went on from there and gave further details, but it's clear that his account of God's activity in his life made an impact. Agrippa, one of his listeners, interrupted and asked him, "Do you think you can persuade me to become a Christian so quickly?" (v. 28). To which Paul, the consummate evangelist, winsomely replied, "Whether quickly or not, I pray to God that both you and everyone here in this audience might become the same as I am" (v. 29).

Telling others about God's activity in our lives can be a powerful tool, but many people will not be convinced by that alone. They might conclude that you're sincere—but that you're mistaking coincidences in your life for supernatural interventions. And some people may even question your sincerity. So let's explore some other ways we can point to the effects of the invisible God in our world by using examples that everyone can access. For the rest of this chapter we'll look at three of the best examples of evidence for God's existence that we can share with our friends: two that are scientific and one that is more philosophical in nature. (Note that other powerful kinds of evidence could be given to support belief in the Christian God, including those from history, archaeology, and the records of prophecies and miracles preserved in the Bible. I do so in my book *Choosing Your Faith . . . In a World of Spiritual Options*,[1] where I present twenty arguments for the Christian faith. Some of that information will come out naturally as we address the other questions in this book.)

As I've been exploring these matters for the last twenty-five years or so, I've come to believe that today, perhaps more than in any other period of human history, the fingerprints of God have become exceedingly evident for anyone who is willing to search for them. Each of these arguments is powerful on its own and has convinced many people of the reality of God. But when considered together, along with our own testimonies of experiencing him in our daily lives, the cumulative case is staggering.

EVIDENCE #1: THE EXISTENCE OF THE UNIVERSE

Throughout history, many people have supposed that the universe always existed. A number of famous ancient thinkers from the East (such as Lao Tzu, a central figure in the Taoist religion) and the West (such as Aristotle) believed that the universe is eternal—in other words, that it never had a beginning. This was a fairly prevalent view among philosophers and scientists up until the twentieth century. They had their reasons for believing this, but there was no effective way to either confirm or disconfirm their beliefs—until recently.

Fortunately, in the last several decades there has been an exponential growth of understanding in many areas of science, especially in physics, astronomy, and cosmology. This third area, cosmology—which is the study of the origin, structure, and development of the physical universe—has seen explosive advancements in recent years. Let's look at one example.

In 1915, Albert Einstein developed the general theory of relativity (which is far too complex to explain in this chapter, even if I could fully explain it!). This theory, which is now almost universally accepted, has certain implications. One is that the universe—defined as time, space, matter, and physical energy[2]—had a starting point in history. And, since it had a beginning, it's not eternal as Lao Tzu and Aristotle believed. As a matter of fact, through Einstein's equations we can trace the development of the universe back to its very origin, back to what's called the *singularity event* when it actually popped into being (what is often referred to as the "Big Bang").

Now, many scientists and others, including Einstein himself, didn't like this result (perhaps because it sounded too much like the biblical account of Creation?). So they tried to find an error in the equations—one that would allow for the universe to be understood as eternal after all. But they didn't succeed. And recent experimental observations have provided even more support showing that Einstein had it right: the universe really did have a beginning.

One of the scientific confirmations of Einstein's theory was provided by the Hubble Space Telescope, named after American astronomer Edwin Hubble. This impressive telescope allowed astronomers to see that the universe is actually expanding—and the farther away the galaxy is, the faster it's moving. This led most scientists to further reinforce their conclusion that the universe had a beginning point from which it began this expansion process.[3]

So how does this Hubble confirmation of the origin of the universe provide evidence for God? Great question! Here's how: if the universe had a starting point in history, then obviously it began to exist. But if it began to exist, then it must have had a cause for its existence. Things don't just begin to exist without a cause. Science itself operates on the principle that all events need a cause. As Einstein once declared, "The scientist is possessed by a sense of universal causation."[4]

But if the universe needs a cause for its coming into being, then that cause must be beyond the universe. As we saw earlier, the universe—by definition—is time, space, matter, and physical energy. So the cause for the universe must be something beyond time and space and matter and physical energy. In other words, the cause must be something uncannily similar to what we commonly refer to as "God"!

Before completely landing on this conclusion, let's look at an objection to it. My friend Chad Meister, who has his doctorate in philosophy and teaches philosophy of religion at the graduate level, told me a story about what happened to him awhile back at a dinner with his wife and others from the company where she was an accountant. The firm was celebrating the end of tax season and had invited the employees and their spouses for a nice dinner at a five-star restaurant. Chad happened to sit next to a pilot for a major airline. As they ate, the conversation eventually came around to spiritual matters, and the pilot said he didn't believe in God—which is not a very good position to take when you're having dinner with the likes of Dr. Meister!

Chad brought up this cosmological evidence from the Hubble telescope, and the pilot responded, "Yes, but how do you know it is *God* who created the universe? Maybe an alien did the creating!" Chad replied, "Maybe so! But let's keep in mind that our alien, whom we can call Bob, is timeless (that is, outside of time), nonspatial (outside of the spatial dimension), immaterial (not made up of any matter), and does not consist of physical energy, yet was powerful enough to create the entire universe—all the billions and billions of galaxies, each of which has billions and billions of stars. In light of that information, you can call him Bob, but I call him Yahweh! This is the transcendent God beyond space and time in whom Christians have believed for two thousand years."

Can you see how powerful this information is—even when people try to escape it with clever stories about things like aliens or elves? Even Richard Dawkins, probably the most prominent proponent for atheism of our times, admitted in an article in *Time* magazine that "there could be something incredibly grand and incomprehensible and beyond our present understanding." When challenged with "That's

God!" he replied, "Yes. But it could be any of a billion Gods. It could be God of the Martians or of the inhabitants of Alpha Centauri. The chance of its being a particular God, Yahweh, the God of Jesus, is vanishingly small."[5]

Against that kind of a diversion we can say, "You can call him what you want, but the evidence from the origin of the universe tells us a lot about what he is like—and the description sounds amazingly similar to what the Bible tells us about one particular God, who actually *is* called Yahweh, the God of Jesus, the Creator of the world."

It's worth noting that the initial reaction of some Christians to the very idea of the Big Bang at the beginning of the universe is negative—but I don't think this is necessary. Yes, many scientists hold that this event was completely natural, unaided by any outside force or intelligence (such as God). But as we've seen, the evidence is against them. The event itself calls for a cause outside of the universe—one that is wise and powerful enough to be able to pull it off. That's why Einstein and many other thinkers in his day and since then have resisted the idea of the Big Bang—they didn't like the theological implications that came with it. But from a Christian point of view, the Big Bang sounds like an awfully compelling scientific description of the biblical doctrine of creation *ex nihilo*—"out of nothing."

One other objection that frequently comes up is this: "Well, if everything needs a cause, then who caused God?" But this is a misunderstanding of the argument itself, which does not say that *everything* needs a cause—just *everything that has a beginning* needs a cause! Science shows, through Einstein's calculations and Hubble's telescope, among other things, that the universe had a beginning—therefore the universe needs a cause. And that cause is the immaterial, eternal God of the universe, who had no beginning and who therefore does not have or need a cause.

We can summarize this cosmological evidence into a concise series of statements:

1. Whatever begins to exist must have a cause for its existence.
2. The universe began to exist.
3. Therefore, the universe must have a cause for its existence.
4. The attributes of the cause of the universe (being timeless, existing outside of space, and so on) are the attributes of God.
5. Therefore, the cause of the universe must be God.

This is precisely what Christians have always believed. The very first words of the Bible, in the book of Genesis, declare, "In the beginning God created the heavens and the earth." In spite of what many people have heard, science is not at odds with belief in God. To the contrary, science actually provides compelling evidence *for* God's existence![6]

EVIDENCE #2: OUR "JUST SO" UNIVERSE

The more I watch the Discovery Channel and read about the amazing intricacies of our world, the more amazed I am at the beauty and complexity of it all. I often ride my mountain bike along the trails near where I live. Sometimes I stop and admire the unique plants growing along the hillsides or down in the ravines; other times I'll enjoy the surprise of an unexpected deer, coyote, or fox as it runs out in front of me. Often I'll reflect on a sunset showering down brilliant colors of red, yellow, and orange. I'm regularly taken aback by what I see. I think often about how much I relate to the psalmist when he says, "The heavens proclaim the glory of God. The skies display his craftsmanship" (Ps. 19:1).

But here's what is amazing: this incredible array of life and beauty and complexity did not spring into existence unaided. Rather, what cutting-edge science is now telling us is that the building blocks of our world—the laws and physical constants that govern all the matter in the universe—appear to be precisely balanced and finely tuned for life to occur and flourish.

These laws and constants were set at the singularity event mentioned earlier. In other words, when the universe exploded into being—the Big Bang—there were a number of variables within the very structure of the universe itself that had to be set exactly as they are in order for life to exist. Scientists have so far discovered about fifty of these parameters and constants that must be "just so" in order for life to be possible anywhere in the universe.

Let's hone in on one particular example of this "fine-tuning." Physicists have discovered four forces in nature, and one of them is the *force of gravity*. Physicists have calculated that the strength of each of these forces must fall within a very specific range or there would be no conscious life possible. If the force of gravity, for example, were to change by one part in ten thousand billion billion billion relative to the total range of the strengths of the four forces in nature, conscious life would be virtually impossible anywhere in the universe.[7]

There are many other parameters and constants that are also finely tuned and that, if changed even slightly, would have disastrous consequences for life in our universe. For example, if the neutron were not exactly as it is—about 1.001 times the mass of the proton—then all protons would have decayed into neutrons or all neutrons would have decayed into protons, and life would not be possible. If the explosion of the Big Bang had differed in strength by as little as one part in 10^{60} (one part in a trillion trillion trillion trillion trillion), the universe would have either quickly collapsed back on itself or expanded too swiftly for stars to form. Either way, life would be impossible. The list goes on and on.[8]

What makes all this even more fascinating is that these finely tuned parameters and constants are independent of one another. In other words, they could all be just right for life except for one, which is off to the smallest degree—and that alone would have precluded me from existing to write this and you from existing to read it. This makes it yet more unlikely that they all came to be just so by chance. In fact, because of this evidence Paul Davies, one of the leading physicists and cosmologists of our day, makes this audacious claim: "I cannot believe that our existence in this universe is a mere quirk of fate. . . . We are truly meant to be here."[9] That's quite a statement for one who doesn't even claim to believe in a personal God!

In addition to the parameters and constants necessary for life in the universe, there are also fascinating characteristics of a *planet* that are necessary for it to support complex life. Recent discoveries demonstrate that there are at least two dozen such characteristics that must be in place for life to be possible on a planet. These include its consisting of the correct mass; being orbited by a large moon, having a magnetic field; manifesting an oxygen-rich atmosphere; orbiting a main-sequence, G2 dwarf star; and being in the correct location in the galactic habitable zone. Each of these factors has to occur in the right place at the right time with respect to the same planet in order for complex life to even be a possibility there. The probability of these factors converging is so infinitesimally small that many cosmologists and astrophysicists now admit that it's more reasonable to believe that a divine designer was involved than to assume it all happened by chance.[10]

Of course, not everyone is happy with this conclusion. Some are working overtime to find alternative theories to explain these phenomena without divine intervention. In fact, there are a few serious objections that we should address. The first is that these highly unlikely events can be explained without God if a very large number of universes exist besides our own, each with its own parameters and constants. If there are a very large number of universes and they were all produced randomly, most of them would surely include parameters that are life *prohibiting*. But if the number of universes is large enough—maybe infinite—then some of them, by sheer chance, might have just the right parameters for life. Luckily for us, the argument goes, our universe happens to be one that has the right parameters.

One big problem with this objection is that there is no scientific evidence that it is true or even possible. It's purely speculative. Science fiction writers are having a heyday with the idea, but the scientific facts are lacking, to say the least.

Another problem is that if there are an infinite number of universes, then those must have been produced by some kind of a "many-universe generator." But this generator itself must be a very sophisticated device in order to produce countless universes. I mean, even my toaster needs to be well designed to toast bread (though I'm not so sure it was really well designed, since it often pops my toast onto the kitchen floor!). How much more so a universe maker who produces countless universes, including finely tuned ones like our own. What kind of an incredible intelligence could account for such an astounding machine or process such as that?

Yet another objection I often hear is this: if the evidence points to a divine designer, then who designed the designer? If we don't need to answer that question, it's argued, then why do we need to worry about a designer of our universe? While this is an interesting challenge, it misses the simple point that the universe is better explained by design than by chance.

Consider this example: suppose you went on a deep-sea expedition and came upon what seemed to be an underwater city. It was unique, like nothing you'd ever seen before. Suppose there were structures apparently designed to sustain oxygen-breathing creatures (like us), including rooms from which water could be evacuated, long tubelike tunnels that could pump in oxygen from above the water, and various inlets that could be used for transportation purposes.

In this scenario, it would seem far more reasonable to believe that there was a designer who created this place than to suppose that it came into being purely by chance. But we would not need to forgo the claim that an intelligent being designed the city just because that intelligent being itself may be in need of further explanation. So the question of whether or not God needs further explanation, though an interesting one, has no bearing on this argument about our finely tuned universe.[11]

So our argument stands: the incredible confluence of the many examples of fine-tuning in the universe—each independently set to the precise measures necessary to support life—points powerfully to the existence of an incredibly intelligent designer who made it all "just so" . . . for us!

Or, as Isaiah 40:25-26, 28 puts it,

"To whom will you compare me?
    Who is my equal?" asks the Holy One.
Look up into the heavens.
    Who created all the stars?
He brings them out like an army, one after another,
    calling each by its name.
Because of his great power and incomparable
        strength,
    not a single one is missing. . . .
Have you never heard?
    Have you never understood?
    The LORD is the everlasting God, the Creator
        of all the earth.
He never grows weak or weary.
    No one can measure the depths of his
        understanding.

Now, someone could object that the characteristics of God just established—that he is timeless, outside of space, matterless, and beyond the physical energy of the universe (from Evidence #1) and that he is a superintellect who fine-tuned the universe to precise measures in order to sustain life (from Evidence #2)—are *some* of the qualities normally attributed to God, but there is an important one missing: how can we know he's a morally good creator?

Fair question. Let's look at one more argument, this one from philosophy, which shows that God is not only the powerful and wise creator of the cosmos but also a morally good being who really does care about good versus evil, right versus wrong.

EVIDENCE #3: OUR MORALLY GOOD UNIVERSE

As an avid news watcher I often get depressed about the bad things that are happening in the world (and in my own city!). In Question 5, we'll address the problem of evil, focusing on how a good and loving God could allow pain and suffering to exist in the world. But what the news reports all too often overlook are the really good things that are happening in our midst.

Here are some examples of goodness I've come across recently:

- A celebrity telethon (*Hope For Haiti Now*) raised $57 million in donations for the Haiti earthquake disaster.

- Parents in Iowa adopted six young special-needs kids now that their biological children are nearly grown.

- A Chicago man donated his kidney to save a local grocery store cashier whom he hardly knew.
- A church in Indiana paid for a poor student's first year of tuition at a private college.
- A group of California students devoted countless hours of work to help displaced children in Uganda.

The list could go on and on. There are countless examples of goodness and virtue in our world. But a question arises: On what basis is something considered good or evil, right or wrong? And where did this basis come from? Did it start with the Big Bang? I can just imagine it: billions of years ago . . . massive explosion . . . galaxies emerging from the fiery blast. And then, out of the gaseous flames, "Thou shalt act altruistically; thou shalt be kind to the underprivileged; thou shalt love thine enemies; thou shalt not steal; and—oh yes—thou shalt maintain a moderately small carbon footprint" (all in perfect King James English, of course).

No one really believes that moral values emerge out of physical explosions. So where did they come from? Atheists are hard pressed to provide an answer for the existence of *objective* moral values. Look at what one atheist wrote in a recent article entitled, "Secularism's Ongoing Debt to Christianity":

> *Although I am a secularist (atheist, if you will), I accept that the great majority of people would be morally and spiritually lost without religion. Can anyone seriously argue that crime and debauchery*

are not held in check by religion? Is it not comfort-
ing to live in a community where the rule of law
and fairness are respected? Would such be likely
if Christianity were not there to provide a moral
compass to the great majority? Do we secularists not
benefit out of all proportion from a morally respon-
sible society?

An orderly society is dependent on a generally
accepted morality. There can be no such moral-
ity without religion. Has there ever been a more
perfect and concise moral code than the one Moses
brought down from the mountain?

Those who doubt the effect of religion on moral-
ity should seriously ask the question: just what
are the immutable moral laws of secularism? Be
prepared to answer, if you are honest, that such laws
simply do not exist! The best answer we can ever
hear from secularists to this question is a hodgepodge
of strained relativist talk of situational ethics. They
can cite no overriding authority other than that of
fashion. For the great majority in the West, it is the
Judeo-Christian tradition which offers a template.[12]

We have, then, what is sometimes called the problem of good. The problem of good is a major challenge for atheism, for within the atheist view there simply is no way to explain or justify objective moral values.

When I read about or travel to other parts of the world, I'm often intrigued by the differences in etiquette. In India, many nationals do not use utensils to eat; they use their fingers instead. It would probably be rude in those contexts to whip out my travel mess kit and eat in front of them with fork and spoon. We should respect the differences in etiquette that have been created by various people groups and societies.

But morals and values are different from etiquette, and we all know it. They are not the creations of human beings. As we've said, they are objective, not relative—so they are above us and our particular laws and practices. If there were a culture, for example, that threw their firstborn male babies into the flames in order to gain the favor of the gods, this would be a morally dreadful act. If there were a culture in which men kept females as slaves and beat and raped them at will, we would be morally outraged. If there were a culture that locked up black people for their color or Jewish people for their heritage or left-handed people for their differentness, we would decry these actions as moral abominations.

If that culture's members objected to our indignation by saying that's just the way people do things in their culture—it's their tradition or custom or preference—we would flat-out reject their answer. We know that murder and rape and bigotry and racism are wrong—really, objectively wrong—regardless of traditions, customs, or preferences. But where did we get this knowledge—this intrinsic sense of right and wrong? If we didn't invent it, if it transcends the realms of culture and politics, if it's something we can't get away from, then what is its source? Could it be that a Moral Lawgiver actually knit those moral standards, along with the ability to understand and operate by them, into the very fabric of what it means to be human?

That conclusion certainly seems to square with logic and experience. It explains why we could boldly tell the Nazis that exterminating Jews was wrong and that they deserved to be punished for such wicked acts. And why we knew that Saddam Hussein was doing evil when he oppressed the Iraqi people, murdered his own family members, tortured and killed those he considered political threats, and ordered the gassing of thousands of Kurds. Our confident conviction about these matters—then and now—shows that morals are objective, not relative.

Unlike the atheist, the Christian has a solid basis for objective moral values, for in the Christian view, God exists as a supreme, transcendent, divine person—the Creator of the universe and everything in it. Goodness flows from God's very nature; moral values are not invented by human beings. They are *discovered* by human beings, but they are *grounded* in the very nature of a good, loving, personal God who made us in his image, implanted a sense of right and wrong in our hearts, and told us to live as imitators of him (see Eph. 5:1). Interestingly, this is also what the Bible tells us in Romans 2:15: "They demonstrate that God's law is written in their hearts, for their own conscience and thoughts either accuse them or tell them they are doing right."

This is powerful evidence for God. We can put this evidence in the form of a simple argument:

1.   If God does not exist, then objective moral values do not exist.
2.   But we know that objective moral values do exist.
3.   Therefore, God does exist.

I'm not saying that atheists cannot recognize moral values or live generally moral lives. I'm certain they can. But recognizing something and even living by it does not mean that one has a real basis for it. The "moral" atheist is simply left hanging in midair on this issue, without any solid footing. Christians, on the other hand, have a rock solid foundation on which to build their beliefs and to live their lives. Our universe is morally good, and it's good because a transcendent and good God created it that way.

As we saw at the beginning of the chapter, God is like the virtue of love in this way: while we can't see love directly, we can often see evidence for it. The same is true about God. In addition to our own experience of him—which is important to talk about—we have looked at three kinds of evidence for him. These arguments provide solid reasons to believe in God: the existence of the universe, the amazing fine-tuning of the universe, and the reality of objective goodness. While each of these *points to* the existence of God, taken together they provide *strong confirmation of* his existence. We could sum it up like this: *the cumulative case for God's existence is more than sufficient for an open-minded person to believe that he really is there.*

God doesn't force his reality on anyone, but if our friends are interested in real evidence and answers, he has not left them wanting. God's fingerprints are dispersed throughout the cosmos. Maybe that's part of why Jesus told us so boldly in Matthew 7:7 to "keep on seeking, and you will find."

SUMMARY OF THE ANSWER

Question 1 asks us, "What makes you so sure that God exists at all—especially when you can't see, hear, or touch him?"

- We believe in many things that we don't see or directly experience with our senses—the virtue of love being a great example. Yet we see evidence of love through its effects. Similarly, we can't see God, but we can believe in him based on his work in us and in the universe around us.

- One of the ways we can know that God is real and active in our world is that he's real and active in our lives—he's our friend! If that's true in your own experience, then talking about him will be a natural part of your answer to people who ask you this question about God's existence.

- Evidence #1: Whatever has a beginning has a cause. Science shows us that the universe had a beginning. It therefore had a cause—one that's outside of itself and is therefore beyond time, space, matter, and physical energy. In other words, that cause has the characteristics of the God of the Bible.

- Evidence #2: Our universe is fine-tuned, with astounding "just-so" precision, in ways that make it a place that can support life. The odds of this happening on its own, by sheer chance, are vanishingly small and thus point powerfully to an intelligent designer—One whom the Bible calls God.

- Evidence #3: Apart from God there can be no objective moral standards. But we clearly live in a world that has objective moral standards. Therefore there has to be a divine moral lawgiver. We refer to that lawgiver as "God."

- Our experience, science, and philosophy all point to the existence of an invisible God, One that fits the descriptions given in Scripture for Yahweh, the God of Abraham, Isaac, and Jacob—and of us, as Christians.

TIPS FOR TALKING ABOUT THIS ISSUE

- Usually people who doubt God have a story to tell about how they got to that point. It's important to ask them questions and to respectfully listen to what they tell you, even though you'll probably not agree with everything they say. That's okay; James 1:19 says we need to "be quick to listen, slow to speak, and slow to get angry." Listening before speaking shows that you care about them, and it earns you the right to talk about your own beliefs.

- It's almost a cliché to say that atheists are angry. But if your friends don't believe in God and do seem angry, ask why. Often you'll discover that something bad happened for which they blame God, the church, or a Christian. Listen with empathy and patience. Agree when you can, but also try to help them see that much of what's done in God's name or in religious circles is not from God but from imperfect people and institutions.

- Share the answers and information in this chapter, but

realize that helping people think in new ways is usually a slow process. Be patient, and be ready to explain it again and again or to talk about additional questions they might want to raise.

- Realize there may be deeper personal issues—beyond what people are talking to you about—that hold them back from believing or trusting in God. These may be lifestyle issues, personal problems, hurts, prejudices, or misunderstandings about what Christians think and stand for. Pray for discernment and sensitivity in sorting out what the real issues are, and then address those issues.

- Refer to the Bible's teachings in talking about your faith, but realize that many people don't accept its authority or truthfulness—especially those who question God's existence. Its message can still have power, but look to other sources of information to reinforce its truths (as we have in this chapter, with science and philosophy).

- The Bible makes it clear that these discussions are not just about logic and good answers—but also about a spiritual struggle. Pray that God will direct your words and attitude and that he'll open your friends up to his love and truth.

- Remember that love draws people, and disagreement can drive them away. So let love be your motivation, and be ready to back off if a conversation gets too heated or combative.

QUESTIONS FOR GROUP DISCUSSION

1. Why might someone think you should believe only in things you can see, hear, or touch? What are some other things you believe in, in addition to love, that you can't see or experience directly through your senses?

2. What are some things you can talk about from your own experience that show you—and might convince your friends—that God really exists?

3. How does the fact that our universe had a beginning or the fact that it's fine-tuned with such exacting precision provide evidence for God?

4. Do you think there could be objective morality apart from God? From where would it draw its authority?

5. How has the evidence for God presented in this chapter affected your faith? Can evidence strengthen one's faith?

CHAPTER 2:

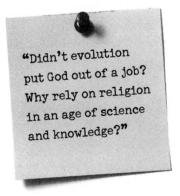

"Didn't evolution put God out of a job? Why rely on religion in an age of science and knowledge?"

Brad had little time—and even less respect—for religion. He had long been convinced that the Bible's teachings had been displaced by insights from science and philosophy. He was a biology student at a major university, an evolutionist, and an atheist, and he loved debating truth with any unwitting Christian he managed to corner.

One day Brad was enjoying a cigarette in the student dining area when he happened upon a table of students talking about spiritual matters. A moth to the flame, Brad was soon in the thick of the conversation. Things got really interesting, though, when a guy whom they hadn't seen before joined them. He was polite, respectful, and articulate—especially when defending his Christian faith.

Raw meat for a good argument, Brad thought. Even though they were all in the discussion, he became increasingly engaged with what this guy was saying, and the more they interacted, the more Brad smoked. Partly interested and partly hoping to shut the guy down, he threw out his best arguments in rapid succession, and then blew cigarette smoke in the poor guy's face while he was trying to answer the questions.

Not only did the fellow endure this abuse, but he showed up for more the next day. The two of them talked again about science, faith, and religion. By the third day the others had left, and it was just Brad and his new friend—talking intensely.

Over the three days a subtle shift took place. Gradually Brad found himself moving from the offense to the defense— an unfamiliar place for him. So rarely had a Christian even tried to withstand his barrage of objections that he was stunned when this guy not only answered his questions but also began prodding Brad to reconsider his own beliefs.

By the end of that third and final conversation, Brad had heard a wealth of information that challenged his long-held opinions. He realized that many of his assumptions were evaporating before his eyes, even if he wasn't convinced on every point. He still believed in evolution, but even that was now mixed with doubt, and he realized the theory didn't explain everything the way he once thought it did. He also walked away with a new view of God—and even of his own life.

That very night, alone, Brad humbled himself and prayed to the God he had long resisted, asking him to forgive his sins and to lead his life. To this day, more than twenty years later, he can't talk about that night without getting choked up—as he is again filled with awe of God's amazing grace.

Has Brad's life changed? Yes—in remarkable ways! He married a Christian woman, and they've raised their three kids as followers of Jesus. He shares his faith with anyone who will listen, and he answers countless questions people ask him about his Christian faith. He's a strong believer in God as the Creator, though it took him a couple more years of study before he modified his evolutionary point of view.

In addition, Brad helped me start an apologetics ministry at our church in Chicago that is still active many years later, and he was an encouragement to Lee Strobel when Lee started working on the material that would later become *The Case for a Creator*.[1]

Also, thankfully, Brad quit smoking—and blowing smoke in people's faces—many years ago!

One of the top questions in our survey of issues Christians hope no one will ask was the title of this chapter: "Didn't evolution put God out of a job? Why rely on religion in an age of science and knowledge?"

Whether it comes from a character such as my friend Brad, an acquaintance at work, a family member, or a young person who is confused by questions that come up in a science class at school, this is an issue that pervades our culture—one we'd better prepare for because it's not going away anytime soon.

It's easy to feel intimidated when you hear the increasingly adamant claims of best-selling authors such as anti-God evangelist Richard Dawkins, who boldly declares, "Today the theory of evolution is about as much open to doubt as the theory that the earth goes round the sun."[2] He also says, "It is absolutely safe to say that if you meet somebody who claims not to believe in evolution, that person is ignorant, stupid or insane (or wicked, but I'd rather not consider that)."[3]

But when we consider the research and conclusions of

other scientists and great thinkers on the subject, as we will in this chapter, the problem won't seem so daunting. The evidence *for* a creator is actually much more compelling than for a universe without one.

As the question indicates, many people assume that, if evolution is true, then science has already explained the mysteries of the origin of life and there's no longer a need for a divine creator. Is that conclusion true—has Darwinian evolution really put God out of a job?

The answer to the question is, in a word, *no*.

Charles Darwin, and the evolutionary theory that flowed from his work, doesn't even try to answer the question of where life came from. His book is called *The Origin of Species*—referring to the successive origins of each new species as it gradually grew out of other previous, more primitive, ones. The theory entails that all species would eventually trace back to one original ancestor—to the trunk, in his classic tree illustration—but how *that* being first came to life was beyond the scope of Darwin's focus. Its existence was obviously implied, but never really explained.

DEGREES OF CHANGE

Darwin was right at least in this: living things do change and adapt over time—everyone agrees that's true to some degree. That is, virtually no one denies that *microevolution* occurs—meaning the adaptations that happen over time within the assorted species. There are lots of examples: the variations in the beaks of finches in the Galapagos Islands that Darwin himself reported; the lightening or darkening of the famed peppered moths in Britain as they adapt to their fluctuating environment; the gradual increases in the size of horses, as well as changes in various breeds of dogs over the centuries.

The question of whether examples of microevolution really provide evidence for Darwin's grand scheme of *macroevolution*—species gradually growing into other species, all beginning with one common ancestor—is one of the great challenges to his theory. For example, the finch with the adapted beak is still a finch; the peppered moths, whether light or dark, are still peppered moths; the horses are still horses (and not dogs—and vice versa), regardless of their size; and so forth. So it's worth noting that most of the evidence offered for evolution is really just evidence for microevolution—which Christians and non-Christians alike acknowledge as happening—but it's a leap to say this proves the much larger claims of Darwinian macroevolution.

THREE MISSING ELEMENTS

Where did life come from in the first place? Did it mysteriously emerge out of the proverbial primordial soup? Even if that answer could be defended, where did the ingredients for the soup come from? Further, where is the recipe that explains how those ingredients all fit together?

There are at least three major building blocks that Darwin's theory relies upon—but which it can't account for: (1) the formation of a universe in which all organic life would reside along with the "ingredients" it would consist of; (2) the origin of the first life itself; and (3) the encoding of information that makes all organic life possible. Let's look at each of these more closely.

1. Matter matters

Let's start by discussing the ingredients themselves, as well as the environment in which they purportedly came together. There is a joke that is popular on the Internet that's worth repeating here:

> One day a group of scientists got together and decided that humankind had come a long way and no longer needed God. So they picked one scientist to go and tell Him that they were done with Him. The scientist walked up to God and said, "God, we've decided that we no longer need you. We're to the point where we can clone people and do many miraculous things, so why don't you just go on and mind your own business?"
>
> God listened very patiently to the man. After the scientist was done talking, God said, "Very well, how about this? Let's say we have a people-making contest," to which the scientist replied, "Okay, we can handle that!"
>
> "But," God added, "we're going to do this just like I did back in the old days with Adam."
>
> The scientist said, "Sure, no problem," and bent down and grabbed himself a handful of dirt.
>
> God looked at him and said, "No, no, no. You go get your own dirt!"

In a similar vein, agnostic astronomer and author Carl Sagan once conceded, "If you wish to make an apple pie from scratch, you must first invent the universe."[4]

You see, evolution could never have gotten off the ground without all the necessary ingredients already present and accounted for. But to say this happened on its own, by mere chance, is a *huge* leap. It's like declaring, "In the beginning . . . the stuff was already here—the heavens and the earth. And the stuff rattled around, bumping into itself, and over eons of time it ultimately got its act together. Randomly, without cause or purpose or outside help of any kind, it arranged itself into the exact elements and order necessary to cause self-replicating and upwardly evolving life to suddenly leap into existence."

Again, where did the vast supply of raw "stuff" come from in the first place? As we saw in the last chapter, most scientists say that all matter came into existence—along with time itself—at the Big Bang. It was out of that cataclysmic explosion (the "singularity event") that the entire universe sprang from an infinitesimal point into what would become the vast expanse of solar systems, stars, galaxies, and constellations that we now gawk at in the dark of night.

But here's what is interesting: it's possible to *name* an event—call it the Big Bang or whatever—without *explaining* how or why it happened. That, I believe, is exactly what scientists (that is, the ones who deny God's existence) have done. They've described something that, when you really understand it as it was detailed in the last paragraph, was a metaphysical as well as a physical event; put a scientific label on it; and then claimed to know that this astounding turn of events happened in the complete absence of any outside mind or creative designer.

How do they know that?

Simply put, they don't. They've just ruled God out of the equation by definition, saying—as modern science now characteristically does, under the influence of *philosophical naturalism*—that only natural (non-supernatural) explanations will be considered as possible causes or influences, regardless of the topic or the strength of the evidence presented. In effect, this is an attempt to decree that science will be, from this point forward, atheistic.[5]

But we don't have to accept that decree or the conclusions that go with it. Most of the great scientists of the past were strong believers in God, and many are today as well. A recently published book by the assistant professor of sociology at Rice University, Elaine Howard Ecklund, called *Science vs. Religion: What Scientists Really Think*, shows this to be the case. As one reviewer summarized, "Ecklund surveyed nearly 1,700 scientists and interviewed 275 of them. She finds that most of what we believe about the faith lives of elite scientists is wrong. Nearly 50 percent of them are religious."[6] *Discover* magazine said the book will "seriously undercut some widespread assumptions out there concerning the science-religion relationship."[7]

Further, John Polkinghorne, former professor of mathematical physics at Cambridge University, insists, "Science and religion . . . are friends, not foes, in the common quest for knowledge."[8] And more specifically relevant to our discussion, a document on a Web site has been created with the heading "A Scientific Dissent from Darwinism"[9] for credentialed scientists who would like to sign it as a way of affirming these statements: "We are skeptical of claims for the ability of random mutation and natural selection to account for the complexity of life. Careful examination of the evidence for Darwinian theory should be encouraged." Already about eight hundred scientists have signed their names to that public document.[10]

Science is not—or at least it does not have to be—an atheistic enterprise that rules out the possibility of influences from intelligent sources beyond the normal order of nature. We can stay open to *all* of what science shows us—not limiting our conclusions to merely naturalistic ones.[11]

So, again, just to get started, evolution would have required the presence of matter and the universe as a whole, which modern science can't account for apart from the Big Bang. And the Big Bang, according to a scholar who is renowned as the world's greatest observational cosmologist, Allan Sandage, "was a supernatural event that cannot be explained within the realm of physics as we know it."[12]

Put another way, it was a supernatural event that is best explained by the cosmological argument that we looked at in chapter 1:

1. Whatever begins to exist must have a cause for its existence.
2. The universe began to exist.
3. Therefore, the universe must have a cause for its existence.
4. The attributes of the cause of the universe (being timeless, existing outside of space, and so on) are the attributes of God.
5. Therefore, the cause of the universe must be God.

And this squares perfectly with the first book of the Bible, Genesis, where the opening verse says, *"In the beginning God created the heavens and the earth."*

In addition, there is the evidence from the incredible fine-tuning of the universe that we discussed in chapter 1. This shows that the Designer precisely shaped the environment in a way that was "just so," making it the exact kind of place that could uniquely support and sustain life—including yours and mine. This kind of evidence alone has convinced spiritual skeptics that there must be an intelligent designer behind the physical universe; in fact, this evidence was instrumental in former atheist Patrick Glynn's concluding that God does exist.

Glynn wrote about his spiritual journey in his book *GOD: The Evidence,* including how this information helped convince him that what "cosmology had come up with was something of a scientific embarrassment: a universe with a definite beginning, expressly designed for life. Ironically, the picture of the universe bequeathed to us by the most advanced science is closer in spirit to the vision presented in the Book of Genesis than anything offered by science since Copernicus."[13]

Summing up the points in this section, Darwin's theory does not explain the origin of the "stuff" that makes up the environment we live in (the universe), or even the matter of which we're made. Scientists try to explain these with the theory of the Big Bang. This theory, when properly understood, sounds much more like a miraculous event than a scientific explanation—thus inadvertently giving support to the Genesis concept of God creating the heavens and the earth out of nothing (*ex nihilo*). Many scientists are fine with that and are in fact religious themselves. Others who don't like that outcome have tried to resist that conclusion and define anything that is beyond the realm of ordinary naturalistic explanation as being nonscientific. But this is arbitrary and ultimately unsuccessful, since true science must follow the facts wherever they lead. And in this case, they seem to lead quite persuasively back to God and his creative activities.

2. The origin of the first life

The second prerequisite for Darwin's *Origin of the Species* model to get started, as mentioned earlier, is the *origin of the original species*—the very first life on the planet—which purportedly then evolved into all the varieties of living beings. But Darwin never even gave serious treatment to the question of how that first life began.

Many other scientists over the decades have proposed a variety of theories about the original inception of life—from sheer chance, to the (later disproved) inherent attraction between the building blocks of living matter, to life "riding in on the backs of crystals,"[14] to a theory known as *panspermia*, which says that life was planted here by beings from outer space. One of the discoverers of the structure of the DNA molecule, Francis Crick, toyed with a version of this theory, and even Richard Dawkins mentioned it as a possibility in an interview with Ben Stein in the movie *Expelled: No Intelligence Allowed.*[15] But as Michael Denton, in *Evolution: A Theory in Crisis* observed years ago, "Nothing illustrates more clearly just how intractable a problem the origin of life has become than the fact that world authorities can seriously toy with the idea of panspermia."[16]

Most evolutionists today, including the most ardently atheistic ones, won't even venture a serious guess as to how life began on this planet. Biochemist Klaus Dose concludes, "More than thirty years of experimentation on the origin of life in the fields of chemical and molecular evolution have led to a better perception of the immensity of the problem of the origin of life on Earth rather than to its solution. At present all discussions on principal theories and experiments in the field either end in stalemate or in a confession of ignorance."[17]

Many scientists simply accept that life is here, acknowledge that they don't know how it got here, and assert what they think they do know: that it arrived on its own, apart from any supernatural guidance or help. But this unexplained arrival of the first life represents another huge leap in the naturalistic scientists' theories about the world we live in.

More than that, there are strong clues that the first life did not come through gradual, successive steps, as the theory of Darwinian evolution demands. Mathematician William Dembski, writing with Sean McDowell, discusses the fossil record and sums up the evidence like this:

> The first life form emerges suddenly. *According to standard dating, this first emergence of life was around 4 billion years ago. For the first 500 million years, the earth was too hot and turbulent for any life form to exist. And then, shortly after the earth was cool enough,* certain types of bacteria appear suddenly and abundantly.[18]

What this means is that, contrary to what we'd expect according to the principles of Darwinian evolution in which the earliest life-forms should have been traceable back to smaller and simpler component parts, the fossil record shows early life just showing up—bam!—unannounced and fully formed. (And as we'll see later in the chapter, this was true of later life-forms, as well.) So not only did Darwin fail to explain how life got here in the first place, the life that did get here first did so in ways that didn't fit his theory. Rather, it was almost as if a creative designer had just made and placed these life-forms here—supernaturally!

Also, consider the incredible complexity of even the "simplest" early life-forms and the overwhelming odds against those coming together by chance. Biochemist Michael Denton, in his book *Evolution: A Theory in Crisis,* poses the problem like this: "Is it really credible that random processes could have constructed a reality, the smallest element of which—a functional protein or gene—is complex beyond our own creative capacities, *a reality which is the very antithesis of chance,* which excels in every sense anything produced by the intelligence of man?"[19]

Cambridge-trained philosopher of science Stephen Meyer elaborates:

> *Consider what you'd need for a protein molecule to form by chance. First, you need the right bonds between the amino acids. Second, amino acids come in right-handed and left-handed versions, and you've got to get only left-handed ones. Third, the amino acids must link up in a specified sequence, like letters in a sentence.*

*Run the odds of these things falling into place
on their own and you find that the probabilities of
forming a rather short functional protein at random
would be one chance in a hundred thousand tril-
lion trillion trillion trillion trillion trillion trillion
trillion trillion trillion. That's a ten with 125 zeroes
after it!*

*And that would only be one protein molecule—
a minimally complex cell would need between three
hundred and five hundred protein molecules. . . .*
To suggest chance against those odds is really to
invoke a naturalistic miracle.[20]

I wouldn't bet those odds even if I *were* a gambling man! You may not have known that amino acids come in left- and right-handed versions (though being a southpaw myself, I appreciate that the left-handed versions are apparently more useful in building protein molecules). And we may not be able to fathom the size of the numbers Dr. Meyer was citing in his quote above. But rest assured of this: neither the scientific record nor the statistical chances point to the conclusion that life could have arisen on this planet spontaneously without the aid of some kind of a creative guiding force.

But if life didn't happen on its own, then what kind of intelligence or power—or both—helped it come into existence? Might it be an incredibly wise designer who helped put the necessary elements together to pull off the Big Bang (without a hitch) in the first place? As Christians I think we've got the best answer to that question!

3. The origin of information

There's one other element that needs to be in place for evolution to have even a chance of getting off the ground: *information*. Dembski and McDowell explain this clearly:

> *The key feature of life is* information—*specified complexity. Even the most simple bacterial cells teem with vast amounts of information. A single primitive cell would require hundreds of thousands of bits of information precisely sequenced in its DNA. . . . In the entire history of the universe, chance can only produce 400 bits of prespecified information, equivalent to Shakespeare's famous lines "To be or not to be, that is the question. Whether 'tis nobler in the mind to suffer." The first primitive cell is therefore far beyond the reach of chance-based mechanisms.*
>
> *Because there is not evidence of simpler life forms from which bacteria could have evolved . . . evolutionary biologists are left with a mystery.* Here is the key question: How could nature, without intelligent guidance, take the massive informational jumps needed for life to originate? These hurdles simply cannot be cleared without information. *This is why a growing number of scientists today are turning to intelligent design as the best explanation for the origin of life.*[21]

And if one "primitive" first cell required that immense volume of information, what about the human body, with all its millions of advanced and specialized cells? How much information does *it* require? That's exactly what Francis Collins and the team he led at the Human Genome Project discovered as they mapped the entire DNA sequence of the human species. Collins describes the information contained in our DNA like this:

> *This newly revealed text was 3 billion letters long, and written in a strange and cryptographic four-letter code. Such is the amazing complexity of the information carried within each cell of the human body, that a live reading of that code at a rate of three letters per second would take thirty-one years, even if reading continued day and night. Printing these letters out in regular font size on normal bond paper and binding them all together would result in a tower the height of the Washington Monument. For the first time on that summer morning this amazing script, carrying within it all of the instructions for building a human being, was available to the world.*[22]

You might want to go back and read that last paragraph another time or two; the truth it reveals about the information encoded into our every cell is simply astonishing. It's so breathtaking that Collins aptly named his book about it *The Language of God*—a title that echoes the words President Bill Clinton used when he stood next to Collins and announced that the amazing genome project had been completed: *"We are learning the language in which God created life."*[23]

Why did they use this theological language at a press conference for a scientific breakthrough? Because that scientific breakthrough unveiled the incredible scope of the biological language in which information—literally, the library of recipes by which living organisms are put together—is contained and conveyed.

But here's what is important to note about information: it is never recorded or communicated by nature alone. One popular illustration contrasts two different patterns on a beach: one formed by the waves, and the other, the words *John loves Mary* written in the sand. The wave-drawn patterns may be interesting to look at, but they're randomly formed by nature. The words *John loves Mary*, however, would never be mistaken for something random. Clearly they had at least *some* level of intelligence behind them. They comprise a message intended to communicate an idea—one to which John hopes Mary will be receptive!

But if something as simple as "John loves Mary" is obviously intelligent communication, how much more so is the life-giving, unimaginably complex "message" of human DNA, which is, as Francis Collins puts it, "3 billion letters long . . . written in a four-letter code . . . [and is] our own instruction book, previously known only to God"?[24]

So powerful is this evidence that Dean Kenyon, a biophysicist from San Francisco State University who had coauthored a book trying to explain the emergence of life apart from any supernatural involvement, later made a dramatic turnabout. "Kenyon . . . repudiated the conclusions of his own book, declaring that he had come to the point where he was critical of all naturalistic theories of origins.

Due to the immense molecular complexity of the cell and the information-bearing properties of DNA, Kenyon now believed that the best evidence pointed toward a designer of life."[25]

Kenyon summarized his own conclusion by saying, "This new realm of molecular genetics [is] where we see the most compelling evidence of design on the Earth." Kenyon's words echo the opinion of many other leading scientists and thinkers around the world—and one I hope we can help convince our friends of as well: the information encoded in DNA points powerfully to an intelligent designer.[26]

So we see that Darwin's theory of evolution—to even have the chance of getting started in the first place—relies on three essential events that design-oriented views best explain: the origin of the universe, the origin of life, and the origin of information.

THE "EVEN IF" APPROACH

You may have noticed that I've said very little in the way of direct criticism of Darwin's actual theory of evolution. Instead I've shown that his theory can't even get off the ground without three preconditions that neither Darwin nor broader science has been able to explain:

1. How did the universe and matter in general get here? (Yes, I accept some version of the Big Bang, but naming it doesn't explain it; the entire universe exploding out of one infinitesimally small point . . . sounds to me not like a *scientific explanation*, but like a *miracle of God*.)

2. How did life originate in the first place? (Science offers no real answers.)

3. Who wrote the informational instructions—the DNA "recipes"—that are required for life to form or replicate? (Information always emanates from intelligence.)

I've taken this approach to show that, far from evolution putting God out of a job, Darwinian evolution—if it is true at all—relies on these three factors (and probably more) that need God for their explanation! Or, putting it in the positive, all three of these points powerfully demonstrate, from a scientific perspective, the need for an intelligent designer.

The other reason I've taken the approach I have is because I don't think we necessarily have to change people's minds about evolution itself in order to lead them to faith in Jesus. In fact, trying to do so can actually put up an additional barrier for someone who might have been otherwise ready to hear and respond to the gospel message. That is, unfortunately, what some Christians inadvertently do with the people they talk to—making it seem that they'll need to go through two conversions in order to come to Christ: first to a particular scientific viewpoint, and then to a new spiritual one.

My friend Cliffe Knechtle, who has ministered with InterVarsity Christian Fellowship on countless university campuses over the years, told me about a professor he met and tried to share Christ with. The man explained that he could never become a Christian because he disagreed with the positions of certain creationists he had interacted with years earlier. Cliffe explained to him that Bible-believing Christians have a variety of views and interpretations on that matter and that he didn't have to accept their scientific position in order to trust in Jesus for salvation. But the man could not be convinced, so sure was he that Christianity and that particular view of origins were vitally linked.

In keeping with Cliffe's efforts, our goal, as we discussed at the beginning of the book, is to lead people to faith in Jesus Christ—not to change their minds about every conceivable question or topic we might discuss with them. Even in the Great Commission, Jesus told us to "go and make disciples . . . baptizing them . . . teaching them to obey everything I have commanded you" (Matthew 28:19-20, NIV). Notice that *making* disciples comes first, then the ongoing *teaching* of those disciples.

And remember Brad's story at the beginning of the chapter, where he "realized that many of his assumptions were evaporating before his eyes, even if he wasn't convinced on every point. He still believed in evolution, but even that was now mixed with doubt, and he realized the theory didn't explain everything the way he once thought it did." In spite of not being fully convinced concerning his long-held views about evolution, he still "humbled himself and prayed to the God he had long resisted, asking him to forgive his sins and to lead his life." Then, over the next couple of years, his views of evolution began to change as well. But if he'd been forced to change his point of view in these areas in the reverse order—becoming some form of a creationist first, and then a Christian—he probably would not have done either.

So my advice is to not make Darwin's theory the primary topic of discussion. Rather, focus your efforts on going after the anti-supernatural biases that many scientists harbor today in the viewpoint of *philosophical naturalism*, which we discussed earlier. From this viewpoint, everything that happens must do so by natural causes, which effectively squeezes God and his activities out of the very equation. Show how that bias is actually unwarranted prejudice and that it fails to explain the things we've examined: the origin of the universe, the origin of the first living being, and the origin of information encoded in the DNA of every living cell.

So *even if* Darwin's *Origin of the Species* were correct about how new species develop out of previous ones, that fact still would not hurt the truth that God exists, that he is the intelligence and power that created and sustains all things, and that he wants everyone to come to him for his forgiveness and leadership.

Here is how evangelical philosopher William Lane Craig argued this at the celebrated debate on "Atheism vs. Christianity" that Lee Strobel and I hosted at Willow Creek Community Church years ago:

> *Now, what about the question of evolution? Let me submit to you that this is a complete red herring. The theory of evolution is irrelevant to the truth of the Christian faith. Genesis 1 permits all manner of interpretations and Christians are not necessarily committed to special creationism. . . .*
>
> *And I want to emphasize this is not a retreat*

caused by modern science. St. Augustine, in the
300s, in his commentary on Genesis, argued that
the days needn't be taken literally, nor need the
creation be a few thousand years ago. He didn't
even envisage special acts of creation. He said the
world could have been made by God with certain
potencies that unfolded in the progress of time. This
interpretation was enunciated 1,500 years prior
to Darwin, and therefore this is a position that is
consistent with being a Christian.

Any doubts that I might have about the theory
of evolution really are not biblical but scientific. *Namely, what the scenario envisages is just*
so fantastically improbable. In their book The
Anthropic Cosmological Principle, *Barrow and*
Tipler lay out ten steps necessary to the course of
human evolution, each of which is so improbable
that before it would occur the sun would have
ceased to be a main-sequence star, and would have
burned up the earth!

Now it seems to me that if evolution did occur
then it would have had to have been a miracle. In
other words, evolution is literally evidence for the
existence of God![27]

DIFFERING CHRISTIAN VIEWS

As you're surely beginning to see, Christians can and do
have differing views on the finer points of this complex issue
of origins. What are the various positions that Christians
tend to take? A book called *Three Views on Creation and*

Evolution[28] lays out the major viewpoints, the first of which is called Young Earth Creationism.

> *The main distinguishing features of the recent creation position are*
>
> 1. *An open philosophy of science [which they describe later as the free inquiry of ideas].*
> 2. *All basic types of organisms were directly created by God during the creation week of Genesis 1–2.*
> 3. *The curse of Genesis 3:14-19 profoundly affected every aspect of the natural economy.*
> 4. *The flood of Noah was a historical event, global in extent and effect.*
>
> *Other distinctive aspects of the recent creation position (e.g., a historical Adam and Eve, directly created by God as the original parents of humankind) follow from these cardinal claims.*[29]

This position is also characteristically associated with the belief that the age of the earth is much younger than is generally believed in scientific circles—usually stated to be as recent as eight to twelve thousand years old.

The second major position discussed in the book is Progressive Creationism (also called Old Earth Creationism). Here's how one of its advocates describes it:

> *As an old earth creationist I understand that the earth and the universe were created far more than just a few thousand years ago as has been*

*the traditional belief among Christians. Rather
I think the earth is some four or five billion years
old and the universe some ten to twenty billion
years old.*

*As an old earth creationist I believe that
unguided evolution is not capable of producing the
features we see in our universe—not the universe
itself, life, its actual variety, not humankind. Nor
do I think that God-guided evolution is the way
God chose to create, at least not to produce the
large-scale differences between the various plants
and animals, nor to make humans. Presumably
God is capable of creating everything we see either
by means of miracles in just a few days (even no
time at all!) or by guiding purely natural processes
over a long period of time. But I don't think the
biblical or scientific evidence we have suggests that
he used either of these means exclusively. Instead,
it seems to me that God used some combination
of supernatural intervention and providential
guidance to construct the universe.*[30]

The third position discussed in the book is Theistic Evolution (also described as Fully Gifted Creation):

*I believe that the entire universe (everything that is
not God) is a creation that has being only because
God has given it being, from nothing, and that God
continues to sustain it in being from moment to
moment.*

. . . I believe that God has so generously gifted the creation with the capabilities for self-organization and transformation that an unbroken line of evolutionary development from nonliving matter to the full array of existing life-forms is not only possible but has in fact taken place.[31]

These are three very different views by people who are all devoted followers of Christ but who interpret the Bible and the data of science in very different ways. The first sees the earth as very young and the days of creation as literal twenty-four-hour periods of time in which God made all things. The second believes that the earth is quite old but that God intervened at various points along the way ("days" in Genesis is usually interpreted as eras or ages) to supernaturally create life. The third holds that God worked actively but behind the scenes through an evolutionary process to bring about life as we see it today (this view would see the "days" and descriptions in Genesis as largely allegorical).

Should every Christian feel comfortable with all three? *Not at all—I don't feel comfortable with all of them!* But can I accept my brothers and sisters in Christ who hold to them? *Absolutely!* I see this as the kind of issue that fits broadly into the message of Romans 14, where God's Word admonishes us to "accept other believers . . . and don't argue with them about what they think is right or wrong. . . . They are responsible to the Lord, so let him judge whether they are right or wrong. And with the Lord's help, they will do what is right and will receive his approval. . . . *You should each be fully convinced.* . . . If you serve Christ with this attitude, you will please God, and others will approve of you, too. So then, let us aim for harmony in the church and try to build each other up" (vv. 1, 4-5, 18-19, emphasis mine).

Timothy Keller sums it up well when he says this in his powerful book *The Reason for God: Belief in an Age of Skepticism*: "Since Christian believers occupy different positions on both the meaning of Genesis 1 and on the nature of evolution, *those who are considering Christianity as a whole should not allow themselves to be distracted by this intramural debate*."[32]

FOR THE RECORD

We've seen that Darwinian evolution, if true at all, is dependent on three factors—all of which point back to God: the origin of the universe and of all matter, the origin of the first life, and the origin of complex information encoded in DNA. We also discussed the "even if" approach that says, *even if* we were to accept evolution as true, the scientific evidence still points to a Creator God who had to create the conditions and potentialities for that process to work. And we explored three different broad positions Christians take on the scientific and biblical data. All of that being said, before we end this discussion it's worth pointing out that the actual arguments for Darwinian evolution are flawed and incomplete for a number of reasons.

First, there is an almost complete lack of hard evidence for Darwin's so-called Tree of Life. Many people within the scientific community are so used to believing in it that they hold onto it with religious zeal, seeing everything through its filters. As an example, they note similarities between two species and rush to call it *common descent*, when in reality it could be the work of a *common designer*.

For instance, there's a reason you generally know a Picasso painting when you see one. It's because Pablo Picasso, like most artists, had a characteristic style that marked his artwork and that was readily recognizable to even the casually aware observer. Why would it be any different if God were the artist that sculpted every creature on the planet? Wouldn't we expect to see similarities in his designs, whether in their outward appearances, their skeletal structures, or even in their genetic makeup?

And what about the fossil record itself? Even Darwin himself recognized that the record did not support his thesis, and he even conceded that the lack of transitional examples was one of the greatest objections to his model—but he was confident that further research would eventually fill in the gaps. If he had been right, then surely all the searching and digging over the 150 years since he first published *The Origin of Species* would have yielded countless transitional fossils. Yet to this day there is a complete lack of solid, undisputed examples.

What does the fossil record actually show? Revealed during what is known as the Cambrian era is what has sometimes been referred to as a *biological* Big Bang, during which an astonishing array of new, fully formed life-forms rapidly appeared. Then these new species exhibited what scientists refer to as *stasis*—the absence of evolutionary change. This "event" is commonly called the Cambrian Explosion—and it has befuddled evolutionists to the point where they've entertained, embraced, and then retreated from a variety of theories to try to explain in naturalistic terms how new life forms can appear so quickly.

In light of all this, we can stand back and gently ask, "Might this not be evidence that a divine Creator somehow made and placed these creatures on our planet, just as the book that claims to be the Word of that Creator so clearly explains?"

God said, "Let the water teem with living creatures, and let birds fly above the earth across the expanse of the sky." So God created the great creatures of the sea and every living and moving thing with which the water teems, according to their kinds, and every winged bird according to its kind. And God saw that it was good. . . .

And God said, "Let the land produce living creatures according to their kinds: livestock, creatures that move along the ground, and wild animals, each according to its kind." And it was so. God made the wild animals according to their kinds, the livestock according to their kinds, and all the creatures that move along the ground according to their kinds. And God saw that it was good.

Then God said, "Let us make man in our image, in our likeness, and let them rule over the fish of the sea and the birds of the air, over the livestock, over all the earth, and over all the creatures that move along the ground."

So God created man in his own image,
  in the image of God he created him;
  male and female he created them.
God blessed them.

(Gen. 1:20-21, 24-28, NIV)

Sometimes the simplest and most straightforward answer is the best one. But embracing that answer requires each of us—*and each of our friends*—to humble ourselves and to be willing to acknowledge the presence, power, and divine prerogative of the One who made us.

SUMMARY OF THE ANSWER

Question 2 asks us, "Didn't evolution put God out of a job? Why rely on religion in an age of science and knowledge?"

- The story at the beginning of this chapter, which shows how Brad became slowly convinced of the reality of God by a Christian who patiently listened and respectfully conversed about difficult topics—including this chapter's question—demonstrates how God's love and truth can break open even the most closed hearts.

- Darwin's theory does not account for the origin of the universe and all that's in it, the origin of the first living organism, or the encoding of complex information in DNA. Even if his theory were true, it would be dependent on these other things—all of which point to a creative intelligence outside the universe.

- The explanation by many scientists for how the universe began is the Big Bang theory. However, this event goes beyond physics or science, and it points to an intelligent cause outside of itself, as we saw in the first chapter.

- While some have attempted to put God and science at odds, many of the greatest scientists in both past and present have been strong believers in God. Science is not inherently atheistic.

- Our greatest opponent is not science or even evolution, but *philosophical naturalism*, which is the view many scientists hold that says only naturalistic (non-supernatural) causes can be considered. Rather, good science should follow the scientific facts wherever they lead—including to an intelligent designer.

- Unless our friends view evolution as incompatible with belief in God, we should focus on introducing them to the Savior. Bible-believing Christians hold a variety of views on this matter, and a person doesn't have to subscribe to a certain position before being able to trust Jesus for salvation.

TIPS FOR TALKING ABOUT THIS ISSUE

- The topics discussed in this chapter are more technical than most of the others in the book. Therefore we should approach them with humility, being careful not to pretend that we know more than we do. Sometimes Christians come across as dogmatic in these areas in ways that can hurt our credibility and influence.

- When talking to people who don't believe the Bible, we're wise to focus at least initially on the broader evidence that backs up what we believe as Christians. We've done that in this chapter, and we will throughout the book—looking to the findings of science, history, philosophy, archeology, and current events to help our friends see the truths that are also revealed in the Bible.

- As we build up the Bible's credibility through the broader evidence mentioned in the last point, we can increasingly use it as an authoritative source of truth. (For us as Christians, it already is that—but to convince our friends, we're generally wise to draw from areas they already trust, like science and history, and show how the truths found there square with the teachings in the Bible.)

- Try not to overreact to what your friends say they believe. A strong commitment to the teachings of evolution, for instance, can mean different things to different people. As always, ask questions and really listen to their answers. Do they believe just in microevolution (adaptations within the various species) or in macroevolution, too?

- If your friends do believe in the full Darwinian view (macroevolution), it's *still* important to find out if, in their minds, that excludes God. If not, then it's probably better to focus your energy on helping them to see that this God, regardless of how he got it done, must be incredibly wise, powerful, and creative—to cause the universe and life in all its complexity.

- If your friends say that evolution rules out the existence of God, ask them to explain why—and while they're at it, ask them how the universe got started on its own, how life began independently, and how the information in DNA came into existence without any intelligence behind it. If they can answer those questions, they're ahead of the scientific community as a whole!

QUESTIONS FOR GROUP DISCUSSION

1. Why do people tend to separate God and science as if the two cannot coexist?

2. The theory of evolution is just that—a *theory* that has never been proven in all its claims. Why, then, do so many people treat it as fact?

3. Some have said that it takes more faith to believe that there *isn't* an intelligent designer than to believe that there *is* one. What information from the chapter would support this statement?

4. This chapter describes three "missing elements" that have to be in place for Darwin's theory to even be a theoretical possibility: the origin of the universe (and all matter), the origin of the first living organism, and the encoding of information in DNA. Which of these could you best use to point your friends to God?

5. React to the statement, "Our goal . . . is to lead friends to faith—not to initially change their minds about every conceivable question or topic we might discuss with them." What other social or scientific topics might this relate to? In what ways can Christians focus on Jesus and salvation first?

6. Briefly describe the differences between Young Earth Creationism, Old Earth Creationism, and Theistic Evolution.

How can we move past these differences when we talk to our friends who don't know Christ?

7. How would you describe the problems in the fossil record related to evolution?

CHAPTER 3:

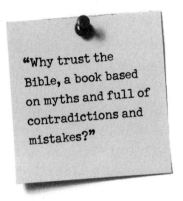

"Why trust the Bible, a book based on myths and full of contradictions and mistakes?"

Some time ago the mother of a dear friend of ours was killed. We first learned of her death through a trusted mutual friend, who reported that our friend's mother had been standing on a street corner waiting for a bus, had been hit by another bus passing by, was fatally injured, and died a few minutes later.

The man who received this report was one of my first professors in graduate school, Dr. Kenneth Kantzer. While he and his family were reeling over this sad news, they received further details about the tragedy, this time from a different source:

Shortly thereafter, we learned from the grandson of the woman who had died that she had been involved in a collision, was thrown from the car in which she was riding, and was killed instantly. The boy was quite certain of his facts, relayed them clearly, and stated that he had secured his information directly from his mother—the daughter of the woman who had been killed.[1]

For a long time that's all the information Dr. Kantzer had—which put him in a dilemma: *Who was right? Which story should he believe?* Had the woman been a pedestrian killed by a bus, as the friend clearly reported? Or had she been riding in a car and killed when she was ejected from the car due to a collision, as the grandson had clearly stated?

This dilemma is similar to the way many people feel about Scripture, as conveyed in our question for this chapter: "Why trust the Bible, a book based on myths and full of contradictions and mistakes?" Often this distrust comes not from any particular concerns, but from general rumors that there are problems with the Bible that can't be resolved. Other times it stems from very specific issues—much like the seemingly contradictory reports that said a woman died standing on a street corner *and* that she died riding in a car. Whether from general or specific causes, this question tied for third place in our survey, in which we had asked Christians what questions they most feared being asked. It's clearly an important one, not just because of how it ranked in our poll, but because of how foundational it is to our beliefs and faith.

ALLEGED GOSPEL CONTRADICTIONS

When people first begin exploring stories about Jesus, they are often perplexed with why there are four different accounts of Jesus' life and teachings. Isn't one Gospel enough, especially when there seems to be so much overlap? And to make things more confusing, they find some details that differ from story to story, making them wonder if these are errors in the Bible. For example, here are a few of the better-known Gospel "contradictions" that people come across—ones our skeptical friends often point out:

Case #1: What was really written on the cross above Jesus' head? Every Gospel says something different.
- Matthew 27:37 says, "This is Jesus, the King of the Jews."
- Mark 15:26 says, "The King of the Jews."
- Luke 23:38 says, "This is the King of the Jews."
- John 19:19 says, "Jesus of Nazareth, the King of the Jews."

Case #2: How many angels were at Jesus' tomb after the Resurrection?
- Matthew 28:2 mentions one angel.
- Mark 16:5 says there was "a young man" in the tomb.
- Luke 24:4 mentions two men clothed in dazzling robes.

Case #3: How many blind men greeted Jesus outside Jericho?
- Matthew 20:30 says two, and neither is named.
- Mark 10:46 mentions one, named Bartimaeus.

Case #4: How many demon-possessed men did Jesus meet in the region of the Gadarenes?
- Matthew 8:28 says Jesus met two.
- Mark 5:2 mentions one.

Case #5: How many donkeys did Jesus ride on as he entered Jerusalem?

- Matthew 21:7 mentions two, a donkey and a colt.
- Mark 11:7 and Luke 19:35 only mention one, a colt.
- This raises another issue: is the prophecy in Zechariah 9:9 wrong because it mentions both a donkey and a colt, and therefore supports Matthew but seems to contradict Mark and Luke?

Case #6: Did the centurion outside Capernaum ask Jesus to heal his servant, or was it someone else who came to Jesus?

- Matthew 8:5 says it was the centurion.
- Luke 7:3-6 says the centurion sent two Jewish elders, then some friends, to speak to Jesus on his behalf.

Case #7: How did Judas die?

- Matthew 27:5 says he went out and hanged himself.
- Acts 1:18 tells us he fell, and "his body split open, spilling out all his intestines."

RESPONDING TO ALLEGED CONTRADICTIONS

How should we answer people who bring these or similar issues to our attention? We should begin by realizing that we're only getting limited perspectives on the story—with an incomplete listing of the details the original eyewitness noticed or thought to tell others (or to write down). Often by getting a fuller version of the story we'll realize that what initially looked like contradictory elements actually fit into the broader picture of what really happened.

For a modern-day example, let's go back to the two reports that Dr. Kantzer received about his friend's mother who was tragically killed. He was left with two seemingly conflicting accounts—from two supposedly reputable sources. It would have been easy for him to have just thrown up his hands and said, "Somebody's lying here! Which of you is telling the truth, and who's making things up?" But he didn't do that. Instead, he chose to live with the tension of the two accounts, to trust the integrity of both people, and to find out more information when it became available.

Sometime later he was finally able to get the friend and the grandson in a room together and probe further into the story in order to find out what really happened. Here's what he discovered:

> We learned that the grandmother had been waiting for a bus, was hit by another bus, and was critically injured. She was then picked up by a passing car to rush her to the hospital—but in the haste, the car in which she was being transported to the hospital collided with another vehicle. She was thrown from the car and died instantly.[2]

Both of his sources had been right—but incomplete! This true story gives us a glimpse into the nature of both history and of eyewitness accounts in general: we never get all the details, and those we do get sometimes seem to conflict. We therefore are wise, following Dr. Kantzer's example, to suspend judgment and look for more information—especially when the conflicting sources seem to be reliable—to see if there might be a way to harmonize the accounts without grasping for far-flung alternate explanations. Clearly this approach served him well. Here's how he summarized his own conclusions as they relate to the question we're discussing in this chapter:

> I submit that this story from my own experience presents no greater difficulty than that of any recorded in the Gospels, not even excepting the two divergent accounts of the death of Judas. Such coincidences occur repeatedly; they are inherent in independent accounts of any event. The only significant difference between this story and the accounts of the four Evangelists is the fact that we cannot cross-examine the Gospel witnesses. We live 2,000 years too late.[3]

In light of that understanding, let's go back to our list of alleged biblical contradictions to see what we can learn—and what we might be able to share with our questioning friends.

Case #1

If the sign on the cross over Jesus actually read in full, "This is Jesus of Nazareth, the King of the Jews," then the Gospels are all correct but simply incomplete, because each accurately records a *part* of that statement—and all of them have the primary element, "the King of the Jews." Also, John 19:20 adds the detail that the sign was written in three different languages. Could some of the Gospel variations be on account of each recording only one of the three translations, which could have slightly varied from the others? We don't have to know for certain which of these options (or others) is correct in order to see that this is not a real problem.

Cases #2–5

I walk out of a room and say, "There's a chair in there." You walk out of the same room and say, "There are ten chairs in there." Our statements don't conflict with each other—you're just giving more detail than I was. Notice that I did not say, "There's *only one chair* in that room," just that "There's a chair in there." If there are one hundred chairs, we're still both right; we're both just telling part of the story.

Remember your first grade math: "one plus one equals two." In the story of the Resurrection, where two angels appear, there is obviously also one angel present; the text doesn't say "one *and only one* angel." Matthew and Mark, who mention one angel speaking, are giving *partial* details; Luke adds a bit more by also mentioning another angel. And when Mark says "a young man," he's describing one angel's appearance (Luke does this as well when he mentions "two men . . . clothed in dazzling robes"). Although this kind of "math" is not required to figure out the vast majority of the biblical accounts, it does help make sense of a few passages, like those mentioned in this chapter: two blind men equals one plus one other, two demon-possessed men equals one plus one more, and so forth. And a donkey and its colt are still two donkeys.

Case #6

If the centurion sent delegates and they were speaking on his behalf, the centurion can be described as "saying" what his delegates said. This is common even today. It's often reported that a president or head of state said something, when it was actually a press secretary or other emissary who said it on his or her behalf—and nobody questions it. Notice also an interesting aspect of the context: the centurion uses the analogy of how chains of command work—about how all he has to do is "say the word" and those under his command do his bidding. He knows that Jesus, like he himself, has power over others and that when they are ordered to act, they become an extension of his will. In this case, his very communication through delegates is a perfect example of the spiritual principle he's talking about when it comes to Jesus' authority.

Case #7

The question of how Judas died—and the apparent contradiction between the two accounts given in the New Testament—is considered by some to be one of the greatest challenges to the accuracy of the biblical record. But our opening story illustrates how seemingly irreconcilable testimonies are often harmonized once we learn the full story. In the case of Judas, for example, here's what could have happened:

> Realizing that he had betrayed the very Son of God and refusing to come to God for grace and forgiveness, Judas decided to do the unthinkable. He went out to a field and found a tree at the top of a rocky cliff, hastily threw a rope over a branch, secured one end of the rope to the tree, and tied the other end around his neck. As his final destructive act, he swung

himself out over the precipice. [This squares with the account in Matthew 27:5.] But then, whether before or after dying of strangulation, either the rope or the branch broke, and his body went tumbling down onto the rocks below, disemboweling him in the process and ensuring his demise if he hadn't passed away already [thus explaining the record in Acts 1:18].

That is not a pretty picture, I know, but it's one that plausibly fits the facts given by both Matthew and the writer of the book of Acts, who was Luke. This sampling of the way many so-called contradictions could be reconciled demonstrates how a fair reading of the text overcomes hypercritical inclinations to find errors. And here's an interesting thought to point out to a skeptic: during the centuries before printing presses, scribes could—but did not—artificially harmonize such variations (or in those rare instances where they tried to, it became clear what happened through the comparing of manuscript copies and is flagged in the footnotes of your Bible). That's a strong argument for how carefully the biblical text was transmitted throughout the centuries and is another reason why we can trust its accuracy.

Even when you or the friends you're trying to reach are still confused, don't despair. There are many great reference tools available, such as Norman Geisler and Thomas Howe's *The Big Book of Bible Difficulties* (Baker Books, 2008) and Gleason Archer's *New International Encyclopedia of Bible Difficulties* (Zondervan, 2001), which help immensely in clearing up many of these issues. As you do more study, your confidence in the amazing harmony of the Bible will only deepen. And then, when someone points out a "mistake" like one of these we've looked at—calling it a contradiction (and people will)—you can help the person see that it's probably not what it at first appeared to him or her to be.

REAL QUESTIONS OR SPIRITUAL SMOKE SCREENS?

On a practical level, before trying to answer every concern that people might conceivably raise about the Bible, I believe we're wise to call their bluff by asking them to be specific. You can do that with a question of your own: "You say the Bible is full of mistakes and contradictions. I'm curious: Which ones bother you the most? What mistakes and contradictions have *you* found?"

Nine times out of ten your friends won't have any specific issues in mind—they've just heard there are problems (if they do raise real questions, the answers and resources listed above and in the rest of this chapter should assist you in helping them find answers). However, in many cases— *truth be told*—they secretly hope that the problems do have some substance, thinking this will let them off the hook in terms of needing to respond to the challenging messages of the Bible. This reminds me of the candid statement of Mark Twain: "It ain't those parts of the Bible that I can't understand that bother me, it is the parts that I *do* understand."

If you sense that your friends are more motivated to find biblical problems than biblical solutions, it can be helpful to gently point that out, asking them if there may be some reason they're hoping that the Bible *isn't* true. Sometimes I'll ask, "Is there something in your life that you're afraid you'd have to change or give up if the Bible turns out to be what it claims—the Word of God?"

This is a very personal question, so it should be asked with care, generally during private conversations, along with the prayer that your friends will be open with you—and honest with themselves. In a sense you're shining a flashlight into the dark corners of their souls. But I've found that, under the Holy Spirit's guidance, many people will let down their guard and begin to open up about what is holding them back spiritually. When that happens, be sure to listen intently and then sensitively talk with them about the issues they've raised—all in an effort to help them understand, in comparison to whatever they're clinging to, "the surpassing greatness of knowing Christ Jesus" (Phil. 3:8, NIV).

MYTHS ABOUT BIBLE MYTHS

There is a broad and growing skepticism in our culture today—one that is understandable. Gone are the days of believing everything we're told by authority figures. Whether it's a government official caught in a scandal, a spiritual leader found to be living a secret life, or a loved family member breaking a sacred trust, we seem to be a society of double-speak and undependability.

So it's no surprise that people would project onto the Bible the same skepticism, partly out of a simple fear of being disappointed. Yet what's interesting is that of all the "truth sources" people can turn to—the latest guru, the consensus of scholarly opinion, something on the Internet—the Bible has withstood the test of time and shown itself to be more current than the latest research and more timeless than any ancient wisdom.

Most of the objections that come up in conversations are fairly easily explained. In addition to the alleged contradictions we've already discussed, let's look at eight common objections to the Bible and consider some ways we can effectively respond to them—all with the goal of encouraging our friends to see that the Bible can be trusted and to reconsider its message for themselves.

Objection #1: The Bible is very old and was written by gullible, illiterate people; therefore, we can't trust it
DISCERNING THE TRUTH If it fits your personality, a response presented winsomely along these lines might be effective: "Yes, they were simpletons all right—that's why people of that age memorized huge portions of every conceivable kind of literature; rabbis formed schools to train young men in theology, who would then pass on that learning verbatim to successive generations; ancients had detailed calendars that kept track of the movement of the planets, the changing of the seasons, and the timing of upcoming solar and lunar eclipses; the circumference of the earth had already been calculated (despite a spherical earth being a topic of debate); and people navigated land and sea without detailed maps or GPS systems—while we, in all our modern wisdom, can't find our car keys, figure out what day of the week it is, or remember how to get to the doctor's office!"

The truth is that societies in any age have both gullible as well as discerning people. Our churches have both gullible and discerning people. The scientific community has both gullible and discerning people. So the fact that the Bible originated in ancient times really has no bearing on whether or not it was created by gullible people or, ultimately, on whether or not it is actually true.

TELLING THE TRUTH   Consider this statement from 2 Peter 1:16-18, and ask yourself if the author seems to know the difference between passing on an untested story and sharing verified truth:

> We were not making up clever stories when
> we told you about the powerful coming of our
> Lord Jesus Christ. We saw his majestic splendor
> with our own eyes when he received honor and
> glory from God the Father. The voice from the
> majestic glory of God said to him, "This is my
> dearly loved Son, who brings me great joy." We
> ourselves heard that voice from heaven when we
> were with him on the holy mountain.

And when the apostle John writes the following (in 1 John 1:1-4), don't you get the sense that he is careful about what he reports to us as "truth"?

> We proclaim to you the one who existed from the
> beginning, whom we have heard and seen. We
> saw him with our own eyes and touched him with
> our own hands. He is the Word of life. This one
> who is life itself was revealed to us, and we have
> seen him. And now we testify and proclaim to you
> that he is the one who is eternal life. He was with
> the Father, and then he was revealed to us. We
> proclaim to you what we ourselves have actually
> seen and heard so that you may have fellowship
> with us. And our fellowship is with the Father and

with his Son, Jesus Christ. We are writing these
things so that you may fully share our joy.

Also consider this: in the years when the New Testament was being written, the church was not widely accepted.[4]
Many people lost their lives because of their associations with
Christianity, their bold statement that "Jesus is Lord," and
their refusal to confess the state-mandated "Caesar is Lord."
Though it's true some people die believing in errors, these
folks were close enough to the events to actually know that
what they believed was true. Almost all of Jesus' companions
lived lives of deprivation and suffering and died martyrs'
deaths, believing Jesus had really risen from the dead and
appeared to them after his resurrection. Who dies for something they *know* is false? Nobody—yet these early followers
of Christ kept proclaiming these truths, even as they were
being fed to lions or burned at the stake.

*Objection #2: The Bible was written too far after the
events actually happened to be considered reliable*

EARLY CREED This objection comes at us from a variety
of sources—including many of the reports done on the
"historical Jesus" in news magazines and television documentaries. But let's look at an early New Testament document: 1 Corinthians, widely accepted as being written by
the apostle Paul no later than AD 56. Though Paul was
not one of the original Twelve, he died about AD 64 (non-
biblical sources say he was beheaded in Rome by Nero during a persecution around that time), so all his writings were
penned within the lifetimes of those who had walked and

talked with Jesus. Notice what he says in chapter 15 of that book (vv. 3-9):

> I passed on to you what was most important
> and what had also been passed on to me. Christ
> died for our sins, just as the Scriptures said. He
> was buried, and he was raised from the dead on
> the third day, just as the Scriptures said. He was
> seen by Peter and then by the Twelve. After that,
> he was seen by more than 500 of his followers at
> one time, most of whom are still alive, though
> some have died. Then he was seen by James and
> later by all the apostles. Last of all, as though
> I had been born at the wrong time, I also saw
> him. For I am the least of all the apostles. In
> fact, I'm not even worthy to be called an apostle
> after the way I persecuted God's church.

Paul is quoting a formal creedal teaching that he had received. He didn't invent the story of the Resurrection; it was so well-known that a formalized statement of it had been developed and taught to him—a primitive catechism. For Paul to pass on "what was most important and what had also been passed on" to him, that creed (vv. 3-7) must have been taught well before AD 56. In fact, according to New Testament expert Michael Licona, "Many scholars believe Paul received this creed from Peter and James while visiting with them in Jerusalem three years after his conversion. That would be within five years of the crucifixion."[5] And the fact that it had already been formulated into a creed pushes it even closer to the actual event. In fact, eminent New Testament scholar James D. G. Dunn boldly states, "This tradition, we can be entirely confident, was *formulated as tradition within months of Jesus' death.*"[6] No wonder former atheist and journalist Lee Strobel often refers to it as "a news flash from ancient history."

Notice the mention that most of the witnesses to the Resurrection were still alive when Paul wrote (in addition to Paul himself). They were available to corroborate these claims—which was another powerful piece of evidence that Jesus' death and resurrection were historical events.

Take also the Gospels. Matthew and John were written by two of the twelve original disciples; they lived through the events they wrote about. The Gospel of Mark was written by the "secretary" of the apostle Peter, so in effect, it is Peter's gospel as transcribed by Mark (insignificant details in many of the stories, such as the mention of "other boats" in Mark 4:36, strongly suggest the recollections of someone who was there at the time). Luke was a companion of Paul, an eyewitness to the resurrected Jesus and someone who had access to Christians from all over the empire as they traveled. Luke functioned as a kind of first-century "investigative reporter" concerning the life of Christ. Notice how he begins his Gospel:

> Many people have set out to write accounts about the events that have been fulfilled among us. They used the eyewitness reports circulating among us from the early disciples. Having carefully investigated everything from the beginning, I also have decided to write a careful account for you, most honorable Theophilus, so

you can be certain of the truth of everything you
were taught. (Luke 1:1-4)

This is not some casual observer or someone who came
along much later and decided to write a fanciful story about
somebody named Jesus. Rather, Luke was a serious scholar
who sought out eyewitness accounts and then carefully compiled what his research uncovered (Col. 4:14 tells us Luke
was a physician, so he was likely well educated). And he, like
all the other Gospel writers, wrote his account well within
the life span of the companions of Jesus.[7]

NOT JUST "THE BIBLE TELLS ME SO" There are also non-
biblical writings that corroborate the New Testament teaching about Jesus. The earliest portrayal of Christ is ironically
a piece of crude graffiti meant to insult Jesus and Christians.
It depicts a man with a donkey's head being crucified and
another man standing to the side, one hand outstretched.
Beneath it is written a caption in Greek, "Alexamenos wor-
ships [his] God." The early Christians' teaching about a crucified Jesus was seen as ludicrous, which explains the image.
But this satire corroborates an important fact: early Christians—strict monotheists—worshiped Jesus. Furthermore,
two inscriptions found on ossuaries dated no later than AD
50 are prayers addressed to Jesus, asking for help from him.
How is it that Jesus—if he never lived or never rose from
the dead—is invoked in prayer a mere twenty years after his
death? There are also non-biblical sources such as Josephus,
Tacitus, and Pliny the Younger who mention facts about
Jesus and his followers that consistently line up with New

Testament teachings. In fact, historian Gary Habermas, who wrote *The Historical Jesus,* lists thirty-nine ancient sources *outside of the Bible* that provide over one hundred facts about Jesus' life, teachings, death, and resurrection.[8]

In addition to that, archaeology has confirmed the claims of the Bible over and over, and continues to do so. As William F. Albright, one of the world's great archaeologists, declares, "All radical schools in New Testament criticism which have existed in the past or which exist today are pre-archaeological, and are therefore, since they were built in *der Luft* [in the air], quite antiquated today."[9]

The conclusion—and there is so much more information that could be brought to bear—is that the central message of the Bible stands strong: Jesus indeed lived; his activities and teachings were written down within the lifetimes of those who knew him (either by those who did know him, or by their close companions); the claim of his resurrection, incredible as the event seems, was made from the very beginning of the spread of Christianity; and Jesus, born a Jew, was worshiped as God.

Objection #3: Even if it was accurate at first, the Bible was copied and translated so many times that it surely has been corrupted

THE FACTS ABOUT TRANSLATION This objection is repeated so often that most people don't really think about what they're saying. I often ask folks with this objection to clarify what they mean—and after a brief pause, they realize that they're not really sure. Those who do have an explanation usually say something along the lines of, "Well, it was first written in Greek; then it was translated into Latin; and then those Latin documents were translated into, say, German; and then those German translations were translated into Old English; and finally, hundreds of years later, they updated that into modern English, giving us what we have today." In their minds, it's like the children's game "Telephone," where a story is passed from one child to the next, through successive retellings, so that by the end of a roomful of kids the story has changed substantially from its original.

Let me just say it: if we had gotten our Bible in that fashion, I wouldn't trust it either! The truth is that all reputable versions begin with the oldest and best Greek manuscripts (New Testament) and Hebrew manuscripts (Old Testament) that we possess, and these are then translated directly into the contemporary language. So other translations that were done in the interim mean nothing to the question of accuracy because today's Bibles are based solely on ancient texts, not intermediary translations.

Therefore, we can be confident in the accuracy of the Bibles we hold in our hands today—given they are one of the main versions that were carefully translated by a broad committee of qualified scholars, and not the work of just one individual or church (or cult or sect).[10]

COMMUNICATION IN THE ANCIENT WORLD In a primarily oral culture, great respect was accorded the ability to relay information accurately when it was not immediately written down. And Jesus' use of stories did make it especially easy to keep intact the information he shared.

As for the things that were finally written down, those

manuscripts were revered from the very beginning. So when additional copies were made, they were made with the highest of care—very often by the clergy or professional scribes who made their living in a "scriptorium," or writing hall.

What happens when you compare the earliest manuscripts to later ones? How much change took place over the centuries in cases where we can compare the two? In the case of the New Testament, what we find in those situations can help us know how things were handled during the "blackout time" between the actual writing (AD 45–90) and the earliest copies or fragments available (AD 125–250).

The record is really quite astonishing. The New Testament contains about twenty thousand lines of text, and of those, only about forty lines are in question. That amounts to about four hundred words (roughly one page of your two-hundred-page New Testament). Most of the variations are insignificant to the meaning of the text: it says about the same thing either way. Of the variations that remain, no major doctrine is affected by or built upon those texts.[11] So everything that really matters to Christianity comes out of well-attested ancient texts.

Objection #4: The Bible has stories that sound like myths; maybe there is truth in there somewhere, like in Aesop's fables, but you certainly can't call it true in a historic sense
Stories such as Noah and the Ark, Moses parting the Red Sea, Jonah being swallowed by a whale (the text actually says "a great fish"), and Jesus walking on water do sound fantastical. But we need to remind our friends: so also do many natural phenomena. Just try to wrap your mind around what

science tells us, for example, about the Big Bang: that our universe existed as a gargantuan expanse, containing trillions upon trillions of stars, galaxies, black holes, antimatter, and "dark energy"—and then try to imagine that all this was once squeezed into an infinitesimally tiny point, unimaginably hot, which then suddenly—*who knows why*—burst forth and began expanding 13.8 billion years ago. Marilyn vos Savant, reputed to have the highest IQ ever recorded, wrote, "I think that if it had been a *religion* that first maintained the notion that all the matter in the entire universe had once been contained in an area smaller than the point of a pin, scientists probably would have laughed at the idea."[12]

I agree! Yes, it sounds like science fiction—but most of us believe it because of the evidence and authorities that support it (not to mention that it sounds like a scientific description of what the Bible says *God* did in Genesis 1). Similarly, we can believe in the amazing things recorded in the Bible because of the supporting evidence, especially that it was seen and reported by credible eyewitnesses (and in many cases hostile witnesses, as well—who rarely deny the miracles but, in the case of Jesus, attack him for doing them *on the wrong day*, thus admitting the reality of the miracles themselves).

The issue comes down to this: If God created the heavens and the earth and everything in them, then is it so hard to imagine he can implant a life in a young virgin, or re-create that life through a resurrection? If God made our bodies, is it really so hard to accept that he at times remakes them? If he made our minds, is it difficult for him to speak his message of love, truth, and guidance into them? Once you grant an omnipotent God, it isn't really hard to imagine him doing any number of amazing things. To a Being like that, these things are like child's play!

So it's possible the things our friends read about and are tempted to laugh at in the Bible are just as true as some of the amazing things that have been discovered in our vast and complex universe. Astronomer Robert Jastrow wrestled with the idea that time and space had a beginning—a truth taught in Genesis and accepted by Jews and Christians long before the scientific community came to the same conclusion in recent decades. He writes, "For the scientist who has lived by his faith in the power of reason, the story ends like a bad dream. He has scaled the mountains of ignorance; he is about to conquer the highest peak; as he pulls himself over the final rock, he is greeted by a band of theologians who have been sitting there for centuries."[13]

Objection #5: The New Testament consists of carefully chosen books, banning others that shed light on the real Jesus of history

"The Bible did not arrive by fax from heaven."

So argues Dr. Teabing in the novel *The Da Vinci Code*. He continues:

> *The Bible is a product of man, my dear. Not of God. The Bible did not fall magically from the clouds. Man created it as a historical record of tumultuous times, and it has evolved through countless translations, additions, and revisions. History has never had a definitive version of the book. . . . More than eighty gospels were considered*

for the New Testament, and yet only a relative few
were chosen for inclusion—Matthew, Mark, Luke,
and John among them. . . . The Bible, as we know
it today, was collated by the pagan Roman emperor
Constantine the Great.[14]

Even though this quote is from a piece of popular fiction (one filled with historical mistakes and misrepresenta-
tions), the thinking behind it is increasingly embraced as
true. Especially with the discovery of the Nag Hammadi
library—a treasure trove of Gnostic writings found in the
middle of the last century—people are wondering if these
books might have more reliable information about Jesus
than the New Testament Gospels.

The simple truth is this: all those so-called gospels
are much, much later than the Gospels in the New Testament—all of them having been written in the second to
fourth centuries, and none of them have ties back to the
apostles of Christ. By contrast, the New Testament was
completed by the apostles (or those they approved) by the
end of the first century and circulated among contemporaries of Jesus and his initial band of followers. Furthermore, those Gnostic documents were created in the very
context in which critics mistakenly charge the New Testament of having been birthed: they are highly sectarian, full
of fictitious events and sayings that have no historical support, and show a dreadful lack of understanding of Jesus'
first-century Jewish context.

A key example is the so-called Gospel of Thomas—
a writing that claims to have been written by Thomas, the

disciple of Jesus. The problem is that it was written about *a hundred years too late* for that to have been possible! Here are a few quotes from that book, supposedly coming from the lips of Jesus himself: "If you fast, you will bring sin upon yourselves, and if you pray, you will be condemned, and if you give to charity, you will harm your spirits" (saying 14). *Huh?* Or here's another one, again attributed to Jesus: "Every female who makes herself male will enter the kingdom of Heaven" (saying 114). Just *try* quoting that one to your female friends! Here's one more: "Blessings on the lion if a human eats it, making the lion human. Foul is the human if a lion eats it, making the lion human" (saying 7).[15]

I don't know about you, but after that I'm ready to go read Matthew, Mark, Luke, and John—to learn again from the real Jesus! Hopefully our friends will be ready as well.

Objection #6: How can one religious book be right and all the others wrong? Isn't it more likely all contain some truth, and all contain some error?

"You Christians don't seem to appreciate the fact that centuries before Christ, Gautama Buddha said, 'Do not do unto others what you would not have done to you.' Can't you see that Jesus is not so unique and that our religion has truth too?" The panelist at our church's world religion event seemed troubled by what she perceived to be Christians' one-sided perception of other faiths. And she was partially right: Jesus' positive version, "Do unto others . . ." does sound similar to what the Buddha said. And we would concede that this particular teaching of Buddhism is true, as far as it goes.

What we as Christians claim for the Bible, however, is

that it is fundamentally different from other "holy books." While there is a measure of truth in many other belief systems, according to Jesus none of those other truths lead to salvation, whatever benefits they may have. It was *Jesus* who said, "I am the way, the truth, and the life. No one can come to the Father except through me" (John 14:6).

The Bible goes beyond giving good advice: It teaches us about a Savior, about the need to rely on his righteousness instead of our own. It breaks down our pride and reminds us we are no better than any other person on the planet. We are all sinners, and so there's no ground for pride in the presence of anyone, much less in the presence of God. It tells us we cannot save ourselves, and so we must accept God's plan for redemption instead of constructing our own.

There are other features that make the Bible unique. Most notably, the Bible has predictive prophecy, which was later fulfilled—to the letter. For instance, if you read Isaiah 53 in its entirety, it will be clear that the whole chapter is an amazing prophecy of the suffering of the Messiah—but it was written more than seven hundred years beforehand. It describes, in advance, how Jesus was to be "pierced for our rebellion, crushed for our sins. He was beaten so we could be whole. He was whipped so we could be healed" (v. 5).

Another prophecy, found in Zechariah 12:10, says that people will look on the one "whom they have pierced and mourn for him as for an only son. They will grieve bitterly for him as for a firstborn son who has died." It's easy to look at the crucifixion of Jesus from our side of history and see clearly how his brutal death fulfilled these prophetic words. But what really shows the divine insight in the words of these prophets is that these words were written not only hundreds of years before the life and death of Christ but also centuries before the Roman practice of crucifixion, with its horrific piercing of the hands and feet with nails that were pounded into the wood of the cross, had even been invented. I imagine that the prophets who penned these words were scratching their heads in bewilderment as they sensed God leading them to write about how the suffering Messiah would be "pierced."

If you read about the Crucifixion as it is recorded in the Gospels (for example, in Matt. 27), it is mind-boggling how these centuries-old predictions were fulfilled in such minute detail. Could any mere human have written such specific history in advance? It seems clear that God's foreknowledge was on display in these predictions—and we've only mentioned a few of the many examples that could be discussed. Others include the place of the Messiah's birth being in Bethlehem (see Mic. 5:2); his being of the lineage of King David (see 2 Sam. 7:12-16); his being born of a virgin (see Isa. 7:14); his claim of deity (see Isa. 9:6); his rejection by his own people (see Isa. 53:3); his betrayal for thirty pieces of silver (see Zech. 11:12); his extreme suffering and disfigurement (see Isa. 52:14); his death on our behalf (see Isa. 53:5-6); his burial in a rich man's tomb (see Isa. 53:9); and his subsequent resurrection (see Ps. 16:10).[16]

Many other examples could be listed, but suffice it to say that no other religion has this kind of prophetic fulfillment. We can respectfully appreciate the limited value of other religious teachings, but we remain confident the Bible is utterly unique and worthy of our trust as the source of God's redemptive truth.

Objection #7: Since ancient mystery religions taught tales of dying and rising gods, isn't it likely Christians borrowed those ideas and invented a Jesus who claimed to do similar things?

This objection is one of the most exaggerated and misleading claims you'll ever encounter, but thanks again to popular literature such as *The Da Vinci Code* and its claim that "nothing in Christianity is original,"[17] encounter it you probably will. Dan Brown, through his character Teabing, claims that by "fusing pagan symbols, dates, and rituals into the growing Christian tradition" there was created "a kind of hybrid religion." This hybrid religion was influenced, he claims, by "the pre-Christian God Mithras,"[18] who supposedly was born on December 25, later died, and then was resurrected after three days.

Sound familiar? It's supposed to, and we're supposed to believe that the whole teaching about Jesus is a myth that is based on earlier pagan religions.

These ideas were thoroughly refuted—well before Dan Brown decided to regurgitate them back onto the unsuspecting public—by many scholars, including Ronald Nash. Here is what Nash said in his powerful book *The Gospel and the Greeks: Did the New Testament Borrow from Pagan Thought?*

> *The significant differences between the death of Jesus and the mythical deaths of the pagan deities must be coupled with the equally serious errors made by those who write of the "resurrections" of the mystery gods.*

> *Which mystery gods actually experienced a*
> *resurrection from the dead? Certainly no early texts*
> *refer to any resurrection of Attis. Attempts to link*
> *the worship of Adonis to a resurrection are equally*
> *weak. Nor is the case for a resurrection of Osiris*
> *any stronger. . . . And of course no claim can be*
> *made that Mithras was a dying and rising god. . . .*
> *The tide of scholarly opinion has turned dramati-*
> *cally against attempts to make early Christianity*
> *dependent on the so-called dying and rising gods*
> *of Hellenistic paganism.*[19]

For his book *The Case for the Real Jesus,* Lee Strobel had the chance to interview Dr. Edwin Yamauchi, Professor Emeritus of History at Miami University of Ohio, about the Mithras claims specifically. He asked him about the December 25 birth date. "That's not a parallel," Yamauchi replied. "We don't know the date Jesus was born. The earliest date celebrated by Christians was January 6."

Then Strobel asked him about the claim that "Mithras was buried in a tomb and rose after three days." Yamauchi replied firmly, "We don't know anything about the death of Mithras. . . . I know of no references to a supposed death and resurrection." Lee later confirmed that fact and reported, "Indeed, Richard Gordon declared in his book *Image and Value in the Greco-Roman World* that there is 'no death of Mithras'—and thus, there cannot be a resurrection."[20] Add to this the fact that, according to Yamauchi, "the earliest mithraea are dated to the early second century" and "most of what we have as evidence of Mithraism comes in the second, third, and fourth centuries AD." Therefore, "the dating disproves that Christianity borrowed its tenets from Mithraism."[21]

The bottom line: the claim that the message of the New Testament is borrowed from mystical religions evaporates when you look into it. If there was any borrowing going on, it was the later mystery religions imitating aspects of Christianity—not the reverse. Add to all of this that the historical evidence for the life, teaching, death, and resurrection of Christ still stands strong, regardless of what other claims or challenges have been thrown at it.

Objection #8: Since you can make the Bible say anything you want it to say, why should we give it any special credence? Doesn't it all come down to subjective opinion, anyway?

This objection points to a real danger. It is always tempting to put our own meanings on verses in the Bible and come up with bizarre conclusions. Just look at the cults, with open Bibles but dangerous doctrines and practices.

The truth is that any message we hear—from any source—can be redefined, manipulated, or rationalized to make it subservient to our own whims and desires. On a daily basis, people reinterpret the law to make it say what they want it to say. This is especially true with rules related to driving—and paying taxes. They tell themselves, *This one doesn't apply to me, It doesn't mean what it seems to mean*, or *Just this once I'm entitled to make an exception for myself.*

They do that, but they can't actually justify it; in spite of their self-serving mind games related to the speed limit, they'll still get a speeding ticket. And rationalizations related to filing taxes may seem to work for a season—but reality will reinstate itself quickly with the first tax audit.

And getting back to the Bible, of course people can "make it say what they want it to say"—at least in their own thinking—for a while. But like any good piece of communication, the Bible is quite clear about its central messages—and it tells us that, much like the case of the speed limit or a tax law, we'll be held accountable to the standards it sets. Romans 14:12 warns us that "each of us will give a personal account to God."

The real point here is that we cannot alter Scripture to suit ourselves. People try, but the results are tragic. Instead we need—and our friends need—to humbly let the text alter us. If we'll let it, it can soften a hard heart; it can convict of sin and bring about repentance and salvation.

THE POSITIVE CASE

We've spent most of this chapter responding to the various challenges people tend to throw at us concerning the Bible—claims that it contradicts itself, that it's not reliable history, that it relays hard-to-believe stories, that it is based on myths, and so forth. It was important for us to address these claims and to see that there are great answers to this raft of popular objections. But before we end, I want to turn the corner and, drawing from many of the elements we've already discussed, present a positive case for the reliability of the Bible (as before, focusing primarily on the New Testament). The case is really quite simple and has three main points:

1. The New Testament is, at minimum, a reliable historical record

As a Christian, I believe it is much more than that. I believe the Bible is the inspired and authoritative Word of God. But we don't have to ask our friends to start there. We just need to help them see it for what it clearly is: a trustworthy account of the life, ministry, and spiritual impact of Jesus Christ. How do we know that? Well, as we've seen, the documents of the New Testament themselves are very early, dating back to the life spans of Jesus' companions—with some parts, such as the creed in 1 Corinthians 15:3-7, going back to within a few years (perhaps even months) of the death and resurrection of Christ.

Certainly people have challenged the historical reliability of the Gospels—such as renowned archaeologist Sir William M. Ramsay, who thought that Luke was foolish as a storyteller because he mentioned so many specific names, places, and dates. These specifics would be easy to check out and refute—assuming, as Ramsay did initially, that they were not true. But after thirty years of studying, searching, and digging, Ramsay famously concluded that "Luke is a historian of the first rank. . . . This author should be placed along with the very greatest of historians."[22]

In addition to the early written records from the followers of Jesus, we have secular historical accounts that in many ways confirm the contours of the New Testament testimony. This includes, as we saw, thirty-nine ancient sources *outside of the Bible* that provide over one hundred facts about Jesus' life, teachings, death, and resurrection.[23] Dr. Craig Evans summed things up well when he said, "There's every reason to conclude that the Gospels have fairly and accurately reported the essential elements of Jesus' teachings, life, death, and resurrection. They're early enough, they're rooted into the right streams that go back to Jesus and the original people, there's continuity, there's proximity, there's verification of certain distinct points with archaeology and other documents, and then there's the inner logic. That's what pulls it all together."[24]

2. The historical record presents Jesus as the unique Son of God

We'll go into much more depth about Jesus' claims and credentials in the next chapter, but suffice it to say that he was very clear about his own divine identity, and he demonstrated that he was the unique Son of God through his sinless life, through his supernatural insights, through how he fulfilled ancient biblical prophecies, through his amazing miracles, and especially through his resurrection from the dead. All this adds up to his having divine credentials that no other spiritual teacher has ever had—before or after him—credentials that should accrue in our minds into incredible respect and trust in all that he did and said.

3. Jesus, the Son of God, taught that the Bible is the inspired Word of God

Jesus had a lot to say about the Bible of his day, the Old Testament. He quoted from it often, and in every case he upheld its authority, accuracy, and trustworthiness. If there had been something wrong with it or there were stories that needed to be corrected, surely he, the Son of God, would have done so.

Rather, Jesus used the Bible with confidence and based his ministry and teachings on its sure foundation. He treated the history parts as historic, the prophecy books as prophetic, and the teaching sections as truth worth following. We trust the Bible primarily because Jesus did. Extrabiblical sources and archaeology tell us the Bible is historically accurate and worth *reading*; Jesus tells us it is spiritually accurate and worth *heeding.*

So we end this chapter with a challenge: as a follower of Jesus, you do not need to shrink back from handling your friends' questions about the Bible. Jesus, the Son of God, said it is true, and it has shown itself over and over again to be true. Almost all major advances in Western civilization, for example, came because people read and believed the Bible's message. Its positive influence for good is unrivaled in human history. Great social movements such as abolition, civil rights, women's rights, sanctity of life, care for the poor, and the rule of law instead of dictatorial tyranny have been energized by those steeped in biblical teaching. And then there are millions—no, billions— of stories of life transformation by individuals who have embraced its core truths. As you've walked with God in your own life I'm sure you've proven it true time and time again.

We need never be ashamed of reading, believing, or living the Bible's powerful message—and we should share it whenever possible with our friends.

I tell you the truth, until heaven and earth
disappear, not even the smallest detail of God's law
will disappear until its purpose is achieved.
                                            —JESUS, IN MATTHEW 5:18

SUMMARY OF THE ANSWER

Question 3 asks us, "Why trust the Bible, a book based on myths and full of contradictions and mistakes?"

- The opening example illustrates how reliable witnesses, viewing the same events, can give accounts that differ or even seem contradictory—though the full story showed that there was harmony between the accounts. In the same way, the four Gospels, written by four different men about the same events, also include accounts that at times differ and seem to contradict but in most cases are fairly easy to harmonize.

- Most Christians believe that alleged contradictions among the four Gospel accounts result from the four writers' seeing the same event but telling the story from their own perspectives. This is the nature of all eyewitness testimony.

- Often people raise the issue of biblical contradictions only because they have *heard rumors* about them, but don't know any specifics. Sometimes they bring up this issue in order to keep the Bible at arm's length, not wanting to face the implications of its teachings for their daily lives.

- There are a variety of myths and misconceptions swirling around in our culture about the Bible. These can seem intimidating at first, but as we've tried to show in this chapter, they have good answers—if we'll study the facts and get the full story.

- Not only can we answer myths and objections regarding the Bible, but we can also present a positive case. We did this by showing that (1) the New Testament is a reliable historical document; (2) the historical record presents Jesus as the unique Son of God; and (3) Jesus, the Son of God and therefore the One with real authority, taught that the whole Bible is the inspired Word of God.

TIPS FOR TALKING ABOUT THIS ISSUE

- When people question the Bible, don't take it personally, and try not to get defensive. God welcomes legitimate inquiry—in fact, he commands it: "Test everything that is said. Hold on to what is good" (1 Thess. 5:21).

- You might want to point out that not understanding something in the Bible puts you and your friends in good company. Even the apostle Peter admitted he had a hard time understanding some of the apostle Paul's letters: "This is what our beloved brother Paul also wrote to you with the wisdom God gave him—speaking of these things in all of his letters. *Some of his comments are hard to understand*" (2 Pet. 3:15-16, emphasis mine). Tell your friends that if one Bible writer had trouble understanding another Bible writer, we shouldn't be surprised when something confuses *us* two thousand years later!

- The Bible is a big book: roughly three-quarters of a million words. No one can master all of it, and you cannot hope to have at your fingertips all the salient information questioners might be seeking. Take the pressure off yourself by admitting it when you don't know—then go find out and get back to your friends with the information.

- At first blush, some questions can feel very intimidating. But remember that people have been reading and critiquing the Bible for centuries. It is doubtful that your friends will be the first to raise a particular issue, and it is certain that the information you need is out there—with a little digging, you'll find it.

- Another approach is to suggest that questioners start reading one book of the Bible, say the Gospel of Mark or the Gospel of Luke, in a modern translation (such as the New Living Translation or another one that is accurate but easy to understand). Tell them to have a notepad handy. As questions arise, they can jot them down, along with the verse numbers. Commit to them that you'll get together when they are done, and agree to go over whatever they write down so you can help them work through whatever doesn't make sense. I love this approach, because it gets people into the Bible directly, reading for themselves the message that is, according to Romans 1:16, "the power of God at work, saving everyone who believes." If your friends are open to this, don't underestimate the power of God's Word to take the conversation to a higher and more life-impacting level.

QUESTIONS FOR GROUP DISCUSSION

1. Have you ever been in a discussion with an unbeliever who argued against the validity of the Bible? How did you respond?

2. Can you think of a time when two people recounted the same event—with two seemingly different scenarios? What is the best way to get at the real picture of what happened? How might this help you explain the so-called contradictions in the Gospel accounts?

3. Have you ever seen someone use arguments against the Bible as a smoke screen to avoid the implications of its teachings in his or her life? How did you respond, or how might you in the future?

4. The chapter quoted Mark Twain as saying, "It ain't those parts of the Bible that I can't understand that bother me, it is the parts that I do understand." What are some examples of biblical teachings that might intimidate people?

5. Why do you think books that are critical of the Bible, such as *The Da Vinci Code,* have such an impact on people's opinions? How can you become better prepared to face these challenges?

6. In the past, how have you faced questions you've had about the Bible? What has most helped you?

7. Paul wrote to Timothy, "All Scripture is inspired by God and is useful to teach us what is true and to make us realize what is wrong in our lives. It corrects us when we are wrong and teaches us to do what is right" (2 Tim. 3:16). How do these words affect your own commitment to learn and study Scripture?

CHAPTER 4:

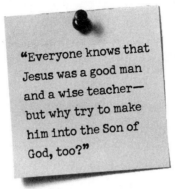

"Everyone knows that Jesus was a good man and a wise teacher—but why try to make him into the Son of God, too?"

He was a man known for his unusual wisdom, which he spent his lifetime trying to instill in anyone who would listen. His efforts were met with great resistance as he pushed against the accepted religious beliefs and authorities of his day. But gradually—against the odds—his teachings caught on, as more and more people were changed by his words and became his disciples. In time his circle of followers grew into a movement, and after his death, that movement became a major world religion.

Over time, however, some of his followers, zealous to honor him in the greatest way possible, began to transform what he had taught into something quite different. The teacher had claimed to be just that: a spiritual guide, with unique insights and wisdom. But they turned him into a savior, and more than that, a divine figure who would be worshiped—ideas that were completely contrary to what he had taught.

Is that an accurate account of what really happened? Yes, it actually is.

Not to Jesus—but to Siddhartha Gautama, otherwise known as the Buddha, the founder of the Buddhist religion, who lived about five hundred years before the time of Christ. He did not want to be considered a savior or a divine person of any kind and, in fact, was actually not interested in discussing the existence of God at all. Many believe that he was an atheist or at most an agnostic (one who thinks we cannot know whether God exists) whose emphasis was on spiritual practices, not theistic belief. Nevertheless, many Buddhists today treat the Buddha as deity and worship him as such.

The question we want to tackle in this chapter is whether or not this is what happened to Jesus as well. It's a common question in our culture, so it wasn't surprising that it came up in our survey. Maybe you've heard it put in a colorful way, as I have: "If Jesus had any idea that people today were trying to turn him into some kind of a god and that they were actually worshiping him, he'd be rolling over in his grave!"

Setting aside for now the question of whether he actually is in a grave, let's explore this important issue. The belief that Jesus was just a good teacher, not the Son of God or the Savior of the world, has been around a long time. Some of the world's most influential thinkers of the past two centuries have actively promoted this idea. Thomas Jefferson notoriously cut up a copy of the New Testament to remove all references to Jesus' miracles or his divinity. In a letter to John Adams, Jefferson claimed that what was left represented the true teaching of Jesus, which he described as "the most sublime and benevolent code of morals which has ever been offered to man."[1]

This is what many people think of Jesus today: a wonderful teacher of good moral values, someone who urged people to be loving, kind, and above all tolerant. They view the claim that Jesus was the Son of God, the resurrected Lord, and the only Savior of humanity as legend or mythical additions to his simple message of "Love thy neighbor."

It is not surprising that non-Christians think of Jesus this way. Buddhists, for example, often reinterpret Jesus to have been a kind of Buddha himself—an enlightened teacher—for the West. Muslims claim that he was a great prophet, but one who would never lay claim to deity or allow himself to be called the Son of God. And many Jewish people consider him to be a good teacher, but certainly not the Messiah or a divine figure of any kind.

What is surprising, though, is how many authors and religious leaders who claim to be Christians are also defending this way of looking at Jesus. They suggest that historic Christianity rests on a big mistake. Jesus, they argue, never made any claims about being the Messiah, the Son of God, or the Redeemer of the world. Instead, he urged people to be good to one another, to be models of God's love, and to work for peace and social justice. Somehow, they say, Christianity lost the pure message that Jesus preached in his Sermon on the Mount and his down-to-earth parables; they say the church replaced it with a message about Jesus as the crucified and risen Savior and Lord. For example, Anglican Archbishop Desmond Tutu—perhaps the most famous and honored religious leader in Africa—endorses the idea put forth by Robin R. Meyers that we need to follow Jesus instead of worshiping Christ.[2]

But this view of Jesus as merely a great teacher and not the divine Son of God is not just that of avowed non-Christians or of a few people on the fringes of the faith. It is an extremely influential view that many religious leaders, university professors, scholars, and media are vigorously promoting. And again, according to our survey, it's one that some of our own friends espouse or are at least curious about as well.

AN EXPLOSION OF DEVOTION TO JESUS

The common claim today is that belief in Jesus as a unique, divine person arose long after he walked the earth. Such books as *The Da Vinci Code* have popularized the notion that it was not until the Council of Nicaea, three centuries after Jesus, that Christians started worshiping him as the divine Son of God. The author, Dan Brown, has his fictional character Teabing declare, "Scholars claim that the early Church literally *stole* Jesus from His original followers, hijacking His human message, shrouding it in an impenetrable cloak of divinity, and using it to expand their own power."[3] This reflects the idea usually put forth—that devotion to Jesus as the divine Savior and Lord evolved over those first three centuries.

Yet as it turns out, the best historical scholarship shows that simply is not the case. For example, Dr. Larry Hurtado, a New Testament scholar at the University of Edinburgh, has argued that devotion to Jesus began so early in the Christian movement that we may speak of a "big bang" of exalted descriptions and reverential devotion and worship of Jesus Christ. The evidence shows that "at an astonishingly early point basic convictions about Jesus that amount to treating him as divine had become widely shared in various Christian circles."[4]

To understand this point, keep in mind that all the New Testament books were written between about AD 50 and 100, roughly twenty to seventy years after Jesus' death in AD 30 or 33—and hundreds of years before the fourth-century Council of Nicaea. The earliest of these were epistles or letters that the apostle Paul wrote beginning about seventeen years after Jesus' death and resurrection—including already established creeds of the church, such as the one in the first part of 1 Corinthians 15, which date back to virtually the beginning. (By contrast, the earliest known writings about Buddha date from roughly three centuries after his death. I say "roughly" because historians aren't even sure in which century he died!)

Paul's epistles and the rest of the New Testament writings reflect the religious beliefs and practices of first-century Christians from Jerusalem in the East to Rome in the West and many places in between, such as Corinth in Greece and Ephesus in what today is Turkey. These writings are excellent sources of information about what Jesus' original followers believed. When we examine these writings, we find that all his followers viewed Jesus as far more than a religious teacher—even far more than a prophet.

First of all, every New Testament writer refers to Jesus as the "Christ," or Messiah (e.g., see Matt. 1:1; Mark 1:1; Luke 9:20; John 4:25-26; Rom. 1:4; Heb. 6:1; James 1:1; 1 Pet. 1:1;

Jude 1:1). As you probably know, "Christ" is not Jesus' last name. The word *Messiah* derives from the Hebrew title meaning "Anointed One"; *Christ* derives from the Greek translation of that title. The title appears over five hundred times and in all but one book of the New Testament (3 John, the shortest book). In the Old Testament, anointment symbolized two main kinds of offices: priests and kings. The New Testament writers, in proclaiming that Jesus was the Christ, were saying that he was the preeminent Priest-King whom God had sent to fulfill his promises to Israel.

That fulfillment would lead, ultimately, to worldwide righteousness and peace. This, at the very least, is who all the earliest Christians believed Jesus to be. Only toward the end of the New Testament era, in the epistles of John, do we find any reference to people who apparently professed to follow Jesus but who denied that he was the Christ (see 1 John 2:22)—an idea that John soundly refuted! So the theory that the earliest followers of Jesus thought of him as just a good teacher, that belief in Jesus as a figure of cosmic importance arose later, has it exactly backward. Jesus' earliest followers thought of him as the Messiah, and it was only later that some people began to view Jesus as just a good teacher.

Second, the earliest and the latest New Testament authors alike use the most exalted titles for Jesus—ones that clearly indicate in their contexts that Jesus is divine. Both Paul (generally considered the earliest author) and John (usually regarded as the latest) speak of Jesus as the Son of God (see Gal. 4:4-6; John 20:30-31), the Savior (see Phil. 3:20; John 4:42), the Lord (see Rom. 10:9-13; John 9:38), and even God (see Rom. 9:5; Titus 2:13; John 1:1; 20:28). The writings of Luke and Peter also use all these titles for Jesus (see Luke 2:11; 9:20; 10:1-2; 22:70; Acts 20:28; 1 Peter 1:1; 3:15; 2 Pet. 1:1, 17; 3:18). All the New Testament authors use the title *Lord* in ways that, given the context, equate Jesus with deity (see Matt. 7:21-22; Mark 5:19; Luke 10:1-2; Heb. 1:10; 1 Pet. 3:15; Jude 1:4).[5]

Third, the earliest as well as the latest New Testament authors also encourage giving Jesus the highest possible divine honors. Jesus' followers are to believe, or trust, in him (see Rom. 10:11; John 8:24), pray to him (see 1 Cor. 1:2; John 14:14), and worship him (see Phil. 2:10-11; Rev. 5:14). The claim that Jesus was not originally the object of Christian faith is simply false. Our earliest Christian writings demonstrate that followers of Jesus throughout a wide area of the known world already believed in Jesus and worshiped and prayed to him within twenty years of his death—and of course, as we'll see in a moment, we believe this evidence points back to the very teaching of Jesus himself.

In fact, some of the evidence for religious devotion to Jesus goes back even earlier than the first New Testament writings, because those writings demonstrate that such devotion had already been well-established. One of the earliest pieces of Christian "liturgy" or corporate prayer is preserved in an expression in Aramaic (the native language of Jesus and his original Jewish disciples) at the end of 1 Corinthians: *Maranatha*, "Our Lord, come" (16:22). This expression was a prayer to the Lord Jesus to return and bring history to its final climax (see also Rev. 22:20). This prayer pushes back our evidence for religious devotion to Jesus, at the latest, into the first decade or so of the Christian movement—again supporting our belief that it originated with Christ.

We have only touched on some of the evidence showing that the earliest followers of Jesus regarded him as a person of a supremely exalted status above all human beings and responded to him with divine honors such as prayer and worship. Here's the key point to remember: there never was a time when the earliest community of followers of Jesus did not regard him as far, far more than a good teacher.

JUST WHO DID JESUS THINK HE WAS?

All right, say some people, very shortly after Jesus' death his followers apparently thought of him as the Messiah and worshiped him as the divine Son of God. But maybe this was simply a colossal mistake on their part. Is there any reason to think that Jesus made such exalted claims for himself? Who did he say that he was?

Answering this question is complicated a bit by the fact that skeptics question whether the Gospels accurately report what Jesus said about himself. We've already talked about the reliability of the Bible in a previous chapter, so we won't repeat that here. Instead, let's look at some ways the Gospels tell us what we can say with confidence about Jesus' own claims, without just assuming (for the sake of the argument with skeptics) that everything the Gospels say is accurate.

Liberal biblical scholars who are engaged in the so-called quest for the historical Jesus use specific tests, or criteria, for determining what material in the Gospels they think most likely goes back to Jesus himself. They regard these as tools for assessing how confident they can be, on rational grounds alone, in determining that a particular statement by Jesus in the Gospels was actually something he said. They also use these criteria to decide which of the actions that are attributed to Jesus in the Gospels they can be confident were actually done by him.

One of these criteria is that if the Gospels report Jesus speaking in ways or saying things that are very unlike what Christian writers typically said, then those sayings are believed by the critics to very likely go back to Jesus. On the other hand, if the Gospels report Jesus saying things that Christians later said, this does not weigh against Jesus saying them first. (I guess they realize Jesus' followers are likely to have repeated at least some of the things he said!)

One good example of these criteria is Jesus' habit in the Gospels of referring to himself as "the Son of Man." This title occurs eighty-two times in the sayings of Jesus throughout the four Gospels, making it by far the most-often used title for him in the Gospels (even more than "Christ"). Yet this title is used for Jesus only three or four times in the rest of the New Testament (see Acts 7:56; Heb. 2:6; Rev. 1:13; 14:14). Why is that? The best explanation is that Jesus really did use the title for himself, but the early church usually did not, perhaps because many of the converts to Christianity would not have understood it.

Now, what did Jesus mean by calling himself the Son of Man? Many modern readers assume that the title simply indicates his humanity. But that's because they didn't live in the first century and understand that he was referring to a visionary prophecy in the Old Testament book of Daniel, in which "one like a Son of Man" was going to be presented to "the Ancient of Days" (God) and receive authority to rule over the whole world forever (Dan. 7:13-14, NASB). That's what Jesus thought of himself! This figure in Daniel has sovereign power and is worshiped by "all the peoples, nations and men of every language"—and only God can legitimately be worshiped. So Jesus was identifying himself as the One who would rule forever over all nations, all peoples, all over the world, for all time. That is a staggering claim for any human being to make.

What's more, in Mark chapter 14, during his trial prior to the Crucifixion Jesus used this title for himself and specifically tied it to the passage in Daniel 7. He was answering a question of the high priest: "Are you the Messiah, the Son of the Blessed One?" (v. 61). To this Jesus replied, "I Am. And you will see the Son of Man seated in the place of power at God's right hand and coming on the clouds of heaven" (v. 62).

These words were astounding to his astute listeners, because by coupling the title "the Son of Man" with the description of his "coming on the clouds of heaven," he was undeniably claiming that he was the divine person described in Daniel 7:13, where it says, "I saw someone like a son of man coming with the clouds of heaven." The group's response said it all: "Then the high priest tore his clothing to show his horror and said, 'Why do we need other witnesses? You have all heard his blasphemy. What is your verdict?' 'Guilty!' they all cried. 'He deserves to die!'" (Mark 14:63-64). If Jesus were merely claiming to be human, he would not have evoked this strongly negative reaction. Clearly, he was making the claim to being deity.

If we stopped right there, we would have sufficient

evidence that Jesus thought he was much more than just a good teacher. Yet there is so much more. Everywhere we look in the Gospels, we find Jesus making audacious claims about himself—even in passages that many people interpret to be presenting Jesus as just a good teacher.

Consider the Sermon on the Mount, for example. If there is any passage where people imagine that Jesus comes across as simply a teacher of high moral ideals, it would be this one. Yet early in this Sermon, Jesus makes this bold statement: "God blesses you when people mock you and persecute you and lie about you . . . because you are my followers" (Matt. 5:11). In some way, following Jesus is personal—it is not just about following his teachings but about being loyal to him (literally, Jesus says, "because of me").

A few sentences later, Jesus claims that he came "to fulfill" the law of Moses and the writings of the prophets (Matt. 5:17, NIV). Other Jewish teachers saw their job description as helping people understand God's Word. Jesus claimed that his job was to bring about the fulfillment of God's Word!

Jesus then launches into his teaching about God's Word in the law of Moses. So yes, he was a teacher, but no teacher had ever taught like this! The standard way that Jewish teachers of the Scriptures taught in those days was to cite the opinions of different teachers about the meaning of a passage and then offer their own viewpoint. In today's vernacular, it would be like a professor standing in front of his class and saying, "Well, Dr. Jones thinks this, and Dr. Smith thinks something else, but here's my take on the matter." However, Jesus did not just offer his thoughts as one more opinion among the many to consider. Instead, he contrasted what the people had heard from their teachers about the law of Moses with what he said, in such a way as to make his the *final interpretation*:

> You have heard that our ancestors were told,
> "You must not murder. If you commit murder,
> you are subject to judgment." But I say, if you
> are even angry with someone, you are subject to
> judgment! (Matt. 5:21-22)

Repeatedly Jesus says, "but I say," shutting the door on any other way of understanding the Scriptures than his own (Matt. 5:22, 28, 32, 34, 39, 44).

Jesus was so confident in his being the final word that he often began a statement by literally saying, "Amen I tell you." Most versions translate these words in ways that show a high degree of certainty, but the English just does not convey the full forcefulness of Jesus' words within that culture. As Christians we traditionally put "Amen" at the end of our prayers, asking God to validate or confirm whatever we prayed according to his knowledge and purpose. Jesus put "Amen" at the beginning of many of his statements when he taught, expressing supreme confidence that what he was about to say was the truth. (By the way, none of the early Christian writers ever prefaced their sentences with the word *Amen*. They wouldn't have dared.) Jesus does this five times in the Sermon on the Mount (see Matt. 5:18, 26; 6:2, 5, 16) and many other places throughout the four Gospels.

Later in the sermon, Jesus warns that he will one day sit in judgment of all people—including people who only profess to be Christians—at the final judgment. To those who claimed to do great things in his name but who actually did evil, Jesus warns that he will say, "I never knew you. Away from me, you evildoers!" (Matt. 7:23, NIV). Imagine if the pastor of a megachurch or a religious teacher on television were to claim that, at the end of history, he was going to decide who would make it into God's heavenly Kingdom and who would not. Or try to picture me telling you, "On Judgment Day, it will all be up to me—I'm going to determine whether you go up or down!" That is something that no ordinary religious teacher would ever say.

Yet at the very end of the sermon (see Matt. 7:24-27), Jesus contrasts two kinds of people: Whoever listens to and applies what Jesus says is like a wise man who builds his house on a foundation of rock. Whoever refuses to do what Jesus says is like a fool who builds his house on sand. Notice Jesus does not say that the wise man bases his life on God's Word, which he, as a good teacher or prophet, is simply explaining to them. No, Jesus is not claiming to be a mere messenger, but the Source of the divine Word that must be the foundation of a person's life if he or she is to survive the Judgment. This explains the reaction of the people when they heard the Sermon on the Mount: "When Jesus had finished saying these things, the crowds were amazed at his teaching, for he taught with real authority—quite unlike their teachers of religious law" (vv. 28-29).

Jesus' claims often shocked his contemporaries, and understanding why will help us answer our friends' questions about him. For example, when people brought a paralyzed man to Jesus in a crowded house, Jesus looked at the man—whom he had probably never seen before—and forgave all his sins. Then, to prove to the religious leaders who were there—who were fretting that only God could forgive sins—that he had the authority to do so, Jesus healed the paralyzed man with a simple command (see Mark 2:1-12). Who has the ability both to forgive sins and to heal broken bodies? Only God alone! Jesus was making his true identity obvious. This is powerful information that we can show our friends in order to help them understand his true identity as well.

In addition, almost all biblical scholars agree that a basic element of Jesus' overall message was the Kingdom of God. References to God's "Kingdom" are characteristic of Jesus' speech in all four Gospels (with about 120 references). Jesus announced that in his ministry the Kingdom of God had drawn near (see Mark 1:15). He compared the Kingdom of God to a wedding—in which he was the bridegroom (see Mark 2:19-22)! In other words, Jesus claimed that the Kingdom of God was about him. Those who wished to gain entrance into that Kingdom needed to come, like little children, to him (see Mark 10:14-15).

Jesus is also the central figure in some of his own parables. For example, in his parable of the wicked vineyard tenants, the owner sent one employee after another to the vineyard to get some of the produce at harvest, but the tenants beat up or killed each of those employees. Finally, the owner sent his son—but the tenants killed him, too. When that happened, the owner went to the vineyard, destroyed the wicked tenants, and gave the vineyard to others (see Mark 12:1-12). In this parable, the vineyard owner represented God; the tenants represented the religious establishment in

Jerusalem; the employees abused by the tenants represented prophets, such as John the Baptist; and the son, of course, represented Jesus himself. Jesus could not have been clearer: he was not just another religious teacher or prophet, not just another of God's messengers, but God's unique "only begotten Son" (John 3:16, NASB), who shared the very nature of the Father.

Skeptics of the biblical view of Jesus have worked for two centuries trying to read between the lines of the Gospels to find a benign, nonthreatening Jesus who thought of himself merely as one of many religious teachers. They can't find one. Jesus saw himself as the King of the Kingdom of God, the Son whom God sent to his "vineyard" to put things right, the Lord whose word on all subjects was final, and the Judge who would determine where you and I will spend eternity.

On top of all this, look at just a few of the other things that Jesus, his disciples, and even his opponents said about his claims to deity in the Gospel of John:[6]

> The Jewish leaders began harassing Jesus for breaking the Sabbath rules. But Jesus replied, "My Father is always working, and so am I." So the Jewish leaders tried all the harder to find a way to kill him. For he not only broke the Sabbath, *he called God his Father, thereby making himself equal with God.* (John 5:16-18)

> [Jesus answered,] "Your father Abraham rejoiced as he looked forward to my coming. He saw it

and was glad." The people said, "You aren't even fifty years old. How can you say you have seen Abraham? Jesus answered, *"I tell you the truth, before Abraham was even born, I AM!"* At that point they picked up stones to throw at him. (John 8:56-59)

[Jesus replied,] *"The Father and I are one."* Once again the people picked up stones to kill him. Jesus said, "At my Father's direction I have done many good works. For which one are you going to stone me?" They replied, *"We're stoning you not for any good work, but for blasphemy! You, a mere man, claim to be God."* (John 10:30-33)

What's interesting is that in all these cases Jesus had ample opportunity to clear up any misunderstandings about what he was really saying (something that any "good teacher" would easily be able to do). He could have said, "Whoa, boys, put down those stones for a minute and tell me what you thought I was saying! . . . What? You thought I was claiming equality with God? Are you kidding? Let me set the record straight right here and now." But he never did that—in fact, he did just the opposite, reinforcing his claims—which further affirms that they really did understand what he was clearly saying: that he was the Son of God, true deity, and equal in nature to God the Father.

Once we see that Jesus made such claims about himself, this fact creates the greatest spiritual dilemma you, I, or our friends will ever face. We can accept the claims Jesus made, which means viewing him not merely as a great teacher but as God's Son and our King, Lord, and Judge. On the other hand, we can reject his claims, but that means rejecting him as any sort of good teacher. After all, anyone who went around making the kinds of claims Jesus made, if those claims were false, would be a terrible teacher and a false prophet—not to mention a flaky human being! C. S. Lewis made this point in one of his most memorable comments:

> *A man who was merely a man and said the sort of things Jesus said would not be a great moral teacher. He would either be a lunatic—on a level with the man who says he is a poached egg—or else he would be the Devil of Hell. You must make your choice. Either this man was, and is, the Son of God: or else a madman or something worse.*[7]

EVIDENCE THAT JESUS' CLAIMS ARE TRUE

We have seen that Jesus' earliest followers regarded him as the Messiah and Son of God and worshiped him as their Lord and Savior. We have also seen that Jesus made such claims for himself. The obvious question is whether these claims are true. Why should we believe them today? One of the best ways to answer this question is to ask another: just what was it that convinced Jesus' followers that he was the Messiah, Son of God, Lord of creation, and Savior of the world?

Ironically, the answer begins with the one historical fact about Jesus that virtually no historian disputes: his death. John Dominic Crossan, cofounder of the notorious Jesus Seminar, a group of scholars who promote highly skeptical views about Jesus, agrees: "Jesus' death by execution under Pontius Pilate is as sure as anything historical can be."[8] What makes the certainty of this historical event ironic is that, for a time, it seemed to be proof positive that Jesus could not have been the Messiah.

Crucifixion was a horrific method of execution that the Romans employed in order to inflict the greatest degree of suffering and humiliation on a victim. From a Jewish point of view, Jesus' death by crucifixion marked him as being under God's curse, because the Old Testament stated that "anyone who is hung on a tree is under God's curse" (Deut. 21:23, NIV). It would have seemed to Jesus' first followers, all of whom were Jewish, that they had been mistaken about Jesus, because anyone dying with God's curse on him could not possibly be the Messiah. They had hoped that Jesus was going to free them from the oppressive rule of the Romans (see Luke 24:21), but instead he had turned out to be yet another casualty of the Roman occupation. No wonder they were initially so down and dejected!

What convinced Jesus' followers that this man, whom God had seemingly cursed, was actually the Messiah, the Son of God? In a word, his resurrection. Just a few days after Jesus' crucifixion, a number of his closest followers, as well as some of his family members, became convinced that Jesus had physically risen from the dead. Jesus' resurrection convinced them that he had suffered his terrible death not because of anything he had done, but in order to free them from the curse that was on them—and on all of us—because of sin. As the apostle Paul put it in one of his earliest epistles, "When he was hung on the cross, he took upon himself the curse for our wrongdoing" (Gal. 3:13). Christianity did not begin with a group of people trying to remember and follow Jesus' teachings even though he was dead. It began with the belief that God had vindicated Jesus as the Messiah by raising him from the dead. This is why one would be completely mistaken to think that Jesus was a good teacher whose followers eventually developed a myth about his being the Son of God. There would *be* no Christian movement today if his original followers had not been convinced that he had really risen from the dead.

More than that, Jesus pinned his own authority on his ability to rise from the dead. See, for example, his response to the religious leaders when they challenged him to do a miracle to prove that he really was from God:

> "All right," Jesus replied. "Destroy this temple, and in three days I will raise it up." "What!" they exclaimed. "It has taken forty-six years to build this Temple, and you can rebuild it in three days?" But when Jesus said "this temple," he meant his own body. After he was raised from the dead, his disciples remembered he had said this, and they believed both the Scriptures and what Jesus had said. (John 2:19-22)

And another time, when they again asked him to prove his authority with a miracle, he replied,

> Only an evil, adulterous generation would demand a miraculous sign; but the only sign

> I will give them is the sign of the prophet Jonah.
> For as Jonah was in the belly of the great fish for
> three days and three nights, so will the Son of
> Man be in the heart of the earth for three days
> and three nights. (Matt. 12:39-40)

In both cases Jesus was alluding to his forthcoming death and resurrection, which, he claimed, would prove that he was who he claimed to be. So this is an important question: How do we know that Jesus really rose from the grave?

REASONS FOR BELIEVING THE REALITY OF THE RESURRECTION

Three facts give us sufficient evidence to conclude that the Resurrection is an actual historical event.

The first is one that no responsible historian denies that Jesus died on a Roman cross. You can forget about those sensational conspiracy theories that suggest Jesus survived the Crucifixion and escaped to another part of the world or that the Romans accidentally crucified the wrong guy or that Jesus never even existed and the church made up the whole story. There wouldn't be a church at all if Jesus had never existed or if any of these fanciful stories were true! Anyone who denies that Jesus was a real person and that the Romans crucified him bears the burden of proof—a burden that nobody can meet because the historical facts are weighted against them.

The second fact is that the tomb in which Jesus' body had been buried was found empty. Skeptical historians try to dispute this fact, but there are excellent historical reasons to accept it:

- All four Gospels report that the tomb belonged to Joseph of Arimathea (for example, Mark 15:43-46), a member of the Jewish court called the Sanhedrin, which had turned Jesus over to the Roman procurator Pontius Pilate for execution. It is very unlikely that Christians would have invented the detail that Jesus' body was buried in the tomb of a member of the council that had sought Jesus' execution.

- All four Gospels also report that the first people to discover the tomb to be empty were female followers of Jesus, including Mary Magdalene, a formerly demon-possessed woman (see Luke 8:2; 24:10). This is another detail that no Christian, making up a fictitious story about the resurrection of Jesus, would have invented— especially not in a culture that was reluctant to accept the testimonies of women because it did not consider them to be reliable witnesses.

- If Jesus' body had remained in the tomb, the belief in his resurrection would have had no credibility. The authorities could have easily exhumed his body and said, "Look, here's your dead Messiah and leader!" And if the whereabouts of his burial site had not been known—that is, if one denies the story of Joseph's tomb—then it is again unlikely that reports of his resurrection would be taken seriously by anyone.

For these reasons, we are on solid ground in concluding that the accounts of Mary Magdalene and other women finding the tomb empty are based on actual fact.

The third fact providing evidence for the Resurrection

is that soon after his death people had experiences that they were convinced were encounters with Jesus, who was alive after being dead. Historians rarely dispute this fact, though of course they may dispute that it was really Jesus those people saw. For example, liberal scholar E. P. Sanders admits, "That Jesus' followers (and later Paul) had resurrection experiences is, in my judgment, a fact. What the reality was that gave rise to the experiences I do not know."[9]

The people who said they saw Jesus alive after he died were a diverse group. It included women such as Mary Magdalene; men whom Jesus had appointed as his apostles (such as Peter and John); some of Jesus' family members, including his skeptical brother James, who had not been one of his original followers; and Saul of Tarsus, later known as Paul. The experience of Paul is especially difficult to explain away, since he was an aggressive enemy of Christianity who had tried to suppress the movement. Then, after what he claimed to be a personal encounter with the risen Jesus, he became Christianity's greatest missionary—spreading the gospel of Christ until he finally gave his life for it.

So, we have strong historical grounds to conclude that

1. Jesus died on a cross;
2. Jesus' tomb was found empty three days later; and
3. the risen Jesus was seen alive by a number of people—including skeptics—and in a variety of settings.

If Jesus' body had been buried in a tomb but later found to be missing, by itself this would be just an unsolved mystery.

The fact that people sincerely thought they saw Jesus alive from the dead might, by itself, be dismissed as hallucinations or religious visions (though these explanations have a hard time accounting for all the facts, especially for Paul's experience). If we put these facts together, however, by far the best explanation for them is that God really did raise Jesus from the dead[10]—and as a result, the Christian movement was launched in the very city where Christ was crucified, becoming what is today the largest religion in the world.

The evidence, then, shows clearly that Jesus was not just a good teacher whose moral values inspired his followers after his tragic death. The exalted view of Jesus in Christianity is not something later Christians made up or a mythology that developed over time. Jesus himself claimed to be a figure of cosmic importance, the Son of Man, destined to return one day on the clouds of heaven to be the Judge and Ruler of the whole world. His death seemed at first to discredit those claims, but then his empty tomb and his appearances to family members, friends, and even one of his most passionate opponents persuaded them that he was alive and really was who he claimed to be. So convinced were they that they dedicated the rest of their lives to spreading the message that Jesus was the Messiah, the true Son of God.

> *For in Christ lives all the fullness of God in a human body. So you also are complete through your union with Christ, who is the head over every ruler and authority.*
>
> —COLOSSIANS 2:9-10

SUMMARY OF THE ANSWER

Question 4 says this: "Everyone knows that Jesus was a good man and a wise teacher—but why try to make him into the Son of God, too?"

- Many people believe this is what happened: Jesus was given a "divine promotion" by his later followers. In other words, today Christians have an exalted view of Jesus that he never claimed for himself.

- History shows, contrary to that belief, that there was an early and dramatic explosion of devotion to Jesus as the divine Son of God—an explosion that points back to him and his teachings as its source.

- The New Testament record, including the earliest written as well as the later books, affirms that Jesus was believed to be the Messiah (or Christ), the Son of God, the Savior, the Lord, and God—and that Jesus' followers trusted in him, prayed to him, and worshiped him as such.

- Jesus affirmed this understanding by repeatedly referring to himself as the Son of Man, which was a clear allusion to the divine figure in the Old Testament book of Daniel, chapter 7.

- Jesus taught with authority like no other human, expected loyalty and devotion to himself (along with the Father), and predicted that he would ultimately judge every person based on what they did with his teachings.

- Jesus made multiple claims to equality with the Father, and he never sought to change the perceptions of his listeners to that end, even when they were hostile and threatening to kill him.

- Jesus predicted that all his claims would be proven true by his impending death and resurrection—and then both of these events actually happened (as evidenced by the empty tomb and his appearances to friend and foe alike).

TIPS FOR TALKING ABOUT THIS ISSUE

- Many people have theories about who Jesus was and what he taught, but they have never really studied these matters for themselves. Their opinions are often based on things they've heard or seen, including fictional sources such as novels, television shows, or movies. We should listen to their views, remembering that many of these views are held deeply, but we should also encourage them to take some time to look into these matters. The best place to start is with the New Testament itself, reading in the four Gospels what Jesus actually taught. My constant plea with people is to "let Jesus speak for himself."

- Beyond reading the Bible, I suggest reading books such as Lee Strobel's *The Case for Christ* and *The Case for the Real Jesus*; Josh and Sean McDowell's updated *More Than a Carpenter*; and my earlier book, *Choosing Your Faith . . . In a World of Spiritual Options*. These books provide good introductions to who Jesus is and how we can be confident in the claims that he made about himself. Also, at a bit deeper level, I recommend *Putting*

Jesus in His Place: The Case for the Deity of Christ, by Robert M. Bowman Jr. and J. Ed Komoszewski.

- In this chapter I've given answers that you can use in talking to your friends. You can repeat those answers, or perhaps ask your friends to read this chapter. Keep in mind that when we quote the Gospels we're presenting them as what they are at minimum: a historical record about the life and teachings of Jesus. That means that your friends can respect and learn from the Gospel report without first having to decide whether the Gospels are the inspired Word of God (we hope that they will someday reach that conclusion, but it's not a prerequisite).

- Even if your friends are skeptical, it's good to encourage them to keep an open mind and even to approach this information with a simple prayer. A good model is the man who vulnerably told Jesus, in Mark 9:24, "I do believe, but help me overcome my unbelief!" God answered that doubter's prayer, and the man received from Jesus what he was looking for.

- It is important for us to remember, and to impress gently upon your friends, that if Jesus is who he claimed to be, then understanding and embracing what he taught is a really big deal. Listen to his sobering words in John 8:24: "That is why I said that you will die in your sins; for unless you believe that I Am who I claim to be, you will die in your sins." Knowing and acknowledging Jesus' divine identity is not an academic theological point. It's the first step toward receiving his salvation!

QUESTIONS FOR GROUP DISCUSSION

1. What did you believe about Jesus as you grew up? Have your views changed? If so, why?

2. What is the most convincing evidence for you that Jesus truly is the Son of God, deity incarnate in humanity?

3. What are the most serious challenges you've heard to the teaching that Jesus really is God in human flesh? What did you do (or can you do) to address those challenges and bolster your own confidence?

4. How might your answer to the previous question prepare you to help your friends understand the reality of who Jesus is?

5. Imagine you're in a conversation with a friend who, after some discussion, finally acknowledges that Jesus seems to be more than a man and probably is the Son of God. What could you say next to help your friend take steps toward actually receiving Christ as his or her own Savior?

CHAPTER 5:

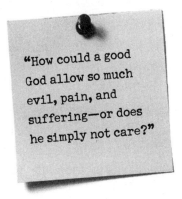

"How could a good God allow so much evil, pain, and suffering—or does he simply not care?"

"Why did this happen to me?"

Emma Jean's question seemed simple enough. Our little toddler was about four years old. She had been skipping happily along the sidewalk in front of our home, thrilled to be wearing the brand new tennis shoes that Heidi and I had just given her. Sadly, though, in the middle of her carefree stroll her shoe caught on an uneven seam in the cement, which sent her tumbling headlong onto the hard concrete surface. I rushed over to see if she was okay.

The look on her face showed shock and disbelief, followed immediately by a display of pain. Then, as the tears began to flow, she blurted out her question: *"Why?"*

Obviously, Emma Jean's trauma was mild compared to the kinds of pain and suffering many people have to deal with—not to mention the truly catastrophic events that devastate or destroy lives every day around our planet, leaving many in their wake wondering, *How could a good God allow so much evil, pain, and suffering—or does he simply not care?*

This issue easily made our top ten list of questions that Christians hope no one will ask, tying with several others for fifth place. But in another Barna survey taken among both Christians and nonbelievers, this one came out number one—by a considerable margin.[1] In fact, this is generally considered to be the number one issue causing people to doubt or disbelieve the existence of God, and it has been so for millennia. How we respond is vitally important for the spiritual progress of a lot of people we'll encounter—including some of our close friends and family members.

THE QUESTION THAT'S NOT ALWAYS A QUESTION

Here's what is interesting. Often people will say words that sound like questions, but they're really not. Emma Jean, for example, asked me several times during her little ordeal, "Why? Why did this happen to me?"—but she really wasn't looking for an explanation.

It wouldn't have helped her much if I had started explaining to her that she had on new shoes that were still rigid and not yet rounded on the front edges of their soles, making them more susceptible to catching the raised edges of the sidewalk, and that she therefore needed to pick up her feet a bit more when skipping down the sidewalk in order to prevent further incidents, and so on. That would have been an accurate description of why this happened to her as well as what she could do to prevent it from recurring, even though it certainly wasn't what she was hoping for! That's because, in effect, she was verbalizing a question but really was crying out for help and comfort—which we immediately gave her in ample measure.

This is a pretty good picture of the situation of many people who are hurting and who almost reflexively raise the question "Why?" My initial suggestion for addressing this topic is to realize that when your friends are experiencing pain they are probably not asking for explanations as much as they're looking for empathy, concern, and tangible expressions of love. They may be asking, "Where was God?" but mostly be wondering, *You say you know God; will you show me his kind of love and care?*

The Bible hints at this issue in James 2:15-16: "Suppose you see a brother or sister who has no food or clothing, and you say, 'Good-bye and have a good day; stay warm and eat well'—but then you don't give that person any food or clothing. What good does that do?" And 1 John 3:18-19 tells us, "Dear children, let's not merely say that we love each other; let us show the truth by our actions. Our actions will show that we belong to the truth."

When someone is in shock and pain because something bad just happened, we're wise to hold off from trying to answer any questions or offering some kind of rationale for why we think God allows such things—valid as those thoughts may be. It's better to delay those conversations by saying something like, "Well, that's a really good question that we can talk about sometime, but I'm pretty sure what you need most right now is not a deep philosophical discussion about pain and suffering. Let's talk about that later. For now, how can I help you get through this?"

Though there's a lot more to discuss about how to approach this issue, I do think it's important, first, to have the philosophical discussion ourselves. The following section, therefore, is for us as Christians to help us gain a deeper understanding of these matters, whether or not all are points that we'll actually discuss in our conversations with our friends.

THE PROBLEM OF EVIL

Here's the way the issue is often laid out, especially by those who have given it some serious thought: There are three teachings in the Bible that don't seem to fit together. The first one is that *God is good,* which means that he is absolutely pure, hates evil, and has to deal with everything that is in rebellion to him. The second is that *God is great,* which means he is all-powerful and he can conquer anything that challenges him. The third is that *evil is real,* which means there are, in fact, things out there that are in rebellion to him and that are at this very moment challenging him.

This is a problem because, as God, he certainly would know about the evil. And if he is really good, then he would condemn and want to do something about the evil. And if he is truly great—that is, if he is all-powerful—then he would follow through and actually do what his goodness demands: destroy the evil.

Do you see the problem? As Christians we believe God is good and he is great, and yet evil still exists—on a grand scale. What are we to make of this conundrum?

There are several "solutions" to this problem that people have proposed. We'll look at four.

Solution 1: Deny God's existence—and, with it, the reality of evil

The first seems simple enough: *deny God's existence.* In

other words, if God is good and great, then he would surely destroy evil, but since evil is not destroyed, there must be no God.

Besides the fact that this conclusion flies in the face of all the evidence for God's existence (see the first chapter), there's another big problem that a lot of people seem to miss: as soon as you throw out the idea of God, you've also thrown out the meaning of evil. In other words, in an atheistic universe there is no actual good or evil, and therefore no absolute standard by which to judge anything as being ultimately right or wrong. So all we are left with are preferences. I have mine. You have yours. Rape and murder may not be my cup of tea, but they may be somebody else's—and who are we to say that what others do is wrong? And who are they to judge what we're doing? In fact, serial killer Ted Bundy said it like this in an interview prior to his execution:

> *I learned that all moral judgments are "value judgments," that all values are subjective, and that none can be proved to be either "right" or "wrong."*
> *. . . I discovered that to become truly free, truly unfettered, I had to become truly uninhibited. And I quickly discovered that the greatest obstacle to my freedom, the greatest block and limitation to it, consists in the insupportable "value judgment" that I was bound to respect the rights of others. . . .*
>
> *Surely, you would not, in this age of scientific enlightenment, declare that God or nature has marked some pleasures as "moral" or "good" and others as "immoral" or "bad"?*[2]

This was from a man who lived out his philosophy by raping and murdering more than thirty women and girls. Christian philosopher Chad Meister quoted these statements from Bundy, then said, "The question I have for the atheist is simply this: *On what moral grounds can you provide a response to Bundy?* The atheistic options are limited. If morality has nothing to do with God, as atheists suppose, what does it have to do with?"[3]

Indeed, atheist writer John D. Steinrucken, whose article "Secularism's Ongoing Debt to Christianity" we quoted in the first chapter, acknowledges this reality when he challenges his fellow skeptics to come up with "the immutable moral laws of secularism," and goes on to admit that there simply are none.[4]

Now, certainly we can and do make up rules and laws to try to help us get along with one another. But if these rules and laws are not grounded in any objective reality or standards beyond mere human opinion, then what makes them right versus wrong? They're just codified human preferences.

And let's not forget that entire societies can go wrong. Adolf Hitler and Saddam Hussein, for example, had their "preferences," which they foisted on their nations. So when Hussein and his henchmen gassed whole villages of Kurds or when Hitler and his Nazi thugs tried to exterminate the entire Jewish race, there's nothing we can say in an atheistic universe that condemns them as genuinely wrong. We can say we don't like it and we can fight to try to stop it, but we're left with the unanswerable question, "Why accept our values over theirs?"

C. S. Lewis was once an atheist who was convinced

that because of the problem of evil there could be no God. But then he realized what we've just said—that if there is no God, then nothing can really be considered evil—and his whole argument against God fell apart. Lewis once asked, "If a good God made the world, why has it gone wrong?"[5] Here's the answer he later gave:

> My argument against God was that the universe seemed so cruel and unjust. But how had I got this idea of just and unjust? A man does not call a line crooked unless he has some idea of a straight line. What was I comparing this universe with when I called it unjust? If the whole show was bad and senseless from A to Z, so to speak, why did I, who was supposed to be part of the show, find myself in such violent reaction against it?
>
> . . . Thus in the very act of trying to prove that God did not exist—in other words, that the whole of reality was senseless—I found I was forced to assume that one part of reality—namely my idea of justice—was full of sense. Consequently, atheism turns out to be too simple. If the whole universe has no meaning, we should never have found out that it has no meaning: just as, if there were no light in the universe and therefore no creatures with eyes, we should never know it was dark. Dark would be without meaning.[6]

And so, ironically, the very problem that had caused C. S. Lewis to disbelieve in God ended up changing his

mind and forcing him to see that there *had* to be a God—
One who established the standard by which we inevitably
know and judge good and evil. This was a vital step in
Lewis's fascinating journey toward faith in Christ.

This is what we can help our friends understand as well.
If all we have is a human race that evolved by chance without
a God in the picture, then there is no absolute standard. And
if there's no absolute standard, then there is no real evil.

Yet we know—unmistakably and undeniably—that
evil is real and that some things, whether legalized and legit-
imized by society or not, are simply wrong. Murder, rape,
confiscating people's property—let alone gassing villages or
committing genocide—are horrors that are impossible to
justify (try as some people or certain regimes might). And
if evil is real, if it truly goes against a set of universal moral
standards (as we show in chapter one), it is a powerful indi-
cator that there must be a transcendent moral lawgiver.

Therefore, it turns out that the reality of evil, rather
than being an argument *against* God, is yet another reason
to believe he *does* indeed exist!

Solution 2: Make evil part of God—thus deifying it

The second proposed solution is to *deify evil*. This comes
primarily through Eastern thought, especially Hinduism and
Buddhism, and through New Age teachings in the West.
Everything is part of God, these religions tell us—so this thing
we call evil is actually, as we saw in the Eastern-influenced
story of *Star Wars*, just the "dark side of the force."

But if everything is part of god—not a personal God
as the Bible teaches, but an all-encompassing impersonal

god as is taught in these pantheistic worldviews—then evil and suffering are part of that god too. This is the very god, or ultimate reality, that Eastern philosophy says we're supposed to become more like and to ultimately merge and become one with. So this becomes a tremendous problem: we're supposed to join with the very thing that contains evil within itself!

Solution 3: Diminish God's power

The third proposed solution is to *deny God's greatness*. This viewpoint says that God does exist but is limited. He is good and he sees the evil, but he lacks the power to do much about it. This teaching often comes through various strains of liberal Christian theology, including a school of thought known as process theology. This teaches that God himself is a growing, changing being who is caught up in the struggle against evil, and he has only the power of persuasion to aid him in his efforts to, hopefully, win out one day over it.

We see this idea that God is not all-powerful at a popular level in the best-selling book *When Bad Things Happen to Good People,* by Rabbi Harold Kushner. Kushner explains his belief: "God wants the righteous to live peaceful, happy lives, but sometimes even He can't bring that about. It is too difficult even for God to keep cruelty and chaos from claiming their innocent victims."[7] Kushner tellingly titled one of the chapters in that book, "God Can't Do Everything, but He Can Do Some Important Things."[8]

There are major problems with this teaching. First, it denies again the evidence that we looked at in the first chapter, which shows that God is a powerful being who created the universe and who built incredible, life-giving order into this universe. It also denies what the Bible tells us—in both the Old Testament (including the Jewish Torah) and the New Testament—about a God who is unlimited in his power; who is unchanging; and who has Satan, the ultimate embodiment of evil, under his feet, ready to crush him at any moment (see Rev. 20). King David said, for example: "Yours, O Lord, is the greatness, the power, the glory, the victory, and the majesty. Everything in the heavens and on earth is yours" (1 Chron. 29:11). And Jesus taught that "with God everything is possible" (Matt. 19:26). In addition, for us personally it creates the tremendous problem of wondering why we should trust and worship a god like Rabbi Kushner's. I mean, are we helping him or is he helping us? How can we know that ultimately there will be any victory over evil? If God is limited, how do we know anything solid about the future? This is simply a weak and unbiblical attempt to explain evil.

Solution 4: Diminish God's goodness

The fourth proposed solution to the problem of evil is to *deny God's goodness*. This viewpoint suggests that God knows about evil and has the power to vanquish it, but apparently doesn't care enough to deal with it. He lacks the goodness to take action, letting evil just go on.

On the face of it, most of us would reject this position—out loud, at least. But truth be told, a lot of people in the midst of pain and suffering are, consciously or unconsciously, tempted to flirt with this idea. They've privately shaken their fists at God and said to themselves, "He must not be good;

he must not care; he must not be loving—why else would I be going through this?"

During those difficult times, it's easy to overlook all the ways God *has* been good to us. It's common in the middle of a drought, for example, to forget that rain is the norm. Or in the middle of a flood to forget that floods rarely happen. Or when bad news comes from the doctor to forget that, for most of us, this comes after many years of relatively good health. In fact, many people ignore God and live for decades as if he doesn't exist, then they encounter a serious problem in their lives and get mad at the God they've been ignoring—as if he owes them something.

Yes, bad things happen, but a lot of good things do, too. Some thinkers have even argued what they call the problem of good, pointing out that if evil in the world is supposed to be evidence *against* God, then life, love, beauty, and blessings in the world are evidence *for* God. Maybe this is one of the reasons the Bible stresses the importance of gratitude—so we'll remember God's many acts of goodness in our lives during those times when we're tempted to focus only on our difficulties or suffering.

As the Scripture says, "Don't worry about anything; instead, pray about everything. Tell God what you need, *and thank him for all he has done.* Then you will experience God's peace, which exceeds anything we can understand" (Phil. 4:6-7, emphasis mine). In addition, we have the recorded revelations all through the Bible (the book with supernatural credentials—see chapter 3) that assure us God is good. And the historical record of God's patient dealings with his people certainly bears out those claims.

LIVING IN THE TENSION

Having looked at the four commonly proposed solutions, I'd like to offer what I am convinced is a vastly better option: to live in the tension and accept that *there is a God*—One who is *good*, who is *great*, and who nevertheless *allows real evil in our world* for a season and for his greater purposes.[9] Put another way, it's preferable to have a *problem* of evil over a *denial* of evil (by denying God's existence—first solution), a *deification* of evil (by making evil part of God—second solution), or a *dumbing down* of what the evidence tells us about God's nature (third and fourth solutions). The smaller problems of biblical belief are far easier to live with than the big problems of any of these denials.

It's also wise to admit to ourselves that we don't have a simplistic solution that wraps this problem up in a neat bow and makes everyone feel good. In fact, there's nothing we can say to make people suddenly okay with the evil around them or the suffering in their lives. Because—let's be honest—we're not okay with it, either!

That said, there are some practical thoughts that we can offer to our friends to show them that Christianity offers the most satisfying answers to this problem. Let's look at those next.

ADDRESSING THE QUESTION WITH OUR FRIENDS

My friend and teaching partner, Lee Strobel, once spoke at a church about this issue of evil and suffering in our lives, and he started his talk with this insightful illustration:

> *Leslie and I were driving to Door County, Wisconsin. We were on Highway 42 at night*

*when it started raining heavily and we hit dense
fog. I could barely see the white stripe on the edge
of the road. I didn't stop, because I was afraid
someone might come along and rear-end us, so
I just crept along.*

*But then a truck appeared in front of us and
we could see his taillights through the fog. He
apparently had fog lights out front, because he was
traveling at a confident and deliberate pace, and I
knew if we could just follow those taillights, we'd be
headed in the right direction.*

*And the same is true in understanding why
there is evil and suffering in our world. We may
not be able to make out all the peripheral details of
why—those may be obscured from our view—but
there are some points of light that can illuminate
a few key biblical truths for us. And if we follow
those lights, they will lead us in the right direction,
toward some conclusions that I believe can satisfy
our souls.*[10]

It's encouraging to know that in the midst of even a
heavy fog of uncertainty, we can find some "points of light"
to give us direction. What are those points of light? Let
me share seven of them that I've found personally helpful
and that have also proven effective in talking with people
who are troubled by these matters. I trust you'll find them
useful in your own conversations, too, as you try to help
friends who feel as if they are also "in the fog" regarding
this issue.

First point of light: the world is as Jesus predicted

Once you've determined that the person who is asking you the question is not giving a cry for help and comfort, as we discussed at the beginning of the chapter, you might convey this simple thought: though the problem of pain and suffering does present challenges to the Christian faith, it's worth pointing out that these problems reflect exactly the kind of world Jesus told us we would live in. He said, "I have told you all this so that you may have peace in me. *Here on earth you will have many trials and sorrows*" (John 16:33, emphasis mine).

I point out to my friends that Jesus was telling the truth—and that the pain and evil they are asking about are actually evidence that show *he was right!* And the daily news proves him right over and over again. This is especially significant when you realize that many religious teachers have gotten this wrong. For example, Mary Baker Eddy, the founder of Christian Science, wrote,

> *Christian Science raises the standard of liberty and cries: "Follow me! Escape the bondage of sickness, sin, and death!" . . . The illusion of material sense, not divine law, has bound you, entangled your free limbs, crippled your capacities, enfeebled your body, and defaced the tablet of your being. . . . If sickness and sin are illusions, the awakening from this mortal dream, or illusion, will bring us into health, holiness, and immortality.* [11]

In Eddy's teaching, sickness, sin, and death are illusory ideas that must be overcome by the mind. This led her to teach her followers to reject medicine and medical procedures—which has, in turn, led many of them over the years to deny reality and with it the very remedies that might have helped or even saved them (and their children).

In a similar vein, New Age gurus teach a "mind over matter" approach to life in general, saying that you can create your own reality by what you focus on in your mind. Deb Bostwick tried to live out that philosophy—and it seemed to be working for her, because for many years she made a living through her highly successful New Age bookstore. Then one day the bookstore burned to the ground. Deb describes her thoughts that day, standing in the ankle-deep, sooty water that had been used to put out the raging fire: "I said, 'Wait a minute; I don't remember creating *this* reality for myself!'" The wake-up call was her first step toward rejecting a philosophy that denied reality and toward embracing the truth and teachings of Jesus. Today she is a committed Christian.[12]

More examples could be given, but aren't you glad Jesus didn't sugarcoat the truth? He just came out and said it like it is. He accurately predicted that we would have "many trials and sorrows"—but he didn't stop there. He also offered his assistance in getting through them: "Take heart, because I have overcome the world" (John 16:33).

Second point of light: evil was not created or caused by God

Some people reason that if God created everything, and evil exists, then God must have created evil. There are several ways to address this challenge, but I think the following is the most straightforward.

God did not create evil, but he did create human beings who could truly love and follow him. And inherent in what it means to be human and able to truly love is the ability to go the other way—to *not* love or follow God. That was the choice humans made, starting with the original couple, Adam and Eve, and that choice has been repeated down through the human race—all the way to you, me, and the friends we hope to reach.

Let's look at this in a little more depth: the ability to love always entails the ability to *not* love. If we didn't have the ability to not love, we would be robots or puppets—preprogrammed to go through the motions, perhaps, of what love would look like, but never being able to express the real thing. For example, the love of my wife, Heidi, means a lot to me because she didn't *have* to love me. There were lots of other guys out there whom she could have chosen and married; however, for some (inexplicable) reason, she chose me—and I'll be forever grateful! Similarly, the love of my parents, the love of my siblings, the love of my children, the love of my friends—all this means so much because they all freely choose to express their love even though they don't have to. The same is true in your life as well.

Real love can never be forced. The idea of "forced love" is actually an oxymoron—a contradiction in terms. Either it's *forced* or it's *love*, but it can't be both because real love is always, by definition, freely chosen. Author and professor Norman Geisler takes this one step further. He explains, "Since God is love, he cannot force himself on anyone against their will. Forced love is not love; it is rape. And God is not a divine rapist. Love must work persuasively but not coercively."[13]

The upshot of this is that God did not create evil, but he did create us as free beings, and thus he created the *potential* for evil. We unfortunately actualized that potential (as did Lucifer and the other fallen angels before us; see Isaiah 14 and Ezekiel 28 for what appear to be allusions to this prior event), and evil entered the human race. God knew this would happen; however, he proceeded with Creation because he also knew that greater good would come of it—including the fact that many of us would choose to turn around and go against the grain of typical human rebellion in order to love and follow him.

Third point of light: the cause behind most suffering is human

A by-product of what we just discussed—that God created us free beings who could choose to follow or not follow him—is that we live in a world where people do what they want to do, and therefore all kinds of sin, abuse, and damage occur. This moral evil leads to untold volumes of human pain and suffering. In fact, a commonly estimated figure is that as much as 90 percent of the suffering in the world comes through human causes: wars, genocide, human trafficking, murders, torture, racial discrimination, domestic abuse, sexual abuse, rape, and the list goes on. God didn't want any of this, and he warns us against it all—in many Scriptures, including the Ten Commandments, which he gave to keep us from sin and to protect us from one another.

In his book *What's So Great about Christianity*, Dinesh

D'Souza explains the hard-to-fathom news that "in the past hundred years or so, the most powerful atheist regimes— Communist Russia, Communist China, and Nazi Germany— have wiped out people in astronomical numbers. . . . Focusing only on the big three—Stalin, Hitler, and Mao—we have to recognize that atheist regimes have in a single century murdered more than one hundred million people."[14] What we humans do to one another truly is mind-boggling. No natural disasters on record have come even close to causing that level of devastation and death.

Interestingly, some people hear these kinds of statistics and say that God ought to just put his foot down and stop all the madness. When I hear someone say this, I like to ask them which freedoms they think God ought to take away from us right now. Usually people get a bit more reflective when they realize that "stopping all the evil" in this fallen, sinful world would entail taking away our human liberty as well as stopping all of us in our tracks—the people who to one degree or another are right now actively participating in that evil that "must be stopped."

So, as the saying goes, people hate the effect but nurture the cause. And until God finally does put a stop to it, as he assures us he will, they continue to perpetuate the problem, wreaking more and more destruction on increasing numbers of human lives.

Fourth point of light: we live in a fallen world

A by-product of the *moral evil* that has infected the human race is the *natural evil* that has affected the world around us. That is, when Adam and Eve sinned, the results were cataclysmic—not just for them and their immediate off-spring, but for the whole of humanity and for the entire cosmos. Genesis 3 tells us that as a result of their sin God cursed the serpent, Eve, Adam, and the ground itself, causing thorns and thistles and intensifying the labor it would take to draw food from it. Beyond those specifics, it becomes obvious when you read about what unfolded after that sadly eventful day that the entire relationship between God and people and the relationships between people and other people were gravely impaired.

In fact, things have never been the same since then. As the apostle Paul describes it, "All creation is waiting eagerly for that future day when God will reveal who his children really are. Against its will, all creation was subjected to God's curse. But with eager hope, the creation looks forward to the day when it will join God's children in glorious freedom from death and decay" (Rom. 8:19-21).

In the meantime, there is death and decay throughout the world from many sources, including hurricanes, earthquakes, tsunamis, tornadoes, floods, fires, and other natural disasters—things the insurance companies have traditionally lumped together under the heading "Acts of God"—as well as unintentional yet harmful accidents and events. These affect people the world over, usually indiscriminately.

We should recognize this natural evil and its roots in the moral failure of humankind—but without ascribing each incident of suffering to a specific sin or action. Often we Christians are tempted to say, "Well, *this* happened because of *that*"—and blame the disaster on the activities of a particular person or on the religion or politics of that particular region. Short of an undeniable prophetic revelation from God himself, we should refrain from making such pronouncements. They almost always discredit the person who says them, and they disturb and hurt a lot of other people with words that may not be true at all—and make them much less willing to listen to the Good News that we are called to share with them.

Jesus corrected this kind of thinking, which was apparently as rampant in his day as it is in ours, in Luke 13:1-5:

> About this time Jesus was informed that Pilate had murdered some people from Galilee as they were offering sacrifices at the Temple. "Do you think those Galileans were worse sinners than all the other people from Galilee?" Jesus asked. "Is that why they suffered? Not at all! And you will perish, too, unless you repent of your sins and turn to God. And what about the eighteen people who died when the tower in Siloam fell on them? Were they the worst sinners in Jerusalem? No, and I tell you again that unless you repent, you will perish, too."

We all live in a fallen world that is not as God intended or originally created it. In this world things go wrong and hurt righteous and unrighteous people alike. Things right now are not normal and, no, life is not always fair. Yes, God can and thankfully sometimes does protect his people from the evils that might have befallen them—but he gives no guarantee that he will always do so. For reasons only he understands, he sometimes allows bad things to happen to his much-loved people.

Fifth point of light: God will finally judge evil

As mentioned earlier, people often assess the evil and suffering in the world and reach the speedy conclusion that if God were good and great, he would certainly extend his strong arm to stop the bad things that are happening. And since he has not done so yet—at least not in a comprehensive way—they conclude that he must not exist or that, if he does exist, he must not be all that good or great.

What they overlook is the fact that God promises he *will* vanquish and judge evil but simply hasn't done so *yet.* The theme of God's justice and of the final day of reckoning at the great judgment is a well-established biblical reality. But mercifully, the Bible also reveals a God who is patient.

For example, God said to Moses, "I am slow to anger and filled with unfailing love and faithfulness. I lavish unfailing love to a thousand generations. I forgive iniquity, rebellion, and sin. But I do not excuse the guilty" (Exod. 34:6-7). And in the Psalms David said of God, "You, O Lord, are a God of compassion and mercy, slow to get angry and filled with unfailing love and faithfulness" (Ps. 86:15).

And why is God so slow to anger? The apostle Peter explains, "The Lord is not slow in keeping his promise, as some understand slowness. *He is patient with you, not wanting anyone to perish, but everyone to come to repentance*" (2 Pet. 3:9, NIV, emphasis mine). Thankfully, the God we worship is good, great, and ready to judge evil when it's time to do so—but in the meantime, he's graciously waiting for more of our friends (including those who ask us such difficult questions!) to reject the evil in their own lives and turn to follow him.

Sixth point of light: God suffered too

It's important to remember—and to remind our friends— that the God who allows us to suffer for a season in this fallen world also came to this world as one of us, in Jesus, and suffered in ways none of us ever will. Paul explains in Philippians 2:6-8 concerning Jesus,

> Though he was God,
>   he did not think of equality with God
>   as something to cling to.
> Instead, he gave up his divine privileges;
>   he took the humble position of a slave
>   and was born as a human being.
> When he appeared in human form,
>   he humbled himself in obedience to God
>   and died a criminal's death on a cross.

It is impossible for us to comprehend what Jesus, who existed in the Godhead as the second person of the Trinity for all eternity, gave up in order to become one of us—let alone to suffer "a criminal's death on a cross" while taking upon himself the sins of the entire world. But suffice it to say that when it comes to human suffering, *he gets it!* He fully understands what we're going through. The writer of Hebrews explains this about Jesus:

It was necessary for him to be made in every respect like us, his brothers and sisters, so that he could be our merciful and faithful High Priest before God. Then he could offer a sacrifice that would take away the sins of the people. *Since he himself has gone through suffering and testing, he is able to help us when we are being tested.*

. . . So then, since we have a great High Priest who has entered heaven, Jesus the Son of God, let us hold firmly to what we believe. *This High Priest of ours understands our weaknesses, for he faced all of the same testings we do,* yet he did not sin. So let us come boldly to the throne of our gracious God. There we will receive his mercy, and we will find grace to help us when we need it most. (Heb. 2:17-18; 4:14-16, emphases mine)

This is great news for us—and for everyone we talk to. The God who cursed the world came to that world and became a curse *for* us[15]—and he offers his comfort and help to all who will reach out to him and receive them.

Seventh point of light: God can bring good out of bad

Finally, the Bible offers us good news related to evil and suffering. God, through the apostle Paul, promises us that he "causes everything to work together for the good of those who love God and are called according to his purpose for them" (Rom. 8:28).

This is one of the most encouraging verses in the

Bible—and also one of the most abused. First, it does not say that everything that happens *is* good. Rather, it acknowledges the reality that many things that happen in our lives are bad, but it assures us that God can use them for good or bring good out of them. Second, it does not promise that God will always let us see the good right away; many suffering people strain for a long time to see anything positive about their suffering, and even then only glimpse it from a distance—if at all. In other words, God can bring out good that we don't recognize. And third, the verse does not promise that God will bring good out of bad for everybody, but only for those "who love God and are called according to his purpose"— that is, for true Christians who are sincerely walking with Christ.

With those qualifiers understood, it is encouraging when we take this promise to heart and realize that God is always at work in our lives as followers of Jesus, taking the things that are bad and bringing good out of their wake, and realize that he offers to do this for everyone we talk to if they'll just turn and follow him as well.

What are some of those good things? Here are just a few examples:

- *He can use pain to deepen our character.* Romans 5:3-4 says, "We can rejoice, too, when we run into problems and trials, for we know that they help us develop endurance. And endurance develops strength of character, and character strengthens our confident hope of salvation."

- *He can use pain to reshape us as his sons and daughters.* Hebrews 12:10-11 assures us that "God's discipline

is always good for us, so that we might share in
his holiness. No discipline is enjoyable while it is
happening—it's painful! But afterward there will be
a peaceful harvest of right living for those who are
trained in this way."

- *He can use pain to give us a more spiritual and eternal
  perspective.* Paul says in 2 Corinthians 4:16-18, "Though
  our bodies are dying, our spirits are being renewed every
  day. For our present troubles are small and won't last
  very long. Yet they produce for us a glory that vastly
  outweighs them and will last forever! So we don't look at
  the troubles we can see now; rather, we fix our gaze on
  things that cannot be seen. For the things we see now
  will soon be gone, but the things we cannot see will last
  forever."

- *He can use pain to protect us from ourselves.* Philip Yancey,
  in his classic book *Where Is God When It Hurts?* reports
  on the discoveries that Dr. Paul Brand made about the
  dreaded disease of leprosy. This sickness conjures up
  images of "stubby fingers, ulcerous wounds, missing legs,
  distorted facial features." Yancey explains that leprosy
  "is indeed cruel, but not in the manner of most diseases.
  Mostly it works like an anesthetic, attacking the pain
  cells of hands, feet, nose, ears, and eyes to produce
  numbness. . . . In virtually all cases leprosy only numbs
  the extremities. Tissue damage results solely because the
  warning system of pain has fallen silent."[16] So, in effect,
  leprosy sufferers damage and maim *themselves*, because
  they lack the warning system that pain normally

provides. This is a strong example of how "the gift of pain" can protect us from greater harm.

- *He can use pain to grab our attention and teach or redirect us in ways that will be important in our lives.* As C. S. Lewis famously said, "God whispers to us in our pleasures, speaks in our conscience, but shouts in our pain: it is His megaphone to rouse a deaf world."[17] God is willing to use pain if that's what it takes to rouse us and the people around us.

- *He can use pain to lead us to himself.* I heard an extreme example of this principle years ago from Ron, a friend at my church, who had visited a man in the hospital with a recently discovered brain cancer. At first bitter and angry at God, this man gradually came to see that he would have never stopped ignoring God were it not for contracting this terrible disease. After several visits and lots of reflection, this man finally gave his life to Christ. He said to Ron, with tears in his eyes, that he could now totally accept the cancer because it was his only way to find God's love. The two men even prayed together, thanking God for the disease that led to salvation. That man is in heaven today because of the pain God allowed to enter his life.

Let's go back once again to Highway 42 and Lee and Leslie Strobel's trip to Wisconsin:

We were following the taillights of that truck, when slowly the fog began to lift, the rain began to let

up, and we entered a town with some lights—and
there, as we rounded a curve, silhouetted against the
night sky, was the steeple of a church and the cross
of Christ.

And it's the Cross that gives ultimate meaning to our suffering, because it tells us we do not have to suffer alone; Jesus suffers along with us. Psalm 34:18 (NIV) says, "The LORD is close to the brokenhearted and saves those who are crushed in spirit."

Questioning the notion that God is full of love
Is a tempting road to take when you forget about
*   His blood.*
But I choose to still believe Him, His heart is kind
*   and just,*
I'm only seeing half the picture, for the other half
*   I'll trust.*

—MUSIC GROUP DAILY PLANET,
"QUESTIONING THE NOTION"

SUMMARY OF THE ANSWER

Question 5 asks us, "How could a good God allow so much evil, pain, and suffering—or does he simply not care?"

- Many times when people ask this question, they are in the midst of great suffering. At that moment they are not looking for a theological treatise; instead, they are asking for empathy, concern, and tangible expressions of love and care. If this seems to be the case, we should hold off with our attempts to answer and simply come alongside to help them through their difficulties.

- It is important to help our friends see that Jesus himself warned us we would all face trials and suffering. This illustrates that Christianity is a real-world faith that tells the truth about the world we live in.

- As Christians, we believe in three seemingly incompatible truths—God is good, God is great, and evil is real. Because these three truths don't seem to go together, many have attempted to solve this problem by denying God's existence (and with it, denying evil), by making evil part of God, or by denying God's goodness or his greatness. But these "solutions" fly in the face of the evidence and of the truth of God's Word.

- The illustration of driving in the fog and following the taillights of a vehicle ahead helps us see that sometimes we cannot understand what is happening around us, but if we focus on the truth that we *do* know, we will stay on a safe path.

- Evil was not created by God; instead, he gave us a

choice. We can choose to follow him, or we can choose sin and evil. Much of the suffering people face in this world has been caused by humans hurting their fellow humans. Sin also affects nature. "Natural" catastrophes occur because we live in a fallen world that is not the way God intended it to be.

- People desire a place without suffering—and God has promised that! One day he will judge all evil and create a new world. In the meantime, he is patient so that many who do not yet know him—including our family and friends—could come to know and follow him.

- God knows about suffering: Jesus suffered in unimaginable ways. He therefore understands what we feel. He desires that we come to him to find grace and mercy to help us in our time of need.

- God can bring good out of all kinds of evil and suffering.

TIPS FOR TALKING ABOUT THIS ISSUE

- I can't underscore enough the point first made in this chapter, that in many cases, people's questions are not really questions, but cries for help. Pray for wisdom and discernment—but lean toward the side of listening and serving before discussing the issues related to suffering and evil. The message of James 1:19 is appropriate in these situations—"Understand this, my dear brothers and sisters: You must all be quick to listen, slow to speak, and slow to get angry." Also, it doesn't hurt to simply admit that you just don't know the answer when they ask for explanations related to what they're going through.

- Don't be dismayed and try not to overreact if your friends blurt out some strong feelings about God or their faith while in the midst of suffering. People in pain often say things that go beyond what they really know or will want to stand by later. My friend Judson Poling once said, "Skeptics argue with each other, but true believers argue with God."[18] If you read the Psalms (Ps. 13, for example), you'll see that it's true. Give gentle encouragement as God leads, but when people are struggling, it is generally best to be sparing with your feedback and admonitions.

- It is better to admit you don't know what to say—or to say nothing—than to talk off the top of your head to someone who is suffering. Far too often Christians repeat clichés that might not even be true, hoping they'll somehow make the person feel better. Usually the effect is the opposite. Don't tell people that loved ones died because "God must have needed them in heaven" or "This must have been God's will." We live in a truly fallen world where evil and calamity touch lives in ways that are not fair and that will never seem right. Yes, God allowed it (in that he didn't intervene to stop it), but that doesn't mean he intended it or that he likes it any better than the person who is grieving.

- In keeping with the last point, we need to realize that it's rarely appropriate to quote Romans 8:28 to people in pain. Yes, if they are followers of Christ, then it's true that "God causes everything to work together for the good"—but they're probably not in the position to see, feel, or appreciate that truth at this point. And even when they do see the good that God brings, they might not like it enough to consider it a fair exchange for what they had to go through. Better to let them discover for themselves the ways God wants to work in their situation. Encourage them, and in the meantime, mostly love, support, and serve them in more general ways.

- Remember that prayer is almost always an appropriate response. Just offer to pray with or for your friends— and do so out loud. But, again, don't say more than you know in the prayer. Rather, admit what you *don't* know, and ask God for help, strength, wisdom, and hope—and for his presence in the midst of their pain. It's generally best, also, to keep the prayer brief and to the point.

- Don't underestimate the encouragement and influence you can have on people's lives by simply being there to love and serve them (and to talk, as appropriate) during their time of pain or crisis. As a friend of mine put it when she explained why she later became a Christian, she said she met a bunch of people "who were like Jesus to me." We can be like Jesus to our friends, as well.

QUESTIONS FOR GROUP DISCUSSION

1. Why do people tend to not think about God when their lives are going well, but then blame him when bad things happen?

2. How would you describe to someone "the problem of good"?

3. Why is it difficult for people to reconcile the three truths that God is good, God is great, and evil is real? Have you ever struggled with any of these?

4. Why does the denial of God leave us with no absolute standards? Why is a standard for judging good and evil vital for life in this world?

5. What does it mean to you that God offers a choice—to love and follow him or to *not* love and follow him? How does that affect your approach in talking to friends about this question?

6. How do the words *not yet* apply to God's dealing with evil and suffering in the world?

7. Describe a time when God brought "good out of bad" in your own experience or in the life of someone close to you.

CHAPTER 6:

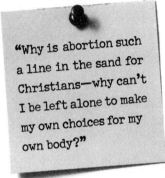

"Why is abortion such a line in the sand for Christians—why can't I be left alone to make my own choices for my own body?"

It was the early 1940s, and Arnie Skeie was driving his car down a rural highway with his young daughter, Jean, by his side. They were just outside their hometown of Leeds, North Dakota, when they noticed something on the pavement ahead of them. Right in the middle of the road sat a medium-sized cardboard box.

As he eased off the gas pedal, Arnie considered what to do. It was tempting to simply steer around the box and let someone else bother with getting it off the road. Some people would have felt compelled to speed up and run it over—just to hear the sound of the cardboard being crushed or to see the carnage in their rearview mirror.

Arnie did neither. He hit the brakes and pulled the car off to the side of the road, near the box. But as he got out of his car and walked onto the pavement to pick it up, Arnie and Jean saw something they would never forget. Suddenly the cardboard flaps flew up and a small child popped his head through the opening, giggling with delight at surprising the strangers in front of him.

After getting over their initial shock, Arnie rescued the boy, and together he and Jean returned him to the safety of his nearby home. Many years later, Jean related this story to me and my wife, Heidi—her daughter—and we experienced some of the emotional shock she and her father had felt so long ago. Jean concluded, "My father told me then what he often repeated in later years. 'You never know what might be inside of something like that. I knew the box could contain things that would be valuable to someone—and that there could even be something alive in it. Whenever you're unsure about things like that, it's always better to give the benefit of the doubt and play it safe. You might be wrong, but you might save someone's life.'"

THE IMPORTANCE OF THE ISSUE

Heidi and I were reminded of this story and its unforgettable lesson when our first child was born at only twenty-eight weeks of gestation, almost three months premature, weighing only two pounds, five ounces, and given just a 50 percent chance of survival. Emma Jean—named after both my mother-in-law and Jean's mother, Emma—could nearly fit into the palm of my hand. After spending her first months struggling for survival in the hospital, she was finally able to be brought home on the very day she had been due to be born. Today, at nineteen years of age, she's still the most precious girl I've ever known, our miracle from God and a beautiful young woman who loves life, learning, friends, music, little children, and following Jesus—and who brings joy to everyone she knows.

Jean's childhood experience finding the box with Arnie as well as Emma Jean's unique birth help answer why for so many people, Christian and non-Christian alike, abortion is a "line in the sand" and is considered anything but a woman's private choice with her own body. Arnie could have done whatever he wanted with the old cardboard box, and my wife could choose to dye her hair, tattoo her shoulder, or do anything else relatively harmless with her body, but neither one of them—nor anyone else, male or female—has the freedom to squash another human life, no matter how small or hidden.

This is certainly not the only issue Christians should care about or address. But since it involves the loss of life for 1.3 million children annually in the United States alone— more *every year* than the combined number of Americans killed in the Revolutionary War; the Civil War; World Wars I and II; and the Korean, Vietnam, Persian Gulf, Iraq, and Afghan wars—what could be more important? This is especially true when we realize that a staggering number of almost fifty million unborn Americans have been killed through abortions in the past forty years alone.[1]

It's hard to hear the details of what really happens in an abortion "procedure"—no one likes to think about them. But regardless of what a person's position is about abortion, it's important that he or she understand what actually transpires.

There is a variety of abortion procedures, including one that tears apart and suctions out the baby's little body (suction aspiration); another that requires the abortionist to insert a knife into the womb and cut the baby into pieces, then to remove and reassemble the tiny body to be sure none of the pieces are left inside (Dilation and Curettage); and other methods that use a combination of chemicals to induce labor or a saline solution that actually burns the fetus, taking about an hour to end the baby's life so the body can be removed.[2]

But the most horrifying method is the one known as partial-birth abortion (Dilation and Extraction or Dilation and Evacuation). For all its coverage in the news, very few people seem to understand what it really is. Here's a description: "Using ultrasound, the doctor grips the fetus's legs with forceps. The unborn is then pulled out through the birth canal and delivered with the exception of its head. While the head is in the womb the doctor penetrates the live fetus's skull with scissors, opens the scissors to enlarge the hole, and then inserts a catheter. The fetus's brain is vacuumed out, resulting in the skull's collapse. The doctor then completes the womb's evacuation by removing the dead fetus."[3]

I'm sorry I had to give you that description. Honestly, just reviewing and writing these details makes me feel much like I did when I visited the Dachau and Buchenwald concentration camps in Germany and heard about the things that had been done in those places to our fellow human beings. Yet it is important that the world understand the atrocities that took place there, and the same is true of abortion. Both my heart and my mind tell me—and I trust yours tell you too—that such things are utterly wrong. For all the political posturing and legal maneuvering that is employed to protect the freedom of women "to choose" to terminate the life of an unborn son or daughter, the actual procedures are horrible to think about—which I'm sure is why most abortion advocates don't like to discuss the details. But that's also a large part of why this practice goes on and on—we too often fail to lift the veil to see what's really happening. Like those living under Nazi rule during the days of the Jewish Holocaust, ignorance seems to be the closest people can get to bliss.

The reasons and information that support the preservation of unborn lives are powerful—yet many of our friends have still never heard or considered them. Even worse, for the women who experience an unwanted pregnancy and are under extreme pressure and confusion about what to do, those who advocate abortion as a morally neutral "choice" deliberately withhold accurate information about these violent procedures and even information about nonlethal alternatives. This means millions of women "choose" abortion in a moment of weakness and vulnerability and then live a lifetime of regret for their own uninformed decision.

I hope that some of the following discussion will help us better answer those who question us about this and, as a result, prevent some of the devastation and regret that abortion brings. Let's review some of the facts that support the preservation of unborn lives and then add the impact of Arnie's argument. In the end we'll be better equipped to point people not only to the truth about preborn human life but also to the Author of life himself.

SCIENTIFIC ANSWERS

We have access to an array of amazing facts about the rapid development of a just-conceived child inside the womb. To help bring these scientific details to life, let's look at them on a calendar, considering a situation just like what Heidi and I experienced when we had Emma Jean, changing it only so that the hypothetical expectant mother asking this chapter's question had become pregnant with her daughter on the first day of the year.[4]

January 1—On the very day of conception, all forty-six chromosomes are present, so a human life has already begun. *This is a unique human being, with a unique genetic makeup, who can never be reproduced or replaced.*

January 22—Only about three weeks after conception, the child's heart begins to beat, pumping her own blood, which is often a different blood type from the mother's.

February 4—In the fifth week, which is around the time many mothers confirm that they are pregnant, the child's eyes, legs, and hands begin to develop.

February 14—By Valentine's Day, which is merely the sixth week after conception, the child's brain waves, which have already been active for some time, are now detectable.

Late February—Only the seventh week from conception, the baby starts kicking and swimming.

Late February—Just under two months into the pregnancy, every organ in the child's body is in place, the bones are taking shape, and fingerprints have already begun to form.

Mid-March—Teeth begin to form, fingernails develop, the baby can turn her head, and she can even frown.

Late March—The baby can grasp objects placed in her hand.

Late April—The baby can start having dreams during REM sleep.

So, tallying up some of this remarkable young child's four-month accomplishments, she has all the human chromosomes in place from day one and is a genetically unique, one-of-a-kind human being; she has a beating heart and her own blood type; she has eyes, legs, hands, fingernails, fingerprints, all her internal organs, bones, teeth, and independent brain waves; and she can kick, swim, turn her head back and forth, make facial gestures, grasp objects, and even have dreams.

We're still less than halfway into the normal nine-month period of fetal development—the mother's "baby bump" is just beginning to show, and the baby's not due until early October—but doesn't that already sound an awful lot like a human being? If she's not a child, then what is she? The scientific data has removed any legitimate doubt about what is growing inside the woman. The baby is not just a "blob," "a mass of tissue," "uterine contents," "birth matter," or "the products of conception"[5]—these are deceptive euphemisms designed to disguise the truth that is now clearly known: she—or he—but not "it"—is a real human child.

As the world famous French geneticist Jerome Lejeune

put it years ago when he testified at the United States congressional hearings, "To accept the fact that after fertilization has taken place a new human has come into being is no longer a matter of taste or opinion. . . . The human nature of the human being from conception to old age is not a metaphysical contention, it is plain experimental evidence."[6] Even the owner of Oregon's largest abortion clinic admitted this when he testified under oath: "Of course human life begins at conception."[7] This isn't new news; it's just overlooked information.

This, by the way, also answers the part of the question that asks, "Why can't I be left alone to make my own choices about my own body?" The simple answer is that we're not talking about the woman's body—we're talking about the separate and distinct body of the baby who is growing inside her.

There's also an extension of that question, which asks, "Why should a woman be forced to go through the hardships of carrying another human being who has invaded her body?" Overlooking the fact that in the vast majority of cases the woman willingly participated in the activities that invited that baby into her body, there are certainly situations in which that was not so. Let's consider an illustration that applies even when there was no cooperation.

Suppose someone broke into your house, left a baby boy in your family room, and then fled the scene. Now you've got a child on your hands that you didn't expect or ask for. What are your options? You might be able to work it out with the state to keep and raise that baby, but more likely you'll turn him over to the authorities to be placed in an appropriate home. Either way, you must not harm the child in the interim. Until he is transferred into safe custody, it is your responsibility to protect and take care of him.

In fact, if you found a doctor to come to your home and dismember, chemically burn, or poison the baby to death, you and your doctor would be guilty of first-degree murder—even though the child is not yours and you did not produce the child, place the child in your home, or even want the child. But what is so sad about abortion is that so many women who are loving, nurturing, and caring individuals are coerced through pressure and ignorance to collude with medical personnel to do exactly that, never really understanding that they are in fact murdering their own children.

The situation with a baby in the house is the same as with a baby in a woman's womb. The woman carrying the baby doesn't have to be the one who ultimately raises him, but she should protect him until he can be safely transferred into the custody of a family that *will* raise him. And, thankfully, there are plenty of loving families waiting to adopt and love every baby who becomes available.

We should add that what the experts prove in their labs and testify to in their hearings a pregnant mother already knows in her heart—and quickly confirms when she has the opportunity to see her developing baby through an ultrasound. As she watches him or her moving around, stretching, kicking, flinching, and in some cases even laughing or crying, the mother knows that what she's seeing is not just a human person—the baby is her own sweet little child. Statistics show that, as a result, 84 percent of mothers decide not to have an abortion after seeing the ultrasound of their babies.[8] It's also interesting to note that most baby books start with ultrasound pictures of "Your Baby" beginning well within the first trimester of pregnancy.

For Abby Johnson, former director of a Planned Parenthood clinic in southeast Texas, it was seeing the ultrasound image of an abortion actually in progress that led her to quit her job, leave the clinic, and become an active supporter of the pro-life movement. "I could see the whole profile of the baby of thirteen weeks head to foot. I could see the whole side profile. I could see the probe. I could see the baby try to move away from the probe." Johnson later explained that this experience changed her forever. "I just thought, *What am I doing?*" she said. "And then I thought, *Never again.*"[9]

In light of the growing avalanche of data that prove what most of us already know, deep down anyway—that fetuses are tiny human beings—and in light of Arnie's argument that wherever human life *might* be involved we must give that life the benefit of the doubt, shouldn't we do everything we can to protect rather than destroy the lives of the unborn?

BIBLICAL ANSWERS

As Christians, it's important for us to point not just to what science tells us about the nature of preborn human beings but also to what Scripture says. Many of our friends and family respect the message of the Bible, especially when the Bible speaks about character and morals. In fact, many who don't claim to be Christians would give serious consideration to its teachings on abortion if we would clarify that abortion is a moral issue, just as compassion, kindness, and love are. (Of course, we can also reinforce the reasons for trusting the

Bible by sharing some of the information we discussed back in our response to Question 3.)

God made us in his image

Let's start by looking at a few passages in the Old Testament. We're told in Genesis 1:26-27 that God created human beings in his own image. This doesn't mean we are like him physically, because he is spirit and not a physical being. Rather, it means that we are like him in other ways—including having rational capacities, moral awareness, and the ability to choose how we'll act upon these things—and this makes us unique among all creation. It also imbues us with a value that is exponentially higher than any animal.

This relates to abortion in two ways. First, unborn children are just as much in the image of God and deserving of life protection as a woman struggling against a rapist or a man defending himself from a robber. Second, men and women who are faced with unwanted pregnancies are also created in the image of God. This means that, whether fathers or mothers, they have the responsibility to make a moral choice concerning an unborn child that affirms their own dignity as humans, leaves their consciences intact, and affirms their moral character years and years after their choice has been made.

That at least partly explains why the Ten Commandments, given by God to Moses and recorded in Exodus 20, tell us, "You must not murder" (v. 13). That prohibition is a command not to kill innocent people. (There are other verses that talk about the mistreatment of animals and there are fines associated with those actions, but they are never on a par with the penalties for mistreating or killing innocent people.) This shows the special protections God wanted to build around us as humans and the special value that he places on us and our children, born or unborn.[10]

God knew us from the womb

Another significant Scripture passage is Psalm 139:13-17, written by King David. Perhaps you haven't read this in the clarity of the New Living Translation, so here it is in its entirety. I encourage you to go through the passage two or three times and let the power of its truth and tenderness soak into your soul:

> You made all the delicate, inner parts of my body
>   and knit me together in my mother's womb.
> Thank you for making me so wonderfully complex!
>   Your workmanship is marvelous—how well
>   I know it.
> You watched me as I was being formed in utter
>   seclusion,
>   as I was woven together in the dark of the womb.
> You saw me before I was born.
>   Every day of my life was recorded in your book.
> Every moment was laid out
>   before a single day had passed.
> How precious are your thoughts about me, O God.
>   They cannot be numbered!

Nothing about this inspired biblical passage hints at the idea that David was of any lower value when he was still in his mother's womb. Quite the contrary! We see God's active involvement and care in the forming and development of his body and personality—and by extension, of our own and of all human beings prior to their births. It seems inconceivable that someone could read this passage, absorb its meaning, and then pretend that God is okay with deliberately and violently ending the life of even one of these little ones who are still in the process of being "made," "knit," "watched," and "woven together" by God, as well as being thought of by him in ways that are "precious."

God's condemnation of abortion is implicit in his other declarations

People sometimes ask, If the Bible is really against abortion, why doesn't it just come out and explicitly condemn abortion? The answer is that the practice of destroying their own unborn children would have been so foreign to the people's thinking at the time the Bible was written that there was no necessity to say so. Theirs was a culture that strongly believed that "children are a gift from the LORD; they are a reward from him" (Ps. 127:3). This is probably similar to the reason the Bible does not explicitly forbid cannibalism, though it mentions it as a detestable act. Some things were—and should remain—simply unthinkable.

Before we move on from the Old Testament, there is one other passage that warrants a brief discussion. Exodus 21:22-25 says,

> Suppose two men are fighting, and in the process
> they accidentally strike a pregnant woman so
> she gives birth prematurely. If no further injury

results, the man who struck the woman must
pay the amount of compensation the woman's
husband demands and the judges approve. But
if there is further injury, the punishment must
match the injury: a life for a life, an eye for an
eye, a tooth for a tooth, a hand for a hand, a
foot for a foot, a burn for a burn, a wound for
a wound, a bruise for a bruise.

Some people have drawn faulty conclusions from this passage based on a mistaken interpretation of the Hebrew
word translated here "gives birth prematurely." They've mis-
translated it "has a miscarriage" and have thought that this
passage places a lower value on unborn babies because it
merely prescribes a fine for causing the death of one through
a miscarriage, versus the much more serious "life for a life,
eye for an eye" penalty to be administered if there is serious
harm to the woman herself. Thus, these people would argue,
the Bible views adults as having high worth, but the unborn
as having much lower worth.

In reality the Bible here—consistent with the other
passages we've reviewed—shows equally high value for both
the mother and the preborn child. The translation I quoted
above is accurate. It gives no indication that the baby dies,
just that labor is induced by the injury and the baby is delivered earlier than planned. For this, the Scriptures say, an
appropriate fine must be paid—probably to pay for the extra
care of the baby who is born prematurely.

The passage goes on to say, "If there is further injury,
the punishment must match the injury: a life for a life, an

eye for an eye." In other words, if the mother *or the child* is maimed or killed, whoever caused it must be punished in like fashion.

So once again we see the Old Testament Scriptures upholding the worth of preborn babies as people made in the image of God, fantastically formed by him. Maybe that's partly why Proverbs 31:8 warns us to "speak up for those who cannot speak for themselves, for the rights of all who are destitute" (NIV). What group of people could this better relate to than the unborn?

Jesus charged us with the care of "the least of these"

In the New Testament, Jesus powerfully reinforced the value of acting on behalf of the needy when he said this in Matthew 25:42-46 (emphasis mine):

> "I was hungry, and you didn't feed me. I was thirsty, and you didn't give me a drink. I was a stranger, and you didn't invite me into your home. I was naked, and you didn't give me clothing. I was sick and in prison, and you didn't visit me."
>
> Then they will reply, "Lord, when did we ever see you hungry or thirsty or a stranger or naked or sick or in prison, and not help you?"
>
> And he will answer, *"I tell you the truth, when you refused to help the least of these my brothers and sisters, you were refusing to help me."*
>
> And they will go away into eternal punishment, but the righteous will go into eternal life.

In this Scripture Jesus was personally identifying with those who suffer, who are mistreated, or who are in need of help or protection. And he concluded this stinging indictment of those who refused to come to the rescue of "the least of these" with a stern warning of their impending judgment. Jesus later identifies "the least of these" as the little ones who trust in him, saying that if anyone causes these children (the original language refers to very young children—those still nursing) to sin, he or she will receive condemnation from God worse than having "a large millstone tied around [their necks]" and being "drowned in the depths of the sea" (Matt. 18:6). If that is how he feels about leading a child into sin, how much more intense will be his judgment of someone who kills a child! Jesus makes it clear that these kinds of evil must stop; we need to do everything we can to protect even the least of the least.

Bible writers believed in life at conception

It's also worth pointing out that consistently throughout the Bible when the writers mentioned their own beginnings, it was with phrases that clearly indicated that they, the persons doing the writing, began at conception and were personally alive within the womb. "You . . . knit *me* together in my mother's womb," David said in Psalm 139:13. He did not say, "You knit *what was going to become me* together in my mother's womb." In Jeremiah 1:5 the Lord is quoted saying this about Jeremiah: "Before *you* were born I set *you* apart and appointed *you* as my prophet to the nations." He didn't say, "Before you were born I set you apart and appointed *what was going to become you* as my prophet to the nations."

In Galatians 1:15 the apostle Paul said, "Even before I was born, God chose *me* and called *me* by his marvelous grace" (emphases in this paragraph are mine). Not *what would become me* or *the potential me*—simply the before-I-was-born-me.

And in the famous account of Mary—already pregnant with Jesus—when she visited her relative Elizabeth—pregnant with John the Baptist—the biblical text says this:

> At the sound of Mary's greeting, Elizabeth's child leaped within her, and Elizabeth was filled with the Holy Spirit. Elizabeth gave a glad cry and exclaimed to Mary, "God has blessed you above all women, and your child is blessed. Why am I so honored, that the mother of my Lord should visit me? When I heard your greeting, the baby in my womb jumped for joy." (Luke 1:41-44)

Again, it's clear that "Elizabeth's *child* [he is already a child] leaped within her" and that Mary's "*child* [again, a real child] is blessed." Further, the "*baby in my womb* [actual baby, not potential baby] jumped for joy." Just think about it: The preborn John the Baptist somehow sensed and responded joyfully to the presence of the preborn Jesus, the Savior of the world!

In light of the consistent biblical message that all human life, preborn and born, is of incredible worth and deserving of our rescue, it certainly seems clear that we have a divine mandate to preserve and protect the unborn.

CIVIC ANSWERS

On July 4, 1776, the following bold words were published for the entire world to see:

> *We hold these truths to be self-evident, that all men are created equal, that they are endowed by their Creator with certain unalienable rights, that among these are life, liberty and the pursuit of happiness. That to secure these rights, governments are instituted among men.*

These are the opening lines of the United States Declaration of Independence, but more than that, they represent a philosophy that provides a foundation for freedom and liberty available for all people—one that formed our nation and that has impacted our world. It is out of this philosophy, and the Judeo-Christian values that undergird it, that we've established a culture in which it is understood that individuals really do matter over and above the state and, therefore, deserve the right of freedom and the government's protection. This clearly sets us apart from communist and fascist regimes that value the government and the nation over any individual person.

Unfortunately, those lofty lines of the Declaration of Independence are easier to write and repeat than they are to live out. Our country, for all the good it has done, has a checkered history of sometimes treating people shamefully, not as being "created equal" or as being "endowed by their Creator with certain unalienable rights." At one time, for example, our government did not consider Native Americans to be legal persons in the sense that it did not grant them the protection of our Constitution. As a result, our officials often felt free to confiscate their land and property. Later, black slaves were "declared to be chattel and property of their masters as a result of the *Dred Scott* decision of 1857."[11] This minimizing of their humanity was then used to justify their ongoing mistreatment and enslavement.

And today, ever since the *Roe v. Wade* ruling of 1973, unborn Americans are refused the status of personhood for the purposes of legalizing abortion—even though they may be considered legal persons as unrelated homicide victims (when they die as a result of the murder of their mothers) or heirs (when they can be included, before they are born, in the estate of people who have died). And, of course, the scientific evidence makes it clear that they are individual human beings who have their own fingerprints, heartbeats, blood types, and brain waves. Yet the arbitrary refusal to acknowledge personhood in the particular case of legalized abortion is used to justify the taking of their very lives.

The U.S. Constitution declares that "no state shall deprive any person of life, liberty or property without due process of law"—yet, as Jean Staker Garton points out in her powerful book *Who Broke the Baby?* we have failed at all three. African-American human beings were denied liberty, Native American human beings were denied property, and unborn human beings are currently being denied life.[12] Garton concludes, "History has proven us wrong about Native Americans. History has proven us wrong about African-Americans. We cannot afford to wait for history to prove us wrong about the unborn."[13]

Regarding Native Americans and African-Americans, we have come far since our highly regretful past. But consider these present-day ironies:

- We are a nation increasingly concerned with social justice, equality, and civil rights for all people, as well as the protection of the weak, the disabled, and the poor—yet we as a society have readily dispensed with the rights and protection due our own unborn offspring.

- We acknowledge that it is wrong to determine a person's rights based on skin color. Yet we regularly determine a person's most basic right—*life*—based on someone else's desire. If a woman desires to terminate her pregnancy, we call it abortion. If someone else does it for her—for example, in the case of an assault—we call it homicide.

- There are those among us who lobby, demonstrate, and even break laws in defense of endangered animals yet at the same time insist that the freedom to destroy unborn humans must remain a legal right up to and including full development at nine months' gestation.

- Many who championed the noble ideals of the Civil Rights Movement— with its strong values of liberty, freedom, and justice for all *and* a firm commitment to nonviolence—have failed to apply these values to the weakest members of our society. Surely the spirit of the Civil Rights Movement would be to speak up for and protect those who can't do so for themselves—the unborn.

As we answer our friend's question about why we are so concerned about abortion, we can point out the scientific data and what it tells us about the true human nature of preborn babies. We can point to what God says in Scripture about the high value he places on human beings from conception onward. And we can remind our friend that we live in a nation that claims to care about and protect every individual, regardless of the person's age, strength, or capabilities; surely we should apply this protection to those who are currently the youngest, weakest, and most limited in our society—but who represent its very future.

IF THERE'S ANY DOUBT

Let's go back to our opening story. When Arnie and Jean saw that box ahead on the highway, how sure do you think they were that there was a human being in it? The answer is, *not at all!* They had no clue that there was a child hiding inside. In fact, if you would have asked Arnie before he got out of his car what he thought the chances were that there was a child in the box, I'm confident he would have given you a very low number. You just don't normally find kids playing in small containers out on the highway.

So, statistically, he might have guessed that the chances were perhaps .0001 percent (one in ten thousand) that there would be a child in that box. Yet even with just those tiny odds, given that he could possibly be dealing with a human life, there was enough of a question in his mind to cause him to give the situation the benefit of the doubt. He played it safe, and he thanked God for the rest of his life that he did. And I'm sure that the boy in the box, given the full story, would join Arnie in giving thanks, since it was his life that was saved!

This leads us to the question we can ask our friends who challenge us about abortion: *In light of all the information from science, Scripture, and the civil rights due all human beings, how sure are you that this is* not *a human life worthy of our full protection?*

Putting it another way, are our friends only half convinced? Okay, if Arnie and Jean saw a box in the middle of the road and thought there was half a chance that there was a child hiding in it, would they ignore or even run over the box? Of course not! Even if they thought there was a one-in-ten-thousandth of a chance, they'd stop and move it. This is precisely what we need to do when it comes to unborn children. We should follow Arnie's example, give unborn children the benefit of the doubt, and protect what the evidence overwhelmingly shows to be real, live human beings, especially since, unlike the child-in-the-box situation, we *do* expect a child to result from a pregnancy—surely we can all agree on that point!

One woman told a friend of mine about the "Arnie moment" that prevented her from aborting her unborn child years ago, even though she thought at the time she would have been justified in choosing abortion.[14] She recalls,

> *As I wrestled with my options, I was leaning toward abortion because I just couldn't see how I could forgive myself if I gave my baby up for adoption and let some strangers raise it. . . . Then it hit me like a sledgehammer—if I couldn't live with giving*

*my child away, what kind of a woman was I to live
with scraping my child off the wall of my uterus?*

*It's been twenty-five years since I gave birth
and my baby was adopted. I've married and had
two other children. Do I wonder about my first
child? Do I regret not knowing him, not watching
him grow up? Of course I do! But I can look my
husband in the eye and know he can trust me with
his children. I can look my other children in the eye
and know I don't have to tell them I killed their
older brother. I can look myself in the mirror and
see a loving mother. And I can run to God's arms
and know he not only forgave me for my careless sex
life, but he also gave me the strength to not kill my
child when everyone around me told me it was the
"easy" way out.*

TRUTH PLUS GRACE

Colossians 4:6 says to "let your conversation be gracious
and attractive so that you will have the right response for
everyone." When we answer hard questions, we should strive
to present the truth but to communicate it in love—always
pointing people back to God's grace. Thankfully, given the
gravity of this issue of abortion and all the pain and guilt it
can bring, we have a God who stands ready to forgive and
heal. No, his forgiveness won't bring back the baby, but it
can bring back life and hope to those who have been part of
the abortion process.

What follows is another firsthand account, from a
woman who knows.

When I was in college, because of lots of bad choices I found myself pregnant at the end of my junior year. At the time, the only decision I could live with was to have an abortion. I couldn't live with knowing how I disappointed my parents. I couldn't live with nine months of guilt and shame. I couldn't live with being responsible for my actions.

The entire day of the ordeal, I knew *I was violating a sacred commandment of God's. I was willingly murdering this life. And I believed with all my heart he could never forgive me.*

Through a friendship, I began coming to church and became immersed in biblical teaching. I heard dozens of messages on forgiveness and repentance and how Jesus died for me to bear my sins. I heard it all—but I never believed it in my heart. I never owned it. How could God forgive me for killing my baby?

I finally made a commitment to Jesus Christ, and that June I felt I needed to take the step of making my faith public through baptism. During the ceremony, there was a big wooden cross on the stage, and we were to write some of our sins on a piece of paper and pin it to the cross just before we were baptized as a symbol that we were forgiven by God.

I remember my fear—the most fear I ever remember—as I wrote as tiny as I could on a piece of paper the word abortion. *I was scared someone would open up the paper and read it and find out it was me. I almost wanted to walk out of the auditorium during the service—the guilt and fear were that strong.*

When my turn came, I walked up toward the center of the stage toward the cross, pinned the paper there, and was directed over toward the pastor to be baptized. He looked me straight in the eyes. I thought for sure he was going to read in my eyes the terrible secret I had kept from everybody for so long.

But instead, I felt that God was telling me, "I love you. You are forgiven. You are forgiven!" I felt so much love for me—a terrible sinner. That's the first time I've ever really felt forgiveness and unconditional love. It was unbelievable, and it was indescribable.

Afterward we all sang "I'm Forever Grateful," and I cried with so much joy and relief. Relief, after all these years.[15]

Consider the powerful words of Romans 5:20: "God's law was given so that all people could see how sinful they were. But as people sinned more and more, God's wonderful grace became more abundant." As Christians dealing with this challenging question, we need to reflect this God-given pattern: Tell the truth about the evils of abortion, but don't forget to add the good news that Jesus died for all our sins, including this one, and he wants us to turn away from whatever we've done and to come to him for forgiveness, grace, and a new life in relationship with him.

Now *that's* good news!

SUMMARY OF THE ANSWER

Question 6 asks us, "Why is abortion such a line in the sand for Christians—why can't I be left alone to make my own choices for my own body?"

- The opening story about the child hiding in the box illustrates that even if we are not fully convinced by the arguments against abortion we should still give unborn children the benefit of the doubt, and thus the right to life.

- In our heart of hearts we know that protecting human lives is honorable and right and that carelessly disposing of human life can haunt us for a lifetime—so we should act accordingly.

- Science shows us that, from early on, unborn babies have a unique genetic makeup; a distinct heartbeat; their own blood type, fingerprints, and brain waves—in other words, they are distinct human beings who deserve our loving protection.

- Scripture shows that God made all humans in his image and that he places a high value on every person, born and preborn—Jesus said we should go out of our way to care for "the least of these."

- The founding values of the United States declare that all humans are created equal and that they are endowed with the God-given right to life, liberty, and the pursuit of happiness—this should be applied to every human, even the smallest among us.

- Those who have already participated, directly or

indirectly, in the abortion of a child can't change the past, but they can come to God and find his forgiveness, grace, the promise of a new life—and a far better future.

TIPS FOR TALKING ABOUT THIS ISSUE

People have deep feelings about this topic, so as James 1:19 tells us, we should "be quick to listen, slow to speak, and slow to get angry." Helping others rethink this issue will almost always be a slow process and entail multiple respectful conversations.

- Using a story or illustration will often draw people in and help them think about an issue in fresh ways. I did this at the beginning of the chapter with the story of Arnie, Jean, and the child in the box. My goal was to help readers realize that, even if they are not fully convinced by the arguments against abortion, they should still give unborn children the benefit of the doubt, and thus their protection. You can use this or similar examples to make the same point.

- Speak boldly about the truth, but as 1 Peter 3:15-16 cautions, do so with gentleness and respect. It is difficult not to get emotionally charged about this issue—but we must manage our feelings in order to deal gently with others.

- Avoid inflammatory terms, especially when talking about what someone has done. It's one thing to believe abortion is murder; it's another to accuse someone of it. Doing so puts up walls. Also, remember that many people have succumbed to the propaganda of the abortion industry and have proceeded with abortions that they were convinced really were just the removal of "lumps" or other euphemisms. They were wrong, and the damage has been done—but they weren't intentionally "murdering their babies." So, again, use gentleness.

- Remember that people will often resist changing their views on issues like this until God first changes their hearts. Many people trust in Christ while still holding pro-choice views and then gradually come to a new understanding. Don't make agreement on this issue a prerequisite to salvation.

- Finally, make it clear that, while you feel great passion and concern about this issue, you would never condone or support the violent actions a few people have taken to fight abortion. Remember that God's way is to "conquer evil by doing good" (Rom. 12:21).

QUESTIONS FOR GROUP DISCUSSION

1. Have you ever had an experience similar to Arnie's? If so, did you "give the benefit of the doubt"? How did it work out?

2. How well-known do you think the scientific data is about the amazing and early development of unborn children?

3. Are there practical steps that should be taken to make that data better known?

4. Reread the Psalm 139:13-17 passage. How does it make you feel about God's attitude toward you? toward unborn children?

5. How do you think the United States is doing in terms of applying its foundational principles of being "created equal" and "endowed with certain unalienable rights" to all human beings?

6. What are some dos and don'ts—whether listed in this chapter, or others you can think of—that you think might help as you talk to others about this important question?

CHAPTER 7:

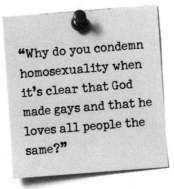

"Why do you condemn homosexuality when it's clear that God made gays and that he loves all people the same?"

Jesus . . . left Judea and returned to Galilee. He had to go through Samaria *on the way. Eventually he came to the Samaritan village of Sychar, near the field that Jacob gave to his son Joseph. Jacob's well was there; and Jesus, tired from the long walk, sat wearily beside the well about noontime.*[1]

WWJD is a popular acronym reminding us that one of the best ways to figure out how to handle confusing situations is to ask ourselves, *What Would Jesus Do?* As we've seen, we have powerful evidence that Jesus is the Son of God and, therefore, has divine wisdom for responding to every issue. Thankfully, we've also seen that in the New Testament we have a reliable record of what Jesus actually *did* do and say— and we can look to that record in order to learn from his example. So as we seek to respond to this difficult question about homosexuality—one that came up fairly often in our survey—we can find guidance in Jesus' own actions and teachings. Let's unfold how he handled a similarly contro-versial issue when he walked on earth.

The account quoted above from John 4 tells us that Jesus "had to go through Samaria." This is an interesting statement, because most Jewish people traveling from Judea up to Galilee did *not* go through Samaria—even though it was the shortest route. Because of their disdain for the Samaritans, who were largely descendants of the Israelites but whom they viewed as political and religious rivals, they would usually go out of their way to avoid passing through that region. We get a glimpse into what was appar-ently a common attitude when in John 8:48 the Pharisees, angered by Jesus' teachings, blurted out this accusation: "You Samaritan devil! Didn't we say all along that you were possessed by a demon?" It was as though being demonic wasn't bad enough—they had to add insult to injury with the term *Samaritan*! Yet Jesus ignored the common prej-udices of his time and resolutely headed north—straight through Samaria.

Why? The answer seems to be revealed in his personal mission statement, which he communicated to his followers after spending time with Zacchaeus, a member of another despised group—tax collectors: *"The Son of Man came to seek and save those who are lost"* (Luke 19:10, emphasis mine). Jesus was driven by an evangelistic vision, and he wasn't pas-sive about fulfilling it. Rather, he actively sought out those who, in his words, were spiritually "lost," in his desire to do what was needed to reach out and "save" them.

What compelled him to do this? We're told in the most famous verse in the Bible, John 3:16: "God loved the world so much that he gave his one and only Son, so that everyone who believes in him will not perish but have eternal life." Jesus "had to go through Samaria" because he was on a love-driven mission to seek and to save what was lost—in this case, a spiritually wayward woman who happened to be a Samaritan.

> Soon a Samaritan woman came to draw water,
> and Jesus said to her, "Please give me a drink."
> He was alone at the time because his disciples
> had gone into the village to buy some food.
>   The woman was surprised, for Jews refuse to
> have anything to do with Samaritans. She said
> to Jesus, "You are a Jew, and I am a Samaritan
> woman. Why are you asking me for a drink?"
> (John 4:7-9)

Jesus, being the Son of God, knew she would be there, what her need would be, and how he would be able to meet it. This is a glimpse of divine intentionality at work: God extending himself to an outcast member of an outcast culture. In fact, I suspect it was more than that she "happened" to be a Samaritan. I think Jesus chose to reach out to her in part *because* she was a Samaritan—as a way to show that all people in all cultures (with all kinds of colorful, sinful, messed-up backgrounds) matter to him and to the Father.[2]

How does this apply to the issue of homosexuality? Stated again, the question asks, "Why do you condemn homosexuality when it's clear that God made gays and that he loves all people the same?"

AFFIRMING AND SHOWING GOD'S LOVE

To begin, I believe Jesus would enthusiastically agree with the last part of the question—God loves all people. The first principle we can draw from Jesus' response to the Samaritan woman is this: *we should affirm God's love for all people*, regardless of their lifestyle or the particular activities or sins they may be engaged in. We can do this through our words, of course, but also by how we reach out in friendship to them.

Jesus was modeling this as he reached out and started a conversation with the Samaritan woman. And again, when Jesus wept outside Jerusalem, longing to gather the rebellious, stiff-necked people there to himself "as a hen protects her chicks beneath her wings" (Matt. 23:37), we see the love of God not just for his followers but for others as well—including spiritual rebels and hypocrites.

The apostle Paul, under the inspiration of the Holy Spirit, later sums it up, "God our Savior . . . wants everyone to be saved and to understand the truth" (1 Tim. 2:3-4). Surely the "everyone" there means . . . well, *everyone*! This doesn't imply that all people would end up actually trusting Jesus as their Savior—just that God wants them to, and he therefore made provision for their salvation through Jesus' death on the cross.

So when Jesus said, "God loved the world," it included people with same-sex attractions. Therefore, I believe Jesus would reach out to homosexual men and women—and indeed all those within the LGBTQ community[3]—with the same kind of love and intentionality that he showed to the Samaritan woman and that he has shown at various points to you and to me, as well.

Likewise, applying the WWJD principle, we should take our cues from Jesus and go out of our way to love and reach out to those who are different from us, including those with a different sexual orientation. As Lee Strobel says in response to this issue, "We can't even begin to comprehend the breadth and depth of God's love toward every person on this planet—including gay men and women."[4] If we believe this biblical value and begin to reflect it through our words and actions, it can open doors of life-giving encouragement and ministry that we can't even imagine.

Let me caution you (and myself) that it's not enough to simply nod our heads in superficial agreement. It's easy to click off a box on our mental checklist of theological obligations, telling ourselves, *Yes, I know I have to try to love gays and others I disagree with—so there,* check, *I guess I really do love them*—while in reality viewing them in much the same way that the Pharisees viewed the Samaritans.

We need to slow down and look again at Jesus, the "author and perfecter of our faith" (Heb. 12:2, NIV). His love was radical and real. He genuinely cared. And he was willing to break the unwritten religious rules of his day, removing himself from the cocoon of like-minded religious people in order to get up close to those who needed his divine love. We should prayerfully reflect on what that kind of extreme love and concern should look like flowing through us today. "Imitate God, therefore," the Bible tells us, "in everything you do, because you are his dear children. Live a life filled with love, following the example of Christ" (Eph. 5:1-2).

Notice that even the Samaritan woman was taken aback that Jesus, a Jewish man who was a religious leader, would come near her, talk to her, even ask her for a drink. But isn't that what Jesus was famous for—touching the untouchables? Lepers, prostitutes, tax collectors, men and women with sinful reputations—Jesus constantly scandalized the religious leaders by hanging out with those they viewed as spiritual riffraff. This upset them to the point that they falsely accused him of being "a glutton and a drunkard" because of what they considered to be bad associations (Matt. 11:19; Luke 7:34). It was this pattern that led them to eventually put a label on Jesus intended to be the ultimate put-down: "He's a *friend of sinners*," they muttered maliciously.

And so he was. And is. And calls us to be, as well. "As the Father has sent me, so I am sending you," he said to the disciples after his resurrection—and to us, by extension (John 20:21). We, like Jesus, must get close to those who need God's forgiveness, regardless of the nature of their sin (including sexual immorality).[5] Like Jesus, we need to become the "friend of sinners," eagerly looking for opportunities to share his love and truth with them. Nothing will cleanse us of prejudice faster than getting into a genuine relationship with a member of whatever group we have tended to look down upon. It's really hard to hate people who have become your friends!

EXTENDING GOD'S GRACE

Jesus replied, "If you only knew the gift God has for you and who you are speaking to, you would ask me, and I would give you living water. . . . Anyone who drinks this water will soon become thirsty again. But those who drink the water

I give will never be thirsty again. It becomes a
fresh, bubbling spring within them, giving them
eternal life."

"Please, sir," the woman said, "give me this
water! Then I'll never be thirsty again, and I won't
have to come here to get water." (John 4:10, 13-15)

In genuine concern for this woman's spiritual situation, Jesus
made sure to move the conversation beyond mere small talk
about water, wells, and the differences between Jewish and
Samaritan beliefs. Rather, he honed in on the all-important
issues of God, his own identity, and the gift God was offering her—symbolized by "spiritual water."

Jesus, the quintessential evangelist, expressed a mixture
of grace and truth—including truth about her moral failures, which he would get to next. People often need to be
shaken up with the sobering realities of their sin and spiritual shortcomings before they'll be motivated to consider the
solutions available through Christ. We see this pattern in the
book of Romans, for example, where the first three chapters
show us our lostness, and then the majority of the rest of the
book presents the solutions available through the gospel. We
also see a microcosm of this pattern in Romans 6:23, where
Paul first presses home the point that "the wages of sin is
death," but then follows with the solution, "but the free gift
of God is eternal life through Christ Jesus our Lord."

It appears that in his divine wisdom Jesus knew this
woman was already well aware of her own moral missteps
and, perhaps, even buried in guilt and shame as a result.
(Some Bible commentators feel that this is why she came to

the well at noon, in the heat of the midday sun—to avoid running into the other women.)[6] That's probably why Jesus chose to start with the grace part of the message, capturing her curiosity first, and then building on her deepening interest.

Keep in mind, as we've discussed in other contexts, the primary goal—both Jesus' and ours. It's to bring people to faith in him, that they might receive the salvation and life available through his gospel. Once they come to know him and the Holy Spirit indwells and empowers them, then *he* can lead them into a greater fullness of doctrinal clarity as well as personal purity. Yes, they need at least a rudimentary understanding of who it is that they're putting their trust in, and there should be an attitude of repentance that says, "Here I am, a sinner in need of a Savior. I don't know everything you'll ask of me, but with an open heart and open hands I humbly ask for your forgiveness and leadership." At the time we receive Christ, none of us are aware of all our sins; what we need is a willingness to cooperate as God begins to conform us to his standards of morality.

So don't focus on trying to reform people from the outside in, but rather on sharing the life-changing gospel, which reforms us all from the inside out. People usually come to Christ by responding to the general message of God's love and Jesus' payment for their sins on the cross—then the Holy Spirit begins to indwell them, applying the teachings of the Bible and guiding them into his fuller truth and a lifestyle marked by purity. All of us must "come to Christ as we are"—often with mistaken ideas and messed-up morals. But that's what grace is for! That's what the sanctification process is designed to deal with. What God looks for is a humble, contrite heart from a person who is willing to be made new.

We must not ignore or excuse sin. Equally, we must keep it in the right perspective—whatever it is, whether of a sexual nature or something else—knowing that "when we were utterly helpless, Christ came at just the right time and died for us sinners" (Rom. 5:6). He "justifies the wicked" (Rom. 4:5, NIV), not the people who think they're all right without him. His specialty is dealing with rebels like us in order to root out the moral decay in our lives and to conform us to the image of Christ.

AFFIRMING GOD'S MODEL FOR HUMAN SEXUALITY

Now we come to the point in Jesus' exchange with the Samaritan woman at which he turned the corner to establish God's standard of purity and, by contrast, to illuminate her sin:

> "Go and get your husband," Jesus told her.
>
> "I don't have a husband," the woman replied.
>
> Jesus said, "You're right! You don't have a husband—for you have had five husbands, and you aren't even married to the man you're living with now. You certainly spoke the truth!"
>
> "Sir," the woman said, "you must be a prophet." (John 4:16-19)

Don't you love how winsome Jesus was in getting to the serious spiritual matters at hand? He could not ignore the issues of God's holiness and this woman's spiritual shortcomings, but he also understood that he needed to apply the truth with gentleness. There were undoubtedly a number of ways he could have gone about this, but he chose to focus on her marital situation and let it illustrate how far she'd drifted from God's will. So he told her (already knowing the situation) to go and get her husband; she reluctantly admitted that she didn't have a husband.

Even then, in the midst of her incomplete confession, Jesus seized on the chance to affirm her for telling the truth. "You're right!" he said to her. "You certainly spoke the truth!" But between those two affirmations he revealed to her, with penetrating insight, that he knew the whole of her situation—that she'd had five husbands and that the man she was currently living with was not her husband. In other words, he put his divine magnifying glass on the reality of her sin, and she instantly knew he had prophetically revealed the unvarnished truth about her life.

This leads to a second principle we can draw from Jesus' example: *we should affirm God's model for human sexuality.* Jesus does this implicitly here—but explicitly elsewhere— in clear support of the biblical model of marriage. What is that model? It was initially revealed at the beginning of the human race, right after God created the first man and woman. Genesis 2:24 says, "This explains why a man leaves his father and mother and is joined to his wife, and the two are united into one."

This simple statement in Scripture sets very clear parameters: How many people? *Two.* Which genders? *Both*—but only one of each. This is the norm, the biblical standard. If there are exceptions that are allowed or encouraged, we ought to find them clearly delineated—but we don't. Since that's the case, this foundational passage should remain the controlling Scripture for understanding God's design for marriage.

In fact, Jesus himself restated this text with that clear intention in Matthew 19. When addressing the hotly debated issue of divorce, he pointed out that later regulations permitting the breaking up of a marriage (for reasons other than marital unfaithfulness; see v. 9) were in fact violations of God's design, allowed not because it was a good idea or God's way but as an acquiescence to sinful people:

> "Haven't you read the Scriptures?" Jesus replied. "They record that from the beginning 'God made them male and female.' And he said, 'This explains why a man leaves his father and mother and is joined to his wife, and the two are united into one.' Since they are no longer two but one, let no one split apart what God has joined together."
>
> "Then why did Moses say in the law that a man could give his wife a written notice of divorce and send her away?" they asked.
>
> Jesus replied, "Moses permitted divorce only as a concession to your hard hearts, but it was not what God had originally intended." (Matt. 19:4-8)

Notice that Jesus here reaffirms the norm of one woman and one man united in marriage for life. He reiterates the necessary "maleness and femaleness" of the relationship— and points out that we can understand marriage biblically not by looking for loopholes but by going back to the guiding text, the first marriage and the design of God, in Genesis 2. He thus establishes once again the biblical norm of sexual intimacy only between a man and a woman, and only within marriage.

And if that's not clear enough, the apostle Paul reiterates this biblical norm of one-man-and-one-woman relations, forbidding expressions of sex in any other context:

> As the Scriptures say, "A man leaves his father and mother and is joined to his wife, and the two are united into one." . . . So again I say, each man must love his wife as he loves himself, and the wife must respect her husband. (Eph. 5:31, 33)

> Don't you realize that your bodies are actually parts of Christ? Should a man take his body, which is part of Christ, and join it to a prostitute? Never! And don't you realize that if a man joins himself to a prostitute, he becomes one body with her? For the Scriptures say, "The two are united into one." But the person who is joined to the Lord is one spirit with him.
> Run from sexual sin! No other sin so clearly affects the body as this one does. For sexual immorality is a sin against your own body. Don't you realize that your body is the temple of the Holy Spirit, who lives in you and was given to you by God? You do not belong to yourself, for

God bought you with a high price. So you must
honor God with your body. (1 Cor. 6:15-20)

That biblical backdrop creates a proper framework for
assessing all other sexual activity. It is easy to conclude that
sex that doesn't express this "one fleshness" between one
man and one woman in marriage is wrong. Therefore pre-
marital sex is out, adultery is out, polygamy is out, orgies
are out, bestiality is out, pedophilia is out, and sexual relations between same-sex partners are out. If anyone—of gay,
straight, or any other sexual persuasion—is engaging in sex
outside of marriage, he or she is violating God's plan. If you
accept the Bible's teaching on sex, you are left with this—
and only this—option.

If you are married, sexual expression between you
and your spouse is encouraged and even celebrated as a gift
from God. But outside of that, there are no examples of sex
condoned by God. Absolutely none. Of course violations
happen, but that is what they are: *violations*. This point is
not biblically controversial or unclear. Sex and marriage go
together, and sex without marriage is forbidden in all cases
in Scripture.

Even the troubling case of polygamy—yes, unfortunately there were examples of this recorded in the Bible—
does not void God's principle: sex is to occur only with one's
spouse. Even when powerful leaders had multiple concu-
bines and wives (again, this practice was in opposition to
God's stated design and purposes), those women were "off
limits" to anyone else, and the man was required to establish their legal status in marriage before he could be sexually

intimate with them. There have always been boundaries around sexual expression, and in the Bible, without exception, God approves of sex only for married people.

TELLING THE TRUTH ABOUT GOD'S WILL

The third principle we can learn from Jesus' example is this: *we need to lovingly tell the truth about what God says regarding sexual relations.* Jesus did this with the Samaritan woman by bringing up the subject of her husband and then revealing what he knew about her current situation. Clearly, she got the message.

You may have noticed what is conspicuously absent from this chapter so far: I have not quoted any of the scriptural texts that speak of homosexuality or that directly address same-sex behavior. That is intentional.

My reason is twofold: first, to make clear that the Bible's position is not based on isolated verses regarding homosexual practices but, rather, is based on the broad biblical teachings about God's design for sex and marriage. I believe that we as Christians need to focus primarily on making the case *for* biblical sexuality, not *against* gay sex. That's why I think Jesus' interactions with the woman at the well are so relevant to this discussion. Second, those who see this issue differently often try to explain away the texts that do seem to prohibit sex between members of the same gender. Therefore we risk getting embroiled in the particulars of interpreting those texts instead of putting the issue back into the broader context of God's stated purpose for sex, which is within the sanctity of marriage.

But in the interest of completeness, we do need to

point out that there are, in fact, a number of verses in the Bible—both Old and New Testaments—that clearly prohibit same-sex practices. Though some of these passages have been declared irrelevant or even mocked by critics because of other prohibitions included in their contexts, these verses do detail various kinds of forbidden sex—including homosexual acts—within ancient Israel, in the New Testament era, and into modern times.

I share these not in the desire to "condemn homosexuality," as this chapter's question suggests, but rather to be faithful to the God I seek to follow and to show his warnings to us as humans about things *God* says are outside his will. So in a spirit of love and humility I share these challenging biblical truths.

Old Testament

In the Old Testament the Bible says, "If a man practices homosexuality, having sex with another man as with a woman, both men have committed a detestable act" (Lev. 20:13; see also 18:22; Deut. 23:18). Some have argued these verses only prohibit homosexual acts by heterosexuals (not by those who are, according to these people, "by nature gay") or that homosexual acts are just prohibited in a ritual context—that the text says nothing about gay sex between loving, committed partners. Those are interesting arguments, but remember what we've already shown: "loving, committed" relationships don't qualify all *heterosexuals* for having sex (they need to be married, not merely in love); so by what standard could a person justify sex among gays in a situation in which it is forbidden between heterosexuals? Furthermore, though these texts would also clearly forbid ritual sexual practices, their contexts (including these prohibitions and the others mentioned in those contexts) are not discussing ritual circumstances. This adds weight to the understanding that such sexual practices, ritualized or not, are forbidden.

New Testament

Although Jesus does not explicitly address the issue of same-sex practices, could someone possibly make the case that he actually endorses it just because of a *lack* of specific prohibition? Jesus doesn't reiterate the Old Testament's prohibition against bestiality; should we suppose his silence means he is okay with it? He never speaks out against slavery, child trafficking, or the oppressive occupation of his homeland by Roman authorities. Are we to therefore think those are unimportant to him? And look at how he does handle the subject of marriage; as we saw above, his interpretation of its sacredness was even stricter than that of the scholars of his day. So why would we think him lax about sexual behaviors outside of marriage?

When he encountered the woman who had been caught in the act of adultery, for example, he was loving and engaging but certainly not permissive. Before parting ways, he told her clearly to "go now and leave your life of sin" (John 8:11, NIV). And again, in Jesus' interactions with the Samaritan woman we've already seen how he shone a light on her sexual sin of living with a man with whom she was not married (see John 4). If "love and commitment" form a sufficient context for legitimizing sexual relations (homosexual or heterosexual), then why would Jesus point out her status as unmarried?

Jesus was masterful at helping her see the way her evasive use of words ("I have no husband") failed to cover up the sinful circumstances she was living in (in effect, she had said, "I am sexually active with someone I am not married to"). Jesus was both gracious and telling. I believe he would do the same if he met a gay couple today: he probably wouldn't start with their sin but would build a rapport first, as he did with this Samaritan woman, and then at the right time and in a sensitive way help them understand how they are violating God's design for their sexuality.

Also, in other places in the New Testament, the apostle Paul speaks about same-sex acts specifically. He writes in Romans 1:24-27 about people who were doing things outside of God's will:

> God abandoned them to do whatever shameful
> things their hearts desired. As a result, they
> did vile and degrading things with each other's
> bodies. They traded the truth about God for
> a lie. So they worshiped and served the things
> God created instead of the Creator himself, who
> is worthy of eternal praise! Amen. That is why
> God abandoned them to their shameful desires.
> Even the women turned against the natural way
> to have sex and instead indulged in sex with each
> other. And the men, instead of having normal
> sexual relations with women, burned with lust for
> each other. Men did shameful things with other
> men, and as a result of this sin, they suffered
> within themselves the penalty they deserved.

Paul also lovingly but clearly warns about same-gender sexual sins (among others) in 1 Corinthians 6:9-11:

> Don't you realize that those who do wrong will not inherit the Kingdom of God? Don't fool yourselves. Those who indulge in sexual sin, or who worship idols, or commit adultery, or are male prostitutes, or practice homosexuality, or are thieves, or greedy people, or drunkards, or are abusive, or cheat people—none of these will inherit the Kingdom of God. Some of you were once like that. But you were cleansed; you were made holy; you were made right with God by calling on the name of the Lord Jesus Christ and by the Spirit of our God.

Notice that these acts *had been* committed by the Corinthian believers in their pre-Christian life, but no longer. Paul was clear that though Christians may have engaged in these acts in the past—including not just homosexual acts but also greed, drunkenness, dishonesty, and adultery—and might have been tempted to do so again, God expected them not to. And, thankfully, he makes it clear that these are all things we can be cleansed from—that there is still the opportunity to be "made holy" and "made right with God by calling on the name of the Lord Jesus Christ and by the Spirit of our God." So although this is a challenging warning, it is also filled with hope and promise.

Finally, Paul also spoke of homosexual practices in 1 Timothy 1:8-11:

We know that the law is good when used correctly. For the law was not intended for people who do what is right. It is for people who are lawless and rebellious, who are ungodly and sinful, who consider nothing sacred and defile what is holy, who kill their father or mother or commit other murders. The law is for people who are sexually immoral, or who practice homosexuality, or are slave traders, liars, promise breakers, or who do anything else that contradicts the wholesome teaching that comes from the glorious Good News entrusted to me by our blessed God.

The matter-of-fact way in which Paul includes homosexuality in this list must mean people at that time were familiar with the practice. Also, notice again that he doesn't limit it to a pagan ceremonial context but puts it among other sins that occurred generally in that society. This flies in the face of the common counterargument that says it is not same-sex practice in everyday life that is condemned in the Bible but only same-sex practice that goes on in pagan religious ceremonies.

ADDRESSING A MISGUIDED ASSUMPTION

Having seen what the biblical norm is for sexuality as well as the biblical prohibitions against homosexual practices, we need to address a common but faulty assumption that is implicit in the question we're addressing. It says, in part, "It's clear that God made gays." Many people combine the idea of

God's creation of people with the fact that some people have same-sex desires—and they conclude that God must have created those desires, which must therefore be good. In other words, "God made me this way, with these desires, so he must have intended me to have and to fulfill these desires."

But there are major problems with this thinking. First, all kinds of desires occur in people: the desire for food, the desire for recreation, the desire for significance, just to name a few. Unbridled, every one of our desires leads to excesses that produce harm. The desire for food can turn into gluttony, and that, unrestrained, can lead to obesity. The desire for recreation can turn into hedonism and pleasure seeking over and above productive activity, which can lead to obsession or laziness. The desire for significance can turn into grandiosity and abuse of power. The list goes on. Desires *can* be from God; but every desire must be limited in appropriate, God-honoring ways or we may end up losing ourselves in the untethered pursuit of that desire.

Second, not every desire is from God. Just try applying the logic of "I was born with it; I can't change it; therefore, it must be from God" to homophobes who naturally hate gay people! Would we say that because their hatred is natural it must be from God and is therefore right and acceptable? Of course not! It might seem natural to them—but it's wrong just the same. This would be true of people born with tendencies toward anger and violence, those with the propensity to become addicted to drugs or alcohol, and even the person who is inclined to get involved with pedophilia.

We are fallen human beings with all kinds of seemingly natural yet illicit desires. For example, the fact that some people are naturally inclined to alcoholism, outbursts of anger, or the sexual abuse of children might help *explain* their behavior—but it certainly doesn't *excuse* it! Those desires need to be curtailed or contained—no matter how natural they may seem to the person experiencing them. This fact, therefore, discredits the arguments of those who seek to justify same-sex behavior based on their desires for it seeming natural.

TEMPTATION DOES NOT EQUAL SIN

There's a lot of debate these days about whether a gay person's sexual orientation is caused by a "gay gene" or some other physical cause. It's the age-old nature vs. nurture argument—and the truth is that we don't have a conclusive answer. I think it's unwise for us as Christians to argue based on a supposed conclusion. Even if there is some physical or chemical cause someday proven that inclines people toward homosexuality, that doesn't mean that the person must go that route or is justified in doing so. Many believe alcoholism has a physiological cause, but that just means a person with that problem needs to fight the pull toward an alcoholic lifestyle all the harder.

The simple fact seems to be that some people are—*by no choice or action of their own*—more inclined and pulled toward homosexual temptation. So in this sense they may indeed have a homosexual orientation, which would mean they're going to be *more tempted to sin* in that direction. But desire by itself is not sin. So the problem is not with homosexual inclination *per se*, but with homosexual behavior—when the inclination is acted out in either a mentally (lustful) or physically illicit way.

It's the old lesson that being tempted to steal something is not the same as actually stealing it. Temptation itself is not sin: even Jesus "faced all of the same testings we do, yet he did not sin" (Heb. 4:15). That's why he, in spite of his sinless and holy nature, "understands our weaknesses" (v. 15). And it is also why we are encouraged to "come boldly to the throne of our gracious God. There we will receive his mercy, and we will find grace to help us when we need it most" (v. 16).

Jesus wants to help us overcome all our temptations and destructive tendencies. He wants to do that with me and with you and with everyone who struggles in any area, including the pull toward same-sex involvement. People may or may not be able to get rid of those attractions completely, but either way they can say no to illicit same-sex activities. With God's help they can stay celibate and pure (just as every single person is called to do) or, as some formerly gay people have experienced, even grow a natural and healthy attraction to those of the opposite sex that ends in marriage and life with a family. I'm not trying to be simplistic or to pretend that this is easy; just that it *is*, with God's empowerment, entirely possible. It's happening right now in the lives of thousands of men and women who have turned to him for strength and help.

GOD IS LOOKING FOR TRUE WORSHIPERS

Sexual purity is very important. But it is important as part of a real and growing relationship with God. That's what was central in Jesus' teaching. And God's grace is available to all people, including our gay friends, just as it was to the Samaritan woman. Jesus, after raising the issue of the immorality in her life, turns their discussion back to a hope-filled spiritual emphasis:

> "The time is coming—indeed it's here now—when true worshipers will worship the Father in spirit and in truth. The Father is looking for those who will worship him that way. For God is Spirit, so those who worship him must worship in spirit and in truth."
>
> The woman said, "I know the Messiah is coming—the one who is called Christ. When he comes, he will explain everything to us."
>
> Then Jesus told her, "I Am the Messiah!" (John 4:23-26)

Far from belittling this Samaritan woman or distancing himself from her, Jesus chose her as the sole person to whom he would overtly reveal his true identity as the Messiah! You've got to love his vision for wayward people—he found a woman whom everyone else had written off and he offered her salvation, told her who he was, and built vision into her for her life as a true worshiper of God. What compassion and grace he lavished on one who had been so spiritually distant!

MAKING THE CHURCH A PLACE OF GRACE

> Just then his disciples came back. They were shocked to find him talking to a woman, but none of them had the nerve to ask, "What do you want with her?" or "Why are you talking to her?" (John 4:27)

I don't want to unduly disparage the disciples, but their response seems to be at least a shadow of the kinds of misunderstanding and mistrust that we'll sometimes feel from other Christians when we seek to show the love of God to people who are far from Christ. Sometimes Christians simply lack evangelistic vision, as seems to be the situation here, but other times they'll even express downright disdain for those they don't trust or agree with. These are pharisaical tendencies we must push back against—whenever and wherever we see them.

It's interesting, too, that the woman's reaction was to leave her water jar and clear out of the area. While the text indicates that this was due to her excitement to run and tell her friends about what she'd just experienced, it's still interesting that she seemed to feel comfortable being with Jesus but not with his friends, at least initially. Similarly, people today often like Jesus, and they might like you, but they're turned off to the church and to other Christians.

Many times that's because we're doing things that make them feel uncomfortable. These things can include everything from smug, self-righteous attitudes to a simple lack of warmth and hospitality—as it seems to be in the case of the disciples. Instead of wondering, *Who's your new friend?* they asked themselves, *"Why are you talking to her?"* This was hardly an accommodating attitude nor one that exhibited an owning of Jesus' mission "to seek and save those who are lost" (Luke 19:10).

This is a trap all of us can fall into. We must therefore constantly, as we discussed earlier in this chapter, ask God to give us the mind and heart of Christ—including the ability to love and extend grace to people who are different from us and whom we believe to be engaged in sinful activities. Probably nowhere is this more needed than in the church's approach toward people involved in homosexuality. It's interesting—and disheartening—that when young people are asked today what they think of the church many of them respond, "Oh, that's a place that is against the gay community."[7]

Even with the legitimate biblical concerns that we've outlined above, is that really what we want to be known for? It reminds me of the reputation of the church among much of the previous generation: "Oh, that's the place that's down on smoking and drinking," they'd say. Well, smoking and drinking cause their problems—but I want to be part of a church that, as the full-orbed body of Christ, reflects the radiant beauty and attractiveness of God's love, grace, forgiveness, salvation, and hope, for this life and for an eternity of fellowship together with one another as well as with him!

We need to work hard to shift the church's focus back to that positive position and much less on trumpeting our convictions about what are sins and who is committing them. It's not an either/or—but a biblical, Jesus-like both/and balance of prioritizing the proclamation of God's good news while still having the courage to lovingly explain to people the truth of what God's Word says about sin. We also must make sure our own churches are centers where people can come with their struggles—including same-sex attractions—and find from us what they find from Jesus: "mercy and grace to help them when they need it the most" (adapted from Heb. 4:16).

GOD USES REDEEMED SINNERS OF EVERY STRIPE

> The woman left her water jar beside the well
> and ran back to the village, telling everyone,
> "Come and see a man who told me everything
> I ever did! Could he possibly be the Messiah?"
> So the people came streaming from the village
> to see him. . . .
>
> Many Samaritans from the village believed in
> Jesus because the woman had said, "He told me
> everything I ever did!" When they came out to
> see him, they begged him to stay in their village.
> So he stayed for two days, long enough for many
> more to hear his message and believe. Then they
> said to the woman, "Now we believe, not just
> because of what you told us, but because we have
> heard him ourselves. Now we know that he is
> indeed the Savior of the world." (John 4:28-30,
> 39-42)

A friend of mine, Bill Hybels, often quips that we're called as Christians "to turn atheists into missionaries." Another friend, Lee Strobel, is a former atheist who, by God's grace, is now both a minister and a missionary to the very world of skeptics that he came out of.[8] God seems to delight in turning unlikely candidates into uncanny instruments of his love and truth. Just think: anti-Christian Saul became the apostle Paul. And under Jesus' influence that's what we see happening in the Samaritan woman's life. Not only did she receive God's salvation, but she also received his commissioning into an immediate ministry of evangelistic influence on her friends and community. In fact, it was through her efforts that the church was launched in Samaria. Talk about an unexpected adventure![9]

It's this kind of adventure and impact that God made every one of us to experience. But not just we who are already in the church—he wants to enfold everyone through the hope-giving, life-changing, eternity-altering gospel message, which is "the power of God at work, saving everyone who believes" (Rom. 1:16).

It is with that image in mind—and the example of Jesus' efforts to reach the wayward Samaritan woman, who turned into a missionary for him—that we should answer people's questions about homosexuality. And it's with Jesus' vision "to seek and to save" that we must reach out with God's love and truth to everyone, whatever background or lifestyle they happen to be coming from, who is willing to listen.

SUMMARY OF THE ANSWER

Question 7 asks us, "Why do you condemn homosexuality when it's clear that God made gays and that he loves all people the same?"

- The story of Jesus' interactions with the Samaritan woman in John 4 provides a helpful model for how we can express God's grace and truth as we answer friends' questions about homosexuality.

- One of the first and most important things Jesus modeled for us was the need to affirm God's love toward all people—including men and women ensnared in any kind of sexual immorality. When we love like Jesus does, it will show up in our attitudes and actions.

- Our primary focus should be on affirming the positive model God gives us for sexual expression within a biblical marriage—between one man and one woman, for life.

- We should also be honest about God's clear prohibition against homosexual behavior expressed in both the Old and New Testaments of the Bible. It isn't listed as being worse than other sins, but it's clearly on the list. As followers of Christ we need to tell people what God says about it.

- We must correct the idea that because a desire seems natural it must be from God and is therefore okay. As fallen humans we all have many desires that seem natural to us but that are not from God.

- Next, we need to explain that someone's orientation toward or temptation by same-sex attractions is not in and of itself sin. The problem, biblically defined, is not with homosexual *inclinations*, but with actual homosexual *behaviors*. However, many people with these inclinations do, with God's help, find ways to honor God either through celibacy or eventual heterosexual marriage.

- Through his treatment of the woman at the well, Jesus shows us that God wants all kinds of sinners to come to him for salvation, to become his true worshipers, and to become his instruments of love and grace in a world that desperately needs him.

TIPS FOR TALKING ABOUT THIS ISSUE

- The first tip is actually for what to do *prior* to talking about this issue: try to gain Jesus' loving perspective toward sinful people of all kinds. Each of us—me, you, and the gay activist who may right now be shaking his fist at God—mattered enough to the heavenly Father for him to send his Son to die on our behalf. We need to seek some serious infusions of that divine love.

- Rid yourself—and to the degree possible help rid your small group, Bible study, and church—of all degrading humor and comments about homosexuals and the gay community. These will only distance you from the people God sent us to reach. Remember the admonition in Ephesians 5:4: "Obscene stories, foolish talk, and coarse jokes—these are not for you. Instead, let there be thankfulness to God."

- When we get into discussions about homosexuality, we need to remember that people's defenses are already up.

The wisdom of James 1:19 is probably nowhere more important. He says, "Understand this, my dear brothers and sisters: You must all be quick to listen, slow to speak, and slow to get angry."

- Because of the actions of some Christians, people often expect us to be uncaring. Surprise and intrigue them with your Jesus-like love and empathy. Try to understand how they think, interacting with them, as 1 Peter 3:16 tells us, "in a gentle and respectful way."

- Speak the truth of God's Word without racing to judgment on individual people. Acknowledge up front that the Bible contains challenges regarding this subject that are hard for many to hear. Also, remind them that this is *God's* revelation, not your personal opinion. You're the messenger trying to be faithful to the God you serve— the One who also knows what's best for us as humans.

- Put your main emphasis on the life-giving message of the gospel—which promises salvation to every person who receives Christ—and not on God's laws about this or that sin. Focus on the truth of Romans 5:6: "When we were utterly helpless, Christ came at just the right time and died for us sinners."

- Realize that as you model Jesus-like grace in your attempts to reach out to those who struggle with homosexuality, there will be people who misunderstand and even malign your efforts. Try to help them get a biblical perspective, perhaps through a passage such as the one we discussed in John 4, but keep doing what God calls you to do, knowing that God's "joy awaits" you (v. 36).

QUESTIONS FOR GROUP DISCUSSION

1. What kinds of examples have you seen from Christians in addressing issues of homosexuality? Did they emphasize truth at the expense of grace—or vice versa?

2. How do you feel about the balance of grace and truth in your own perspective on this issue? Do you need to shore up one side or the other a bit? How can you go about doing that?

3. What can we as Christians do if we've been too strong on one side of the issue, failing to live out the WWJD principle discussed at the beginning of the chapter?

4. What are some practical things your group or your church could do to make it a more accessible and friendly place for serious spiritual seekers who are struggling with this issue?

5. Toward the end of the passage in John 4, after the disciples came back to find Jesus talking to the Samaritan woman, they urged him to eat. Jesus replied, "I have a kind of food you know nothing about. . . . My nourishment comes from doing the will of God, who sent me, and from finishing his work" (vv. 32, 34). Have there been times or eras in your life when you related to Jesus' statement? What could you do to experience that kind of era once again?

CHAPTER 8:

"How can I trust in Christianity when so many Christians are hypocrites?"

"And why are Christians so judgmental toward everyone who doesn't agree with them?"

My friends and I took a trip into downtown Chicago for a play and dinner afterwards. Soon after we found our seats in the theater the house lights dimmed. A hush swept over the audience as the curtain opened and a single actor stepped into the spotlight. Immediately we were transported into a whole other world—one filled with suspense and intrigue. The play lasted well over two hours, but it was so riveting the time flew by quickly.

What made the show extra entertaining were the captivating performances of the actors themselves. They were enthralling. World class. Awardworthy. Particularly the one who just happens to have the same last name as me. The one who, well . . . also happens to be my younger brother.

Obviously, I know Jim really well. I know his personality, I understand his strengths and weaknesses, and I appreciate his unique wit and sense of humor—as well as his consistent quirks. After all, I've known him his entire life. But that night at the play he became, for the span of a couple hours, an entirely different person to me. In fact, several times I caught myself grinning as I had to remind myself that the person on that stage wasn't real, but actually a fictional character portrayed by none other than my very own bro!

After the show, my friends and I went backstage to congratulate Jim on his masterful performance. He playfully responded—in character—and gave us a great laugh as he kept the role going for the next several minutes.

It was all a lot of fun, but I have to admit that later when we walked to a nearby restaurant I felt relieved that he was no longer playing the part. As much as I enjoyed Jim's acting, it was nice to have my own brother back again.

Pretending to be someone we're not isn't a bad thing—if we're actors. It's part of the job description. Audience members would demand refunds if the cast refused to get into character and act out their assigned parts in the play. Actors are supposed to act.

But it's a completely different matter when it comes to everyday life. People in the real world ought to be true to who they say they are. If someone openly claims to adhere to a set of values or beliefs, then that person had better be careful to back that

up with consistent actions and behaviors—espe-
cially if he or she is a Christian. There's no room for
actors on that *stage.*

—Garry Poole[1]

We see the problem all around us—from the headlines announcing the latest case of clergy abuse and subsequent cover-ups to rumors of yet another evangelical leader who has fallen into some kind of serious sin. Whether the information is about someone whose name everybody knows or somebody relatively unknown, when the person is reputed to be a follower of Christ, it's always a tragedy.

Worse, to many of our friends who are trying to decide what to believe and whether *any* form of faith is worth following, it's a travesty—one that can set them back years in their spiritual journey or maybe even turn them 180 degrees to the opposite direction.

Perhaps that's why the issue of hypocrisy and judgmentalism ranked so highly on our survey, in which we asked Christians what questions they'd most like to avoid being asked. Together they tied for fourth place, right next to the question about the Bible, which we addressed in chapter 3. Probably part of the reason our interviewees wished to avoid it was because of the seriousness of the subject, as well as the fact that it may hit close to home in their own lives or in the lives of others around them. But address it we must—if we wish to help our friends keep moving forward in their spiritual journeys toward Christ.

Being called a hypocrite is never a compliment; it's usually uttered in complete disgust. In modern language, *hypocrisy* is "claiming to have moral standards or beliefs to which one's own behavior does not conform; pretense."[2] The label comes from an ancient Greek word that was a technical term for a stage actor. Hypocrites are mask wearers, acting without ever acknowledging that is what they're doing.

The problem is not so much that they sin or fail; it's that they pretend they don't. They're inauthentic, unwilling to admit they're not really who they say they are. Hypocrites are frauds and imposters—people living a lie.

According to Shakespeare, "All the world's a stage." Well, here are some of the not-so-popular players:

- The Bible study leader who teaches moral purity but walks out on her husband and kids and into the arms of another man

- A churchgoing, Bible-quoting boss who cheats on the sales figures "just a little bit" to get a better market rating for his company

- The respected priest, trusted by his parishioners, who preaches piety but covers up his sexual abuse of children

- A charismatic youth minister who calls students to biblical fidelity, but then is caught in a secret life—one checkered with illicit sex and illegal drugs

- That "perfect" soccer dad who sits in the church pew every Sunday but goes home to a hidden habit of alcohol abuse and violence toward his wife and children

- The religious neighbor who pretends in front of others that "every day with Jesus is sweeter than the day before" but in reality is filled with fear, resentment, and jealousy

You can try your own experiment. Ask some non-Christian friends, "Have you ever encountered a hypocritical Christian?" Chances are you'll hear lots of stories—such as, "My daughter's playground friend keeps correcting her behavior, saying 'Jesus wouldn't want you to do that,' but her family is doing things I know Jesus wouldn't want *them* to do either." Or, "That politician claims to be a Christian, but look at how he treats his wife!" Or "My coworker has a Bible on her desk and Christian bumper stickers, but has she even once offered to pitch in when extra help is needed around here?"

Unfortunately, statistics seem to bear out the perception that many Christians often fail to live out their stated spiritual ideals. David Kinnaman and Gabe Lyons, authors of *unChristian: What a New Generation Really Thinks about Christianity*, have done research that shows there isn't much measurable difference between people who claim to be born-again Christians and the rest of the world.

> *Born-agains were distinct on some religious variables, most notably owning more Bibles, going to church more often, and donating money to religious nonprofits (especially a church). However, when it came to non-religious factors—the substance of people's daily choices, actions, and attitudes—there were few meaningful gaps between born-again Christians and non-born-agains. . . . In virtually every study we conduct, representing thousands of interviews every year, born-again Christians fail to display much attitudinal or behavioral evidence of transformed lives.*[3]

That's a sad commentary on Christians and the church. Gandhi once remarked, "I like your Christ, I do not like your Christians. Your Christians are so unlike your Christ." Mark Twain stated, "If Christ were here, there is one thing he would not be—a Christian."

My friend and ministry partner, Lee Strobel, reflects on the impact that hypocrisy had on him when he was a non-Christian:

> Holier-than-thou Christians *repelled me. Smug and self-righteous, they painted themselves as being much better than they really were, and tarred people like me as being much worse than we really were, as if every social problem in the country stemmed from the fact that everyone didn't agree with them 100 percent. That angered me. . . .*
>
> *The other folks who chased me away from the faith were* cosmetic Christians. *They had a skin-deep spirituality that looked pretty good on the outside but didn't penetrate deep enough to change their behaviors and attitudes. . . .*
>
> *Frankly, I don't think anything repulses people like the hypocrisy of cosmetic Christians.*[4]

HALTING HYPOCRISY

In the midst of all these negative reactions to inauthentic believers, many of our friends simply throw up their hands and ask us honestly, "How can I trust in Christianity when so many Christians are hypocrites?"

Our friends are not alone in their harsh judgment of hypocrisy. Jesus dealt with this issue often—and no one spoke more strongly about it than he did. Here are some excerpts of what Jesus said to the crowds in Matthew 23 regarding the religious leaders of his day:

> Practice and obey whatever they tell you, but don't follow their example. For they don't practice what they teach. . . .
>
> Everything they do is for show. . . .
>
> What sorrow awaits you teachers of religious law and you Pharisees. Hypocrites! For you cross land and sea to make one convert, and then you turn that person into twice the child of hell you yourselves are! Blind guides! What sorrow awaits you! . . .
>
> Hypocrites! For you are so careful to clean the outside of the cup and the dish, but inside you are filthy—full of greed and self-indulgence! You blind Pharisee! First wash the inside of the cup and the dish, and then the outside will become clean, too. . . .
>
> Hypocrites! For you are like whitewashed tombs—beautiful on the outside but filled on the inside with dead people's bones and all sorts of impurity. Outwardly you look like righteous people, but inwardly your hearts are filled with hypocrisy and lawlessness. . . .
>
> Hypocrites! . . . Snakes! Sons of vipers! How will you escape the judgment of hell?

Wow! Do you get the sense that Jesus was *serious* in his condemnation of their spiritual duplicity? He hated it enough—but also loved the people it affected enough—to hit them hard with the unvarnished truth about themselves, their attitudes and actions, and the detrimental impact they were having on others.

And that leads to the first point we can make as we answer questions about hypocrisy.

When our friends condemn hypocrisy, they're actually on Jesus' side!

Yes, I understand that many people use this issue to blame God or to resist Jesus, but part of our task is to help them to see error in their thinking. *Jesus agrees with them*—at least on this broad point about hypocrisy. He's their ally. If they'll just read passages like the one above and see the passion with which Jesus railed against spiritual pretense, it might help them open up to him in other areas as well. Their problem isn't so much with God as it is with some of his *people*— or, more specifically, with some of his people's *sin and their unwillingness to own up to it.*

Here's how a conversation with a friend might play out along these lines:

Your friend says, "I could never become a Christian be-cause of all the hypocritical Christians who say one thing and do another."

"That's interesting," you reply, "because you're already taking steps toward following Jesus."

"What do you mean?" he asks you, surprised. "I'm mad

at all the people who claim to be religious but who fail to live up to what they say."

"That's my point! Jesus gets really worked up about the same thing—so the two of you see eye-to-eye on this one. I wonder, How else might you agree with him?"

"I've never thought about it like that before," he says, starting to let his guard down a little bit. "Did Jesus really talk about that?"

"Right here in the Gospel of Matthew, in chapter 23," you answer. "Let's take a look at it and perhaps read some of the other things he said. It wouldn't surprise me if you resonate with a lot of what Jesus talked about."

Our friends naturally see Christians' hypocritical behavior as being unacceptable. But they need help to see that Christ feels the same way. This point may also open them up to the second point we can make.

Jesus is the only perfect example—and therefore the only one who won't disappoint us

This is not to excuse the inauthentic actions of the Christians who have disappointed our friends, but it is the truth—and important for our friends to understand. The Bible claims moral perfection for only one human being, and that was Jesus. Hebrews 4:15 tells us that he "understands our weaknesses, for he faced all of the same testings we do, *yet he did not sin*" (emphasis mine).

And Jesus himself, when he was on trial before his crucifixion, actually challenged his accusers by asking them boldly, "Which of you can truthfully accuse me of sin?" (John 8:46). I would *dare* anybody to present that challenge to his own family, roommates, or friends. Because, well, he would undoubtedly get an earful! The people who know him the best are going to have a whole laundry list of things to say about him—probably a lot longer than he would have guessed—just as my relatives and friends would have for me.

But Jesus could give this challenge because he alone was free from sin, and the response of his opponents ultimately bore this out—since they were the ones who later brought him to trial and "were trying to find witnesses who would lie about Jesus, so they could put him to death" (Matt. 26:59). Jesus' enemies ended up having to manufacture false charges in order to get him out of their way, giving further evidence that he was without sin or flaw. That's just another reason that we need to stop relying on our own moral performance and to "fix our eyes on Jesus, the author and perfecter of our faith" (Heb. 12:2, NIV). He's the One who "suffered for our sins once for all time. He never sinned, but he died for sinners to bring you safely home to God" (1 Pet. 3:18).

Let's look at the first question once more: "How can I trust in Christianity when so many Christians are hypocrites?"

The late Ruth Bell Graham, Billy Graham's wife, spoke about Pashi, a young college student from India. Pashi once told her, "We of India would like to believe in Christ. But we have never seen a Christian who was like Christ." Ruth Graham said that when she consulted Dr. Akbar Abdul-Haqq about what might be the best response to Pashi's challenge, he answered decisively: "That is quite simple. I would tell Pashi, *I am not offering you Christians. I am offering you Christ*"[5] (emphasis mine). Yes, the primary issue regarding the validity of Christianity is not Jesus' followers but Jesus himself—and what he offers to those who follow him.

Ultimately we need to encourage our friends to put their faith not in Christianity—and certainly not in the flawed efforts of frail Christians—but in the powerful and proven person of *Jesus Christ himself.*

The third point we need to make is a very important one.

Many hypocrites are only pretending to be God's people

"Exhibit A" is the group of people Jesus rebuked in the Matthew 23 passage, quoted above. You remember them—the ones he called "Hypocrites! Snakes! Sons of vipers!" These people were playing a high-level religious game, but according to Jesus, it was all for show, completely lacking in spiritual substance. And there are plenty of folks like them today as well. "Such people claim they know God, but they deny him by the way they live" (Titus 1:16). "They will act religious, but they will reject the power that could make them godly" (2 Tim. 3:5).

When we understand that many people who claim to be Christians are not really followers of Christ at all, it helps us—and it can help our friends—to stop blaming the faith for what these faithless people do. By way of analogy, we wouldn't disparage the medical community for something a witch doctor does. He may have "doctor" in his title, but he's certainly not a representative of the medical community. Similarly, the Christian community should not be held responsible for the actions of false Christians.

Admittedly, it is often hard to discern who is pretending versus who is simply falling short of sincerely held beliefs. But that doesn't negate the point. Jesus warned, for example, that "false messiahs and false prophets will rise up and perform great signs and wonders so as to deceive, if possible, even God's chosen ones. See, I have warned you about this ahead of time" (Matt. 24:24-25). The only way they will be able to deceive anyone is by pretending to be the real thing.

In addition to false religious leaders, there are many other spiritual posers, including political and military leaders both now and throughout history, who have committed all kinds of inhumane acts and injustices in Jesus' name. We need to be discerning to see, and to help our friends see, that their crimes are their own and not the fault of the One who told them to love, to forgive, to show mercy, and to help the helpless—regardless of what these imposters may have claimed.

Now, with the fourth point we can make, our conversation starts hitting closer to home.

Hypocrisy comes in degrees—and each of us struggles with some measure of it

The Bible describes the human race as fallen. Television news programs confirm this reality every day. And so do the people around us, not to mention—let's face it—the person *inside* us. The Bible describes us all as sinners who "fall short" of God's moral standards (Rom. 3:23).

As followers of Jesus, we have a high calling. We are forgiven through his grace, yes, but we also have a responsibility to live like we're forgiven. We have the duty to obey Christ and to honor him by turning away from the sin he paid for through his death on the cross. The Bible is clear about this: "As God's chosen people, holy and dearly loved, clothe yourselves with compassion, kindness, humility, gentleness and patience" (Col. 3:12, NIV). There is no question that Christians are called to be holy people, set apart to uphold high values and virtues.

But it would be a mistake to assume that when a person becomes a Christian all his or her problems, trials, and difficulties evaporate. Struggles and temptations do not go away simply because an individual turns his or her life over to Jesus.

This is where the promise of new life can appear incongruous with our actual experience. Though we have been forgiven and called to turn from sin, we still encounter pain, disappointment, hurt, troubles, and temptation, and, yes, we all struggle with sin. This is the dichotomy that is troubling for us, as well as others, to see. God does not wave a magic wand and make all our struggles disappear. The work that he has begun in us has been initiated but not completed. Every true Christian is in the midst of a sanctification process, one in which God says, "Let the Spirit renew your thoughts and attitudes. Put on your new nature, created to be like God— truly righteous and holy" (Eph. 4:23-24). Thankfully, we have also been given the hope that "he who began a good work in you will carry it on to completion until the day of Christ Jesus" (Phil. 1:6, NIV).

Authentic Christ followers understand they are works in progress. They engage in the everyday battle against sin, embrace the victories, and own up to the setbacks and defeats. And all along the way they learn to display the kind of transparency that Jesus describes in John 3:21 (NIV): "Whoever lives by the truth comes into the light, so that it may be seen plainly that what he has done has been done through God."

So in reality, there should be no surprise that Christians are unable to live up to standards they strive to attain—for no one can! We are not perfect. None of us do everything we intend to do. But here is an important distinction: it is one thing to admit to missing the mark and falling short of the goal, but it is quite another thing to deny this struggle altogether or to pretend we're winning when we are not. Herein lies the distinction between an honest sinner struggling to become more like God and a hypocrite who refuses to come clean and acknowledge his or her own flaws.

Jesus died on the cross to pay for and to free us from our sin—including that of hypocrisy

We showed earlier how strongly Jesus condemned hypocrisy, especially in the Matthew 23 passage where he challenged the Pharisees. But before we end this discussion, let me remind you of what we need to convey to our friends: Jesus came primarily to "seek and to save," not to confront and condemn.

Again, the most famous verse in the Bible is John 3:16: "God loved the world so much that he gave his one and only Son, so that everyone who believes in him will not perish but have eternal life." But too often people stop reading there, and miss the great news that comes right after it in verses 17-18: "God sent his Son into the world not to judge the world, but to save the world through him. There is no judgment against anyone who believes in him." This does not deny that ultimately God will bring judgment to those who persist in resisting and denying him. We'll discuss that in the next chapter. But the passage tells us that this was not his goal or his desire when he came and walked on earth.

His desire was to "save the world"—including every imaginable kind of sinner, even the worst of hypocrites, if they would just turn to him. The apostle Paul sums it up well when he says this in 1 Timothy 1:15-16 (emphasis mine):

> This is a trustworthy saying, and everyone should accept it: "Christ Jesus came into the world to save sinners"—and I am the worst of them all. But God had mercy on me so that Christ Jesus could use me as a prime example of his great patience with even the worst sinners. *Then others will realize that they, too, can believe in him and receive eternal life.*

A PERSONAL RESPONSE

So how should we respond to all this? First, we need to start by being honest with—*and about*—ourselves, speaking vulnerably about our own experience. As genuine followers of Jesus, we ought to be able to illustrate the difference that knowing him has made in our lives without glossing over the ups and downs we face in trying to follow him.

Kinnaman and Lyons explain the importance of being transparent:

> *Young people talk these days about the need for authenticity, for "keepin' it real"—not pretending to be something you are not, being open about*

your faults. Young people are searching for this type
of person, this kind of lifestyle. In one survey we
found that "doing what you say you are going to do"
was among the characteristics young people most
admired.[6]

I heard a good example of this when pastor Jim Dixon was interviewed in front of his suburban Denver congregation during the last week of a series he had been teaching on the topic of love. He was asked what he had been learning himself through the series. His answer struck me as refreshingly honest, along the lines of what Kinnaman and Lyons were talking about. "Personally, I know I'm just a sinner in need of grace," Dixon conceded. "So every time I preach, and even during my times of preparation, I feel like God— by his Spirit—convicts me as to where I need to change. And that was true during this 'Love' series. I became very mindful through the five weeks of how I need to grow in love. I know I need to love God more. And I know I need to love people more."[7]

I once heard someone say that people won't want to poke holes in us if we go ahead and poke holes in ourselves first. I think that's partly what Dixon was doing—admitting his own need to grow before someone else felt compelled to point it out to him. That approach helps explain why people have been so responsive to his teaching and leadership over the nearly three decades he has been the pastor of Cherry Hills Community Church.

On the other hand, I wasn't so fortunate once when a friend confronted me for not being honest about my spiritual condition. We were just a year out of high school when Terry, a former classmate, asked me why I claimed to be a Christian when my lifestyle at the time did not reflect that reality. I stumbled around trying to justify and joke about my actions, but he was relentless. Before the conversation was over, he told me pointedly that there was a term for people like me. You probably guessed it—the word was *hypocrite*.

Ouch! Terry made me angry that day, but he also made me think. It was humbling to realize that he was right and that I needed either to stop pretending to be a Christian or to actually start living like one. It took me almost a week to make my decision, but thankfully I ended up making a genuine commitment to Jesus, and with God's help my life began to change in dramatic ways.

Perhaps it is because of those humble beginnings that I've had a pretty good grasp over the years that while my attitudes and actions have changed in many ways, I'm still a sinner in need of the Savior. Living "in the light" before God and before a watching world is an ongoing challenge, one that leads me back often to 1 John 1:9, which tells us, "If we confess our sins to him, he is faithful and just to forgive us our sins and to cleanse us from all wickedness." And about the time I think I'm getting the whole Christian life figured out, I go through a season in which I feel like one of God's sons described in Hebrews 12:5-6, 12: "My child, don't make light of the Lord's discipline, and don't give up when he corrects you. For the Lord disciplines those he loves. . . . So take a new grip with your tired hands and strengthen your weak knees."

When I said earlier that *all of us struggle with some measure of hypocrisy*, I really meant it—and we need to be open about our own experience with it. Think how disarming it would be to just admit to our friends, "Yes, a lot of Christians do struggle with hypocrisy. And you know what? Sometimes *so do I*! Sometimes I fall to the temptation to act like I'm better than I am—to project an image that I've got it all together, when I don't. Thankfully, I've been learning, sometimes the hard way, to be more honest with myself and with others and to admit that living the Christian life is not easy. Sometimes I do that a lot better than at other times. But I'll tell you what: it's liberating to admit I'm a sinner saved by God's amazing grace, and with his help I'm trying to live the kind of life he calls Christians to live. I'm glad he still forgives me when I fail in those efforts."

This kind of vulnerability—without going into unnecessary levels of detail about our actual struggles—is, first of all, just old-fashioned honesty. But it's also attractive to people who are trying to find God in their own broken lives. A friend of mine wrote in a letter about her attitude toward Christians when she was still a spiritual seeker: "I'm not looking for perfect, but I am looking for real."

Hopefully, that's also true of the persons who ask us the question about hypocrisy. If so, then our honesty will help them to become more honest with us. Because once we've set the example by vulnerably talking about our own struggles to follow God, it'll be a lot easier to get our friends to open up as well. It will no longer feel like "us versus them," but more like "us *with* them"—fellow strugglers trying to sort out what's best for our lives.

It's at that point that the stage will be set for us to gently ask, "How about you? Do you ever get that nagging sense that your life doesn't live up to what you know to be right? Can you relate to this question at some level like I can?"

Hypocrisy is a disease that has, to one degree or another, infected the whole human race. It's one that understandably offends our friends, especially those who have been hurt by Christians (or pretend Christians) who have not lived up to their claims. But once we've addressed the issue, acknowledged our own struggles with it, and helped the persons we're talking with see and admit that they're not immune to the problem, either, then we're ready to talk to them about the forgiveness and grace that are available through Jesus.

JUDGING JUDGMENTALISM

Finally, let's look at the second question for this chapter: "Why are Christians so judgmental toward everyone who doesn't agree with them?"

There's no doubt that judgmentalism from Christians is a huge problem in the eyes of spiritually sensitive people who see it. What is doubtful, though, is what exactly that means! Let's examine and analyze a couple of possibilities.

First, it seems that what many people react to is *a haughty and arrogant attitude* that they sometimes see in others—one that says, in effect, "I'm right and you're wrong; I know more than you, I live better than you, and I'm more spiritual and holy than you." Well, arrogance is ugly no matter who exudes it—Christians or otherwise. Make no mistake about it, the Bible is down on arrogance! Pride is considered one of the seven deadly sins, and the Old Testament book of Proverbs lists it first when it says, "There are six things the LORD hates—no, seven things he detests: haughty eyes . . ." (Prov. 6:16-17). The King James Version translates the "haughty eyes" in verse 17 as "a proud look." And a few chapters later this biblical book of wisdom warns us that "pride goes before destruction, and haughtiness before a fall" (Prov. 16:18).

In the New Testament Jesus placed the sin of pride squarely in the midst of an unsavory list of evils that emanate from a fallen human's inner being: "From within, out of a person's heart, come evil thoughts, sexual immorality, theft, murder, adultery, greed, wickedness, deceit, lustful desires, envy, slander, *pride*, and foolishness. All these vile things come from within; they are what defile you" (Mark 7:21-23, emphasis mine).

So there is obviously no place for pride, haughtiness, or arrogance among Christians, and our friends who are down on these things need to know that God is too—and so are we! If they ever see a proud, better-than-others attitude in us, they would be doing us a favor to come and point it out, to help us get our spiritual feet back on the ground.

In fact, when it comes to sharing our faith with others, I've always loved the humility and realism in the description that says, "All we are is beggars telling other beggars where to find bread." We're not smarter than others, we're not better than they are, and we're not more worthy than anyone else—we're just blessed to have found what we have in Christ and are privileged to get to share it with them. That, in my opinion, is the biblical understanding of evangelism.

A second possible explanation of what our friends might have in mind when they condemn judging is *the idea that we should never say we're right and somebody else is wrong.* The verse they often quote to back up this idea comes straight from the mouth of Jesus, in Matthew 7:1, "Do not judge others, and you will not be judged." Interestingly, according to my friend Paul Copan, "That verse has replaced John 3:16 as the favorite verse that people like to quote."[8]

What's fascinating is that the people who condemn Christians for acting as if they're right and others are wrong are, in that very action, acting as if they themselves are right and Christians are wrong. So they are at that moment doing the very thing they say is wrong. When you think about it, it's pretty silly to condemn people for thinking they are right—because aren't you simultaneously thinking *you* are right in saying they are wrong? Or, broadening the point a bit, who in their right mind *doesn't* consistently think that they are right? Seriously, if a sane person thinks he is wrong, doesn't he immediately change his thinking and begin to believe what he now thinks is actually right? If so, then doesn't he once again think he is right and that anyone who contradicts his new belief is, by the very nature of logic, wrong? Don't we all think that way? I mean, really, do you ever think you're wrong while you're in the midst of thinking that very thought? I don't think so; I think as soon as you start to realize your thinking is wrong you change your belief and start thinking differently! Therefore, for two reasons no one should condemn Christians just for thinking they're right and others are wrong: (1) everybody else does the same thing, and (2) Christians might really be right, after all.

If you happen to be a philosophy major, you loved

that last paragraph! If you didn't love it, then let's come at it another way—from the Bible. Jesus couldn't have meant in Matthew 7:1 that we should never judge anything in any way. How do we know? Well, again I'll quote Paul Copan, who went on to explain, "Jesus says, 'Stop judging by mere appearances, and make a right judgment' [John 7:24, NIV]. So Jesus clarifies that it's all right—in fact, it's a good thing—to make *proper* judgments about people. What Jesus condemns is a critical and judgmental attitude or an unholy sense of moral superiority"[9]—in other words, the kind of attitudes we discussed and dismissed under possibility number one, just above.

To clarify further, Erwin Lutzer explains that "the word *judge* means to exercise discernment; at other times it can mean to condemn; and sometimes both ideas are present. But clearly Jesus is not teaching that all judging is wrong. Judging, or discernment, lies at the heart of Christian living."[10] This understanding helps make sense of the rest of the Bible, which tells us in many different ways and with a variety of words that it's not our job to judge (as in condemn) other people, but it *is* our job to judge (as in discern) which leaders are to be followed, which teachers are really teaching truth, which doctrines are to be trusted, which courses of action are wise, and so forth.

One final thought related to this discussion: many people in our culture seem to think that the second possibility—namely, being convinced that we're right—invariably leads to the first one, arrogance. But let's look again at Jesus. He was absolutely convinced he was right. In fact, he even said, "I am the way, the truth, and the life. No one can come to the Father except through me" (John 14:6)—yet he was also known for his gentleness and humility. And to us, his followers, Jesus said, "You will know the truth, and the truth will set you free" (John 8:32); he also told us to serve one another in all humility.

So, yes, we can be fully convinced that what we've found in Christ is completely true, and yet present those truths to others with a humble and patient spirit. That's exactly what Jesus, who was God in human flesh, did—and according to Ephesians 5:1, you and I are to "imitate God, therefore, in everything you do, because you are his dear children."

SUMMARY OF THE ANSWER

The questions for this chapter ask us, "How can I trust in Christianity when so many Christians are hypocrites?" "And why are Christians so judgmental toward everyone who doesn't agree with them?"

- The opening illustration of a man seeing his brother portray a character in a play points out that, while acting like something you're not is the job of an actor, we shouldn't act in real life. How people live should back up the values and beliefs they claim to embrace.

- As harmful as hypocrisy is to Christianity, one doesn't have to look far to find Christians falling into some kind of serious sin. Statistics bear out the sad fact that many who claim to be Christians fail to let their faith significantly affect their lives.

- When people express anger at hypocrisy, they are in good company—Jesus directed some of his harshest words at the hypocrisy of the religious leaders of his day. The problem with hypocrisy isn't with God, but with people. At least on this subject, our friends and God are actually on the same side.

- Jesus alone was free from sin; therefore, he is the only person who is also completely free from hypocrisy. He will never disappoint those who put their trust in him.

- Many hypocrites are only pretending to be Christians. That said, however, hypocrisy is a sin, and believers struggle with some degree of it too. There is a difference, however, between a struggling but honest believer and a hypocrite who refuses to acknowledge any wrongdoing.

- Judgmentalism can refer to an arrogant and unacceptable "I'm better than you" attitude. But it can also refer to Christians' mind-set that we are right in our beliefs and, therefore, others are wrong. Such an attitude is usually just spiritual confidence, which is natural (as long as it doesn't get mixed with pride and arrogance too). Everyone thinks that what they believe is true. Don't make this an argument; rather, point your friends toward the truth of Christ.

TIPS FOR TALKING ABOUT THIS ISSUE

- Be honest about the reality of Christian hypocrisy. Don't give excuses, but let the hard truth of failures stand. The validity of Christianity does not depend on your ability to defend every fallen Christian. It's okay to simply admit the truth that Christians fail.

- Listen in order to understand. If your seeking friends have had a hurtful, angry, or confusing personal experience with hypocrisy, enter into their world and listen with empathy. Really be there for them. Try to agree where possible, and be willing to offer an authentic apology on behalf of hypocritical Christians.

- Be transparent. At the core of hypocrisy are hidden motives, inauthentic actions, and controlled appearances. Your openness about the topic can help remove the barriers that secrets and shame have created.

- It is helpful when we as Christians can be vulnerable (at appropriate levels) about our own struggles to follow God—and this can draw out increasing degrees of openness from our friends as well.

- Redirect. Remember that the basis for evaluating Christ must be Christ, not Christians. Remind your friends that humans are human, but Jesus claimed to be God. The perfect person and teachings of Jesus are the foundation on which to evaluate Christianity.

- Point out to your friends that in condemning hypocrisy they are actually agreeing with Jesus. Encourage them (and help them) to learn more about Jesus. Express your confidence that they'll find other areas of agreement with him.

- Accusations of judgmentalism need to be defined. If an accusation is related to arrogance, we should make sure that it's not true—or else seek to change.

- There's no place for spiritual pride in the church, and it can put up real walls to people who see it. But if people are upset because of our confidence in what we believe, we should help them see that everyone thinks they're right—including they themselves, at that very moment. The question to focus on is, How can we know what is true in the spiritual realm?

QUESTIONS FOR GROUP DISCUSSION

1. Why is the hypocrisy of Christians such a hot button for unbelievers? Why do you think it bothers them so much to see Christians acting in unchristian ways?

2. Why do unbelievers hold Christians to such high standards?

3. Have you ever encountered a hypocritical Christian? Describe the encounter. How did that person's hypocrisy make you feel?

4. Why did Jesus speak so sternly about the hypocrisy of the religious leaders of his day?

5. Can you share a way you have struggled with hypocrisy? What did you do about it? Can you think of a way to utilize that experience to point people to Christ?

6. Explain the statement, "Authentic Christ followers understand they are works in progress." Is that a helpful description or an effort to excuse bad behavior or attitudes? How does this help you talk about hypocrisy with unbelievers?

7. Describe the difference between "judgmentalism" and "judging with wisdom and discernment."

CHAPTER 9:

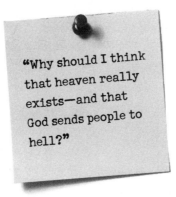

"Why should I think that heaven really exists—and that God sends people to hell?"

"I've just gotta be where the action is!"

That's what Marie Little said to her friends who years ago questioned why a woman her age—already seventy at the time—would choose to go to an upstart, youthful, rock-and-roll-oriented church. She explained to them that people were coming to faith in Christ there, and she had to get in on the excitement.

That's a pretty good description of Marie's life as a whole: she always had to be where the action was. That was true when she was a young missionary in China at the start of the Communist revolution. And when she served in the midst of an exciting new campus ministry called InterVarsity, eventually marrying one of its most dynamic leaders, evangelist, and soon-to-be best-selling author Paul Little. And then when she came to be part of our church and a key leader in our very active outreach ministry, which I was privileged to lead for many of the years she was involved.

But today, in the ultimate sense, Marie is truly in the middle of the action—in the presence of the Lord of the universe, along with his angels; every true believer who has ever died; and, of course, her beloved husband, Paul. I can just hear her saying to us today, "This is where the real *action is, my friends!"*

Like all of you, my family and I miss Marie greatly. It's natural to mourn the loss of our wonderful friend and, for many of you, your dear family member—but let's keep it in perspective. She truly is in a better place. First John 5:13 says, "I have written this to you who believe in the name of the Son of God, so that you may know *you have eternal life." Well, there's no question that Marie believed in him, and that's why she had such confidence about where she was heading next.*

So Marie is in heaven today, with Jesus, and life for her is good. *In fact, she was excited about getting there and for the past few years couldn't stop talking about it. It was like a big upcoming graduation that she could hardly wait to finally experience!*[1]

It was an honor to stand in front of so many of Marie Little's family and friends to give the eulogy at her memorial service. Over the years that Heidi and I lived in Chicago, she had become our "adopted mom," and our kids, Emma Jean and

Matthew, grew up knowing her simply as "Auntie Marie"—
even though we were not actually related to her. Because of
our special relationship, we were naturally sad when we heard
that she had died, yet her memorial service truly felt more
like a celebration than a time of grieving. That wouldn't have
been possible were it not for our confident belief—shared
by virtually everyone who was there—that she truly was in
heaven at that very moment.

But what made us so confident? How can anybody
really know what the afterlife will be like—assuming there
actually will be one? Why were we "sure" that Marie was in
heaven—was it just because we loved her? or because she
was such a great person? or because of her participation in
churches throughout most of her life? Maybe we were just
projecting our personal wishes onto the situation and talking ourselves into believing something for which there was
no real evidence. We felt convinced—but why?

Putting it another way, the first part of our question
for this chapter asks, "Why should I think that heaven really
exists?" We find that there is a lot of curiosity about this
issue in our culture right now, as well as about the related
second part, ". . . that God sends people to hell." In our
survey this question of heaven's existence tied for first place
(next to the topic of God's existence) as one of the questions
we as Christians feel least ready to answer.

How do we know that heaven and hell are real and that
real people can go there? Some interesting approaches have
been taken to try to answer that question. In previous centuries, for example, experiments were done weighing people
right before and after the moment of their death in an attempt

to determine the weight of the soul. The assumption was that as the soul left the body there would be an immediate, though minute, reduction in weight. Of course, such experiments turned up nothing because, in Christian theology, the soul is not a material entity and therefore we wouldn't expect it to register on even the most sensitive of scales.

But therein lies the problem. We're talking about an immaterial component of a human being—a spirit that we can't see, touch, weigh, or measure—and we're discussing whether or not that invisible entity is transported at death, unseen, to an invisible place of which there are no photographs, no YouTube videos, no testimonials from current occupants, or any hard evidence that can be checked out in any remotely scientific manner. When you think about it, it's not surprising that a lot of people question the existence of heaven and that many of us get a bit queasy trying to figure out how to answer them.

Christian philosopher Dallas Willard tells the story of a woman who refused to talk about life beyond death because, she said, she didn't want her children to be disappointed if it turned out no afterlife exists. Willard pointed out to this woman that if no afterlife exists, her children won't have any consciousness with which to feel the disappointment! On the other hand, if there is an afterlife, then her children and any others who enter that next life unprepared may experience far more than mere disappointment.[2]

So, on the chance that people really do face an eternal destiny based on choices they make here on earth, it is definitely worth talking about—and going beyond mere talk to give some kind of reasonable assurance.

MAKING THE CASE

Before we try to help someone else get an answer to this question, it might clarify the discussion to start on a more personal note: why do *you* believe in heaven and, for that matter, in hell? Put another way, what is your own compelling reason for believing that there is an afterlife—one that lasts for *eternity*?

You may reply, "I don't know; I've just always accepted it." But you weren't *born* with this conviction. You must have picked it up somewhere along the way. Many of us first heard the subject taught by a parent, Sunday school teacher, or friend, and it simply "rang true" so we never investigated it further.

But let's turn it around. Imagine someone saying to us, "I don't believe in an afterlife." So we ask, "What is your compelling reason for *not* accepting it?" and the response is, "I don't know; I've just always rejected it." How satisfied would we be with that kind of an answer? How would you view someone who "just *dis*believes things" of such importance without any real study or investigation? Unfortunately, that's how we can sound to others, as well. So let's explore some reasons for believing in an afterlife that go beyond the concept simply ringing true.

Eternity in our hearts

We might point to the universality of people in virtually every culture and era having such a belief. Maybe this is one manifestation of what the Bible means when it says that God "has planted eternity in the human heart" (Eccles. 3:11). Though by itself this fact is not grounds for certainty—especially since the particulars regarding what is believed about the afterlife in those cultures vary significantly—it does seem to point to a divinely infused awareness of realities beyond the everyday here and now.

There is something strange about us humans. Though we are beings of the earth and limited in our perspective, we have a sense of having been made for something more: many of our longings in this life cannot be fulfilled here and now. Yet we go on settling, alternatively struggling against and then giving in to whatever substitutes for ultimate meaning and purpose we can find. As C. S. Lewis famously wrote, "We are half-hearted creatures, fooling about with drink and sex and ambition when infinite joy is offered us, like an ignorant child who wants to go on making mud pies in a slum because he cannot imagine what is meant by the offer of a holiday at the sea."[3] Still, even in the middle of the compromise we sense that the holiday offer is available, beckoning us at the soul level. Could all this be an echo of the "eternity in the human heart"—and evidence that eternity is our true destiny?

Near-death experiences

Or we might argue that people who have had near-death experiences often see a bright light, meet angels, have visions of Jesus, or experience some other manifestation of life beyond death. Isn't that grounds for belief? Contrary to the soul-weight experiments, these eyewitness accounts do seem to add to the evidence for an afterlife, in spite of the fact that these experiences vary in detail and the particulars of their religious references. Christian scholars J. P. Moreland and Gary Habermas argue that "from the kind of scientific and psychological testing that has been done, we see that we can place greater confidence in the evidential value of near-death experiences. These experiences cannot be ignored or slightly regarded. They play an important role in establishing support for life after death."[4]

Ultimate justice

There is also something to be said for the cry of human beings for ultimate justice (though we ourselves commit acts of injustice), our irrepressible moral sense that all is not right in this world, and a longing for a better place that reflects real goodness and righteousness. I think this sense of ultimate justice is inherent in the common complaint that a loving, powerful God would not allow evil to go on and on. Surely that kind of a God would have to *do* something about it. Well, according to the teachings of Jesus and the Bible, he *will* do something about it in the end, at the Judgment. At that time he will mete out justice in ways that finally balance the fairness scales—the ones we sense are so imbalanced in this life. Again, this isn't proof by itself, but it provides additional indicators that God really has given us an internal sense that points to realities beyond our current experience.

Home beyond the horizon

C. S. Lewis—master of profound reflections on these ideas—observed, "If you are really a product of a materialistic universe, how is it that you don't feel at home there? . . . Though I do not believe that my desire for Paradise proves that I shall enjoy it, I think it a pretty good indication that such a thing exists and that some men will. . . . If I find in myself a desire which no experience in this world can satisfy, the most probable explanation is that I was made for another world."[5]

It's interesting that the apostle Peter referred to God's people as "temporary residents and foreigners" in this world (1 Pet. 2:11). And the writer of Hebrews talked about Christians who were martyred for their faith, saying, "All these people died still believing what God had promised them. They did not receive what was promised, but they saw it all from a distance and welcomed it. They agreed that they were foreigners and nomads here on earth. Obviously people who say such things are looking forward to a country they can call their own . . . a heavenly homeland" (Heb. 11:13-14, 16). The Bible consistently tells us what our hearts also confirm: that the earth is our temporary dwelling, but our ultimate home is beyond this world.

However, most of these reflections will probably not connect very well with the younger people you talk to. They often feel enamored with the world and all it has to offer them. With the addition of years, most people begin to see through the empty promises and short-lived pleasures of the current order. They increasingly become aware of what the writer of Ecclesiastes lamented as the pervasive *meaninglessness* in this earthly life. More and more they relate to the sentiment that seems to rise up within all of us after a particularly frustrating day: *"There must be more to life than this!"* Well, there is—and I think our hearts are telling us something about what that "more" will be and that we ought to focus greater proportions of our time and energy preparing for *that* rather than remaining all caught up in *this*.

Eternal perspective with earthly benefits

In his best-selling book *Life after Death: The Evidence*, Dinesh D'Souza argues that having belief in an afterlife can actually improve the overall quality of *this* life. He quotes Duke University's Professor of Psychiatry and Behavioral Sciences Harold Koenig and his summarization of a "wide body of data" pointing to the fact that people of religious faith, who believe in life after death, are not only healthier than their counterparts but also "less likely to suffer from stress and depression, less likely to attempt suicide, less vulnerable to a host of other ailments, and more likely to live longer."[6]

"None of this is particularly surprising," D'Souza concludes, "when you consider the nature of belief: the prospect of an afterlife provides a motive for morality and generosity because it is linked to cosmic justice. These data show that there are immense practical benefits to belief: you are likely to live longer and healthier, be happier in your marriage, and also make a greater contribution to your fellow man."[7]

Perhaps these kinds of earthly benefits were part of what Jesus had in mind when he promised his followers, "Yes, I am the gate. Those who come in through me will be saved. They will come and go freely and will find good pastures. The thief's purpose is to steal and kill and destroy. *My purpose is to give them a rich and satisfying life*" (John 10:9-10, emphasis mine).

GOD AS OUR WITNESS

We have considered some of the broader arguments that we might make for the reality of life after death. But I've saved what I think is the surest and most powerful for last. For all the reasons one might believe in life after death—specifically, that there is a heaven and a hell—the most compelling argument is Jesus' direct and clear teaching on the topic. In all of history, no one else had the credentials he had or, therefore, the ability to authoritatively tell us the truth about these realities.

Jesus' unique credentials

Jesus alone fulfilled the many Old Testament prophecies concerning the Messiah—where he would be born, what lineage he would be born into, the kind of birth he would have, how he would live and minister, and how he would suffer for the people he came to serve. He was also unique in the variety and impact of the miraculous signs he performed—including dramatic healings and even raising people from the dead—and he did these miracles often, in many different settings, and in the presence of hostile witnesses who could not deny what he had done.

He knew the hearts, minds, and thoughts of people as nobody else ever has. He alone lived a sinless life, which even his enemies could not deny or find fault with (so they resorted to bringing false accusations against him). He showed supreme love for the very people who opposed him by willingly laying down his life and dying a cruel death on the cross.

And surely the tour de force that established his credibility was his rising from the dead three days later—just as he had predicted he would. Does not that single event prove that what Jesus, the unique Son of God, said about any topic must be true? More than that, it shows that he alone was in a position to *know*—to speak from actual experience—about what is true and real about life beyond the grave. Literally, he's already "been there, done that" in terms of dying, seeing the other side, and then coming back to talk about it. Not to mention the fact that he, as the eternal God incarnate (as we celebrate at Christmas), along with the Father and the Holy Spirit, created all these realities in the first place (see, for example, John 1:1-5, 14; Col. 1:15-20; Heb. 1:8-12).

Considering who Jesus is and his unique vantage point and knowledge, it's highly significant that he was adamant about the existence of both heaven and hell—holding out the beauty and wonder of the former and warning about the horror of the latter. There is simply no better support for our beliefs than Jesus' clear conviction that these places are real.

"Wait a minute," someone might protest. "You Christians say you believe in heaven and hell because Jesus taught it. But the only way we know Jesus taught it is that it's in the Bible, and I don't accept the Bible. So you really have no argument at all!"

There's a key distinction we need to make (which we touched on in chapter 3, where we discussed why we can trust the Bible). Our case for knowing and believing Jesus' teachings does not rest on the Bible's necessarily being inspired by God; we affirm that it is, but we don't have to start there—nor do our friends. All we need to establish is that the information in the Gospels is *reasonably reliable history*. In other words, we don't have to believe anything about the divine origin of the Bible to make the case that the Gospels are solid historical sources of information about what Jesus said and did. Once we see the record of what he actually taught, as well as how he backed it up with a variety of supernatural confirmations and credentials, we quickly come to understand that *the historical record presents Jesus as the unique Son of God.* Once we know his identity and the authority that goes with it, *we can then trust what Jesus, the Son of God, taught about things such as the afterlife, heaven and hell, the authority of the Bible as a whole, and so forth.*

So there's clear and consistent logic to what we're saying. But for the friends who say they can't trust the Bible, we need to patiently back up to establish those compelling points, starting with the historical nature of the New Testament record and, perhaps, presenting more of the information we discussed in chapter 3.

Jesus' clear teaching

So what did Jesus, the Son of God, actually teach about the afterlife? The simplest way to answer that question is to look at the consistent, repeated ways he spoke about this topic so that no single text is taken as an isolated "proof" by itself. Here is a sampling of Jesus' teachings on the topic from a variety of places throughout the Gospels:

> There is more than enough room in my Father's home. If this were not so, would I have told you that I am going to prepare a place for you? When everything is ready, I will come and get you, so that you will always be with me where I am. (John 14:2-3)

> Jesus replied, "Your mistake is that you don't know the Scriptures, and you don't know the

power of God. For when the dead rise, they will neither marry nor be given in marriage. In this respect they will be like the angels in heaven. But now, as to whether there will be a resurrection of the dead—haven't you ever read about this in the Scriptures? Long after Abraham, Isaac, and Jacob had died, God said, 'I am the God of Abraham, the God of Isaac, and the God of Jacob.' So he is the God of the living, not the dead." (Matt. 22:29-32)

Don't be afraid of those who want to kill your body; they cannot touch your soul. Fear only God, who can destroy both soul and body in hell. (Matt. 10:28)

No one has ever gone to heaven and returned. But the Son of Man has come down from heaven. (John 3:13)

I have come down from heaven to do the will of God who sent me, not to do my own will. (John 6:38)

If your eye—even your good eye—causes you to lust, gouge it out and throw it away. It is better for you to lose one part of your body than for your whole body to be thrown into hell. And if your hand—even your stronger hand—causes you to sin, cut it off and throw it away. It is better for you to lose one part of your body than for your whole body to be thrown into hell. (Matt. 5:29-30)

Snakes! Sons of vipers! How will you escape the judgment of hell? (Matt. 23:33)

What blessings await you when people hate you and exclude you and mock you and curse you as evil because you follow the Son of Man. When that happens, be happy! Yes, leap for joy! For a great reward awaits you in heaven. (Luke 6:22-23)

You people of Capernaum, will you be honored in heaven? No, you will go down to the place of the dead. (Luke 10:15)

Don't rejoice because evil spirits obey you; rejoice because your names are registered in heaven. (Luke 10:20)

This is the way to have eternal life—to know you, the only true God, and Jesus Christ, the one you sent to earth. I brought glory to you here on earth by completing the work you gave me to do. Now, Father, bring me into the glory we shared before the world began. . . . Father, I want these whom you have given me to be with me where I am. Then they can see all the glory you gave me because you loved me even before the world began! (John 17:3-5, 24)

The Son of Man will send his angels, and they
will remove from his Kingdom everything that
causes sin and all who do evil. And the angels
will throw them into the fiery furnace, where
there will be weeping and gnashing of teeth.
Then the righteous will shine like the sun in
their Father's Kingdom. (Matt. 13:41-43)

When the Son of Man comes in his glory, and
all the angels with him, then he will sit upon his
glorious throne. All the nations will be gathered
in his presence, and he will separate the people as
a shepherd separates the sheep from the goats. He
will place the sheep at his right hand and the goats
at his left. Then the King will say to those on his
right, "Come, you who are blessed by my Father,
inherit the Kingdom prepared for you from the
creation of the world." . . . Then the King will
turn to those on the left and say, "Away with you,
you cursed ones, into the eternal fire prepared for
the devil and his demons." . . . And they will go
away into eternal punishment, but the righteous
will go into eternal life. (Matt. 25:31-34, 41, 46)

And perhaps the most compelling lesson Jesus gave about
the realities of heaven and hell came in a parable he told,
recorded in Luke 16:19-31:

Jesus said, "There was a certain rich man who
was splendidly clothed in purple and fine linen

and who lived each day in luxury. At his gate
lay a poor man named Lazarus who was covered
with sores. As Lazarus lay there longing for
scraps from the rich man's table, the dogs would
come and lick his open sores.

"Finally, the poor man died and was carried
by the angels to be with Abraham. The rich
man also died and was buried, and his soul went
to the place of the dead. There, in torment, he
saw Abraham in the far distance with Lazarus at
his side.

"The rich man shouted, 'Father Abraham,
have some pity! Send Lazarus over here to
dip the tip of his finger in water and cool my
tongue. I am in anguish in these flames.'

"But Abraham said to him, 'Son, remember
that during your lifetime you had everything you
wanted, and Lazarus had nothing. So now he is
here being comforted, and you are in anguish.
And besides, there is a great chasm separating us.
No one can cross over to you from here, and no
one can cross over to us from there.'

"Then the rich man said, 'Please, Father
Abraham, at least send him to my father's home.
For I have five brothers, and I want him to
warn them so they don't end up in this place of
torment.'

"But Abraham said, 'Moses and the prophets
have warned them. Your brothers can read what
they wrote.'

"The rich man replied, 'No, Father
Abraham! But if someone is sent to them from
the dead, then they will repent of their sins and
turn to God.'

"But Abraham said, 'If they won't listen to
Moses and the prophets, they won't listen even
if someone rises from the dead.'"

I don't know how Jesus could have been much clearer about
these matters! When you read his consistent and repeated
warnings about the sobering realities of heaven and hell, it
becomes clear that he believed in them sincerely and expects
us to do the same. More than that, especially in this parable
of the rich man and Lazarus, we can see that these realities
drove Jesus forward in his mission to "seek and save those
who are lost" (Luke 19:10)—and as his followers we should
let that be our driving motivation as well.

So our main argument for the reality of heaven and
hell is that Jesus, who was the Son of God and therefore
in a unique position to know what he was talking about,
taught it—clearly and literally. He gave evidence for his
existence prior to the Incarnation, he gave evidence to the
fact that he would (and did) live beyond the grave, and he
gave evidence to being uniquely in touch with the Father
in heaven. Without a doubt, he gave us every reason to
believe he had the experience, credentials, and knowledge
required to tell us with authority what's real beyond this
here-and-now, earthbound life. Through his teaching, the
doors of eternity have been opened to us. We can be confident of the realities he testified to: that heaven is a real

place of joy and reward, and hell a real place of anguish and regret.

> No eye has seen, no ear has heard, and no mind has imagined what God has prepared for those who love him. (1 Cor. 2:9)

QUESTIONS ABOUT THE AFTERLIFE

In spite of Jesus' clear and compelling teachings about the afterlife, the coming Judgment Day, and heaven and hell specifically, we're still talking about an area that is at this point completely unseen—and therefore subject to abundant speculation. So don't be surprised when you get barraged by your friends with a myriad of "Oh yeah?" issues, "What about this?" inquiries, and "But wait a minute!" objections. Some of their queries can be challenging to respond to, but be encouraged that they reveal a certain measure of curiosity as well, if not downright interest.

Let's look next at a few of those disparate questions that are likely to come up.

A vacant hell?

"Okay, I guess there must be a hell, as well. But what if nobody is bad enough to go there—or God forgives everyone so nobody has to?"

The young Christian who asked this question was wrestling with two apparently contradictory beliefs. On the one hand, he was sure that the God of the Bible—the God Jesus spoke of—was loving, compassionate, forgiving, and willing to initiate relationships with the humans he created.

But that same God—the God Jesus spoke of—was also the creator of a place called hell. You couldn't read Jesus' words without concluding both. So how can we put those two convictions together: a loving God who, in this individual's mind, couldn't possibly send people to hell, and a Jesus of history who says it exists?

This young man's conclusion was that maybe hell is real, but nobody is there!

Such speculation doesn't fit the facts. For one thing, why would Jesus warn about the possibility of judgment if it never occurs? And Jesus does seem to teach that people—lots of people, sadly—end up there: "You can enter God's Kingdom only through the narrow gate. The highway to hell is broad, and its gate is wide for the many who choose that way. But the gateway to life is very narrow and the road is difficult, and only a few ever find it" (Matt. 7:13-14).

With a little thought—and lots of honesty—it's actually easier to make the case that we all deserve hell rather than heaven:

- God is perfect, and as a just Judge he has to condemn sin, not overlook it (see Gen. 18:25; 1 Sam. 2:10; Rom. 2:2).

- God doesn't owe anyone a second chance, and yet he gives repeated opportunities to repent, even though people stubbornly refuse (see Rom. 1:18-23, 31-32).

- God has given us this planet, with all its beauty and diversity, and we have abused it as if we had no one to answer to (see Ps. 24:1).

- We treat our fellow humans with disregard, even though everyone on the earth bears the image of God (see Gen. 1:26-27).

- We fool ourselves about where we are on the moral spectrum, but truly we have more in common with criminals and convicts, morally speaking, than we do with Jesus, the sinless Son of God (see Rom. 2:1-4; 3:9-20).

It's no wonder the Bible sums up our situation with these disquieting words: "No one is righteous—not even one. No one is truly wise; no one is seeking God. All have turned away; all have become useless. No one does good, not a single one. . . . For everyone has sinned; we all fall short of God's glorious standard" (Rom. 3:10-12, 23). Thankfully, the story doesn't end there; the passage goes on to talk about the grace of God that is offered to all people.

But if God is love . . .

So we've shown that hell is real and real people go there. But let's get to the second half of our question—one that has many people in our culture perplexed, including perhaps some of our own friends. To put it a little differently, "How can you believe that God sends people to hell?"

The short answer is "*We don't!*"

In spite of our sin and spiritual rebelliousness, hell was never the plan or purpose of God for human beings. Jesus said, "God loved the world so much that he gave his one and only Son, so that everyone who believes in him will not perish but have eternal life. God sent his Son into the world not to judge the world, but to save the world through him" (John

3:16-17). The apostle Paul refers to "God our Savior, who wants everyone to be saved and to understand the truth. . . . He gave his life to purchase freedom for everyone" (1 Tim. 2:3-4, 6). And the apostle Peter boldly declared that the Lord "is being patient for your sake. He does not want anyone to be destroyed, but wants everyone to repent" (2 Pet. 3:9).

So then why does anybody end up in hell? This is hard to hear, but it's because people actually *choose* to go there. They do this by willfully continuing in their sins and by refusing to humbly submit to the God of grace in order to receive his provision of forgiveness and salvation. Romans 6:23 sums up both sides well: "The wages of sin is death, but the free gift of God is eternal life through Christ Jesus our Lord." The people who will face God's judgment

1. are those who have sinned (that's all of us), thus earning their "wages"—which is actually a debt—of spiritual death, meaning separation from God for eternity; *and*
2. who also refuse God's free gift, which is the salvation and eternal life provided through the death of Christ Jesus on the cross, wherein he paid the spiritual death penalty that they had owed.

Hell is the logical consequence of a life lived separated from God. In his justice, God set aside and designated it as a place to quarantine and punish beings, particularly fallen angels, whom he had created as good but who rebelled against him and chose evil instead. As we've shown, God doesn't want people there, and he warns them that they should turn back to him through a variety of means, including their consciences; his power demonstrated in nature; promptings and convictions of his Holy Spirit; and, of course, the preaching of the *gospel*—literally, the "Good News"—of Christ. Most people have ample opportunity to change their ways and acknowledge their need before God. But God stops short of forcing anyone to come to him. At the Judgment, he will simply consign people to the destination where they've already been heading.

The Old Testament prophet Hosea warned the people of Israel during his time. He said they were "like a stubborn heifer. So should the LORD feed her like a lamb in a lush pasture?" (Hos. 4:16). As God dealt with these rebellious people and considered their commitment to false gods, he came to this conclusion: "Leave Israel alone, because she is married to idolatry" (Hos. 4:17). That's a pretty good picture of Judgment Day. God will say and do with us eternally essentially the same he said and did with them temporally: "If you are so joined to your sin that you don't want me and my holiness, then fine. You can have it your way."

Once again, C. S. Lewis sums it up well: "There are only two kinds of people in the end: those who say to God, 'Thy will be done,' and those to whom God says, '*Thy* will be done.'"[8]

So the people in heaven are those who have said to God during their lives here on earth, "Thy will be done." They have let him take over the rule of their lives and surrendered their self-made plans to accept his plan for them instead. They are now eternally bound to God and to his holiness. The people in hell are those to whom God has said, "*Thy* will be done."

He lets those who don't want his interference or guidance in their lives have it their way. They will be consigned to a place where God is silent and where he leaves them alone. It is a place where they get to be their own "god" and follow that "deity" exclusively—such as it is. There, people are eternally bound to their sin and its dire consequences.

So as we answer this question, we need to stress that people are not subject to mere fate or to the whims of some capricious deity. Rather, they are the objects of God's love and targets of his grace—but also the product of the choices they themselves make. Those started with the choice we've all already made—to sin against God. But more than that, it's the choice to go it alone, to try to improve our own lives and earn our own way into God's graces rather than choosing to receive the one provision God has made to pay for sins: the forgiveness available through Jesus and his sacrificial death for us on the cross.

We need to help people see that choice by telling them, "Hell is terrible, and it is also real. The only thing standing in the way of your salvation from that place of punishment and regret is your sin and your will. Your sin makes you deserve it; your will must choose to receive God's provision to keep you out of it. You don't have to end up in hell. God doesn't want you to go there. But it's your decision. What are you waiting for? Why not receive his gracious gift of salvation and eternal life?"

People who haven't heard
"Okay," our friends may say, "that might make sense for those who hear a clear rendition of the message and are given an

opportunity to respond—but that's not most of the world! What about all the people in places who have never had the chance to know about Jesus?"

It's a great question. Let me offer five quick thoughts that might be helpful to you in responding.

First, it's probably worth pointing out that the old perception that the "Christian West" is trying—and failing—to reach the spiritually troubled remainder of the world is way out of date. In fact, in many ways the opposite is true. Look at the startling facts in this recent missions report:

> *One of every eight people on the planet is a practicing Christian who is active in his/her faith. The number of believers in what used to be "mission fields" now surpasses the number of believers in the countries from which missionaries were originally sent. In fact, more missionaries are now sent from non-Western churches than from the traditional mission-sending bases in the West. The Protestant growth rate in Latin America is well over three times the biological growth rate. Protestants in China grew from about one million to over 80 million believers in less than 50 years, with most of that growth occurring in just the last few decades. In the 1980s, Nepal was still a staunch Hindu kingdom with only a small persecuted church. Today there are hundreds of thousands of believers, and churches have been started within each of its more than 100 distinct people groups.*[9]

This means that many of the people we thought never had a chance are already Christians today, and some of them are mobilizing to come and reach some of *us* in the increasingly secular West!

Second, Jesus addressed this issue when he made the following promise: "Ask and it will be given to you; seek and you will find; knock and the door will be opened to you. For everyone who asks receives; he who seeks finds; and to him who knocks, the door will be opened" (Matt. 7:7-8, NIV). Notice he did not limit this to any certain group of people, locale, or time frame. Anyone, anywhere, who keeps on *asking, seeking,* and *knocking* will be led by God to the place where *it will be given, they will find,* and *the door will be opened.*

How will this happen? Our answer is "in many ways"— probably some quite mysterious and unexpected. For example, many Muslims around the world today who seem unreachable with the gospel are having dreams and visions of Jesus, and great numbers of them are coming to faith in Christ. I think of a former Hindu man I had the privilege of meeting a number of years ago, the late Mahendra Singhal. He was raised in a Hindu home in India, grew up going to the temple to offer food to the idols, and was later tutored personally by gurus whose task it was to instill in him the truths of Hinduism. The only problem was that Mahendra kept on asking questions—which caused him to realize that his religion wasn't providing him with real answers. So what did he do? He kept on *asking, seeking,* and *knocking*—until one day he saw an ad in the local newspaper about a Bible correspondence course, which led him to begin a study of the Bible. Not long after that he met some Christians, heard the gospel, and gave his life to Christ.[10]

Third, it's helpful to point out that though not everyone has equal amounts of information or access to the gospel, they are responsible to follow whatever measure of light God has afforded them. For Mahendra, that was asking more and more questions when things didn't make sense and actively seeking truth wherever he could find it—including an ad for a Bible course. For others it might just be seeing God through observing his works in nature. Romans 1:20 assures us, "Through everything God made, they can clearly see his invisible qualities—his eternal power and divine nature. So they have no excuse for not knowing God." So if people will seek out the God who clearly had astounding amounts of knowledge, power, and creativity—who was able to produce a universe filled with living creatures like us—that God, according to the Bible, will go out of his way to meet them in the middle and lead them into his fuller truths, as well as his salvation.

Fourth, here's another point that flows out of the last one. I've found it very helpful to explain to people who are scrutinizing the Christian faith that God is, in fact, a fair judge. That is, he will judge people who reject him according to the amount of light they were given and by what they did with it—the person who has little opportunity and minimal information (and rejects it) will be in less trouble than the person who was given more and rejects that. So, yes, there will be degrees of judgment in the afterlife.

How do we know this? Jesus said, "When someone has been given much, much will be required in return; and when someone has been entrusted with much, even more will be required" (Luke 12:48). The way this is often paraphrased is "to whom much is given, much is required"—and obviously the opposite would be true as well. In fact, Jesus made this very clear by the illustration he gave right before that statement. He said, in Luke 12:47-48: "A servant who knows what the master wants, but isn't prepared and doesn't carry out those instructions, will be severely punished. But someone who does not know, and then does something wrong, will be punished only lightly."

In addition, Jesus often told people that there would be greater judgment for those who heard and rejected him than there would be for earlier groups who had rejected less clear revelations from God (see, for example, Matt. 10:15; 11:21-24; 12:41-42; also see the corresponding passages in the other Gospels).

This biblical teaching can show our friends that God is logical and fair in his approach to judgment. And it militates against what I remember being taught in a church class growing up—that a sin is a sin is a sin is a sin, and they're all equally evil in God's sight. The upshot of that lesson was that the sweet little old lady who lives next door, if she rejects Jesus and dies, will be viewed and judged by God equally to, say, an Adolf Hitler. Even in my young mind as a child I knew this didn't seem right—and the teachings of Jesus prove it.

This news was liberating to me when I first discovered it, and I've found it to be quite freeing to spiritual seekers I've shared it with over the years. It shows them there is thoughtful rationale that goes into God's judgment—though I'm always very careful to make sure they understand that everyone receives at least some information, or "spiritual light," and thus everyone also has at least some degree of responsibility before God (including the proverbial little old lady). Therefore, every person still needs to hear and to respond to the gospel message of Christ.

Finally, without exception, the people who ask us this question *have* heard the message. So after sharing some of the other responses above, I always come back to gently remind them that they themselves *have* received both the information and the opportunity, and—based on what we've just discussed—they are therefore more responsible for what they do with it than any of the people they're asking about. This provides you the opportunity to then ask them, assuming they're not Christians already, what's stopping them from receiving the grace of God that is so clearly and freely being offered to them—even at that very moment.

Who goes to heaven?

For many people, heaven is the place where *everybody* goes when they die. You'll hear it often repeated when someone famous dies. Without regard for what the person believed or how he or she lived life, many people will blurt out sentiments such as, "Well, at least he's in a better place now" or "I'm sure she's a lot happier—smiling down on us from above."

And if people are fairly sure that others are going to heaven, they're usually much more confident that *they* are. An article in the *Los Angeles Times* reported, "An overwhelming majority of Americans continue to believe that there is life after death and that heaven and hell exist, according to a new study. What's more, *nearly two-thirds think they are heaven-bound.* On the other hand, *only one-half of 1% said they were hell-bound,* according to a national poll by the Oxnard-based Barna Research Group."[11] Randy Alcorn summed up these statistics: "For every American who believes he or she is going to Hell, there are 120 who believe they are going to Heaven."[12]

So the majority of people think they're going to end up in heaven—but ask them how they plan to get there and you'll quickly discover that confusion reigns. From my experience, about nine out of ten people think they'll get there because of their own good works, moral behavior, or religious performance. This is in spite of the fact that the Bible teaches repeatedly that "we are made right with God through faith and not by obeying the law" (Rom. 3:28) and "God saved you by his grace when you believed. And you can't take credit for this; it is a gift from God. Salvation is not a reward for the good things we have done, so none of us can boast about it" (Eph. 2:8-9). We also read, "He saved us, not because of the righteous things we had done, but because of his mercy" (Titus 3:5).

The Bible is very clear about this, the central message of the gospel: we can't earn God's forgiveness or entry into heaven. Rather, we must simply and humbly, with an attitude of repentance, ask for it—trusting that Jesus' death paid our penalty and opened the way for us. This, then, should be our goal: not to just give people reasons to believe in the reality of heaven and hell, but to invite them to receive God's salvation, adoption into his family, and the sure hope of heaven when they die.

Let's end with an inspiring story about a Christian who models well how we can winsomely make that invitation.

DIVINE ENCOUNTER

"So you're a pastor. Hmm, interesting."

The discussion started in a good-natured way, two men sitting next to each other on an airplane. They conversed freely about their mutual interest in a local sports team. When the businessman asked the other man what he did for a living, the pastor smiled and in the same good-natured tone said that he worked in a large church. The businessman became suddenly uncomfortable.

"Well, you know, I'm not much of a churchgoing guy—that's more my wife's deal—but I do believe there's a life beyond death, and I think as long as we do the best we can, that's all that matters. Right?"

The pastor responded nonchalantly, "Well, rather than my telling you what I think, I wonder if you'd humor me for a minute. Would you agree that there's a 'preferred place' in the afterlife as opposed to a 'less-preferred place'?"

"Yes, I get what you're hinting at. I believe that too."

The pastor continued. "And do you think everybody gets to the preferred place?"

"Well, no that wouldn't be fair. You can't have ax-murderers and child molesters mixed in with everybody else!"

"So, what about you? Are you going to the preferred place?"

"Look, I may not be religious, but I live a good life. I've been pretty darn faithful to my wife over the years, I've been a steady provider, I'm a good friend to those I hang with, and I keep all my business dealings completely aboveboard. Isn't that what religion is supposed to do for you? Surely that will get me into the preferred place. Right?"

"Well, you've obviously put a lot of thought into this. And it's certainly good you care about these things. But let me show you something." The pastor pulled out a napkin and drew a ladder on it. "Let's say this ladder represents morality and goodness. God is up here at the top, because he's perfect. And let's pretend this ladder is so big every human being who's ever lived could stand somewhere on it. Those that are better go closer to the top, and those who are not so good don't go up as high. Be honest now. Take this pen and write your name on the ladder where you think you belong."

The businessman hesitated.

The pastor continued. "Tell you what. Let me help you out. Who do you think is the best person alive right now—the most moral and kind and selfless?"

It didn't take long for the businessman to answer. "Mother Teresa." (This took place when she was still alive.)

"Well, you know, I happen to agree with you. And I have friends who know her, and do you know what they say she says about herself? She admits she's committed sins and is far from perfect. If she pegged herself on this ladder, she would never put herself at the top—she's way too humble. I bet she wouldn't go any higher than halfway."

The businessman nodded in agreement.

"And closer to home, who do you think is the most good and moral person here in America?"

"I'd say Billy Graham."

"I agree with you—he is a very good man. But in all

his talks, in all his writings, he stresses again and again what a sinful man he is and how much he needs forgiveness. I'm quite certain he would put himself south of Mother Teresa on this ladder."

The businessman stared thoughtfully at the napkin and the names drawn on the ladder.

"Now I want you to take this pen, and write your name anywhere you think it belongs."

He wrote his name near the bottom.

"Where do you think is the cutoff for those who are going to the 'preferred place'? Where would you draw that line? And before you do that, I want to remind you of something you said earlier. You mentioned you were 'pretty darn faithful' to your wife. I have a hunch you're waffling. I bet there is a story—something you'd rather not talk about."

He looked down. "Yeah. There was that night in Cincinnati."

The pastor remained quiet and let the words sink in.

"I guess I'm screwed," the man muttered under his breath.

"Well, welcome to the club. We're *all* in that kind of predicament. And here's the real problem: do you think, if you got really serious and tried to do good for the rest of your life, you could ever hope to climb above Mother Teresa?" He shook his head immediately. "And if she says she needs to be forgiven, how can you expect to get all the way to the top by climbing?"

"Well, what am I supposed to do?"

The pastor smiled. "I'm glad you asked. Christianity says you can't do anything. But it also says this: *God has.*

He made a way for you to be taken up to the top without having to climb it yourself. God comes down the ladder, step-by-step, in the person of Jesus Christ, and meets you at the point of your need. His death for you pays the price, and his perfection is given to you so you are completely forgiven and made pure. That's what Mother Teresa and Billy Graham and I—and all Christians down through the ages—are counting on.

"All we need to do is accept what he has done for us. It's by grace, through trusting God to do it because we cannot. That is the message of Christianity. That's how you get to 'the preferred place.'"[13]

> *Today I have given you the choice between life and death, between blessings and curses. Now I call on heaven and earth to witness the choice you make. Oh, that you would choose life, so that you . . . might live!*
>
> —DEUTERONOMY 30:19

SUMMARY OF THE ANSWER

Question 10 asks us, "Why should I think that heaven really exists—and that God sends people to hell?"

- The opening story of Marie Little's memorial service illustrates the confidence Christians have in the afterlife. The certainty that she was in heaven turned the service into a time of celebration. The question of whether or not there is an afterlife is extremely important, and Christians need to be able to articulate their confidence to questioning unbelievers.

- There is a nearly universal belief in the afterlife. God created humanity with a general awareness of something beyond this earthly existence. We also share a sense that there will be ultimate justice, and stories of people's near-death experiences support the reality of something beyond death.

- Jesus had the experience, credentials, and knowledge required to be able to tell us with authority about the afterlife. He made it clear that heaven is a real place of eternal joy—and that hell is also a real place, but one of punishment and regret.

- Many people have trouble with the concept of a God of love sending people to hell. But God doesn't send people to hell; people choose to go there by clinging to their sins, resisting God's grace, and refusing to turn from their sin to receive Jesus' sacrifice on their behalf.

- God offers heaven to everyone and has made provision for all to be there. He is patiently waiting for people to turn around and come to him. However, he doesn't force anyone to believe. That is a choice each person must make.

- Heaven is reserved for those who have said to God during their lifetime on earth, "Thy will be done." They've received Jesus Christ as their Savior and sought to honor him with their lives. Hell is for those who refused to allow God any say in their lives. To them, God will say, "*Thy* will be done." They have chosen separation from God, so he gives them that—for eternity.

- Many question how God can condemn people who haven't heard the Good News and therefore have had no chance to respond. We can be certain that, because of God's love and grace, no one is left without the opportunity to choose. God works in many ways to draw people to him. People will be held accountable for what they did with the amount of information they had.

TIPS FOR TALKING ABOUT THIS ISSUE

- Our main argument for the reality of the afterlife— including both heaven and hell—is that Jesus, the One with true credentials as well as personal experience, told us clearly that these things were true. Keep in mind when you talk about this that most people do have a built-in respect for Jesus. Unfortunately they often don't know what he said or taught, but we can build on their positive disposition toward Jesus as a way to help them really consider what he actually said about these things.

- A specific example of the first tip is when friends say, as people often do, that they think Jesus "was just a good teacher." Rather than arguing with them about the fact that he's much more than that, we can build upon their words and remind them that good teachers are only helpful if we pay attention to what they actually teach. Jesus was a good teacher, so we should take seriously what he tells us, including what he said about the afterlife, heaven, and hell.

- We need to be aware that the question in this chapter rarely comes at us as a mere intellectual curiosity. Rather, it's often driven by people's concern for someone else, sometimes by fears related to a friend or family member who has died. Or people might be asking out of doubts about their own destiny. So be sensitive to what they're really asking, and don't be afraid to ask them why that issue is a concern for them. Then stop talking and genuinely listen to what they tell you. Ask follow-up questions, too, so you can truly understand their situation, and so you'll know how to provide the best answers for them.

- Resist the temptation to offer an opinion about where their departed loved ones are right now—especially if there were spiritual doubts and concerns. The exception would be if you know they were clear-cut followers of Christ—such as my friend Marie Little. Her beliefs and faith in Christ left no doubt that she's in God's presence in heaven. But even when someone's relatives rejected Christ, I would still refrain from opining about their probably being in hell—not because we're afraid to speak truth, but because we truly don't know. Maybe, like the thief on the cross who died moments after meeting Jesus, they reached out and trusted in him at the very last moment and, like that thief, received the confident hope that, "today you will be with me [Jesus] in paradise" (Luke 23:43).

- It's often helpful to acknowledge to friends that we are not entirely comfortable with the Bible's teachings on hell ourselves. In other words, we understand the fact that a righteous God must punish sin and rebellion, and we're confident he'll be fair in how he does it—but that doesn't mean we have to feel good about it all. C. S. Lewis wrote, quite vulnerably, that "there is no doctrine which I would more willingly remove from Christianity than this, if it lay in my power."[14] Expressing these kinds of thoughts (if they're authentic) can help people understand that we wrestle with the same questions they do—and yet continue to trust in Christ. This can encourage them to follow our example.

- As we mentioned earlier, let the realities of heaven and hell—as well as the finality that death brings in sealing people's eternal destiny (see Luke 16:19-31)—be strong motivators in your own efforts to reach out to people with the love and truth of Christ.

QUESTIONS FOR GROUP DISCUSSION

1. What does it mean that God has "planted eternity in the human heart" as quoted from Ecclesiastes 3:11? How have you experienced that in your own life or seen it in the lives of others?

2. Look back at the verses quoted in the chapter that contain Jesus' teachings about heaven and hell. Which verse means the most to you? Which is most surprising or intriguing?

3. Have you ever experienced the feeling, as Peter writes in 1 Peter 2:11, that you are a "temporary resident" or even a "foreigner" here in this world? How?

4. How do you think most people picture heaven? How do they picture hell? Where do you think they get their mental images of these places?

5. Do you think it is important to talk about *both* heaven and hell when discussing the afterlife with unbelievers? Why or why not?

6. How would you explain to an unbeliever God's fairness and justice in judging?

7. React to this statement made by the apostle Paul: "If Christ has not been raised, then your faith is useless and you are still guilty of your sins. In that case, all who have died believing

in Christ are lost! And if our hope in Christ is only for this life, we are more to be pitied than anyone in the world" (1 Cor. 15:17-19). Why is it so important for Christians to be certain of a resurrection and eternity with Christ in heaven?

CHAPTER 10:

The questions
our friends need
us to ask them

It was one of the greatest verbal comebacks in the history of public discourse, and it may have affected the course of history—not just for the two debaters, but for the entire nation.

During a televised presidential campaign debate in 1984, Henry Trewhitt of *The Baltimore Sun* posed his question to Ronald Reagan:

"You already are the oldest president in history, and some of your staff say you were tired after your most recent encounter with Mr. Mondale. I recall that President Kennedy had to go for days on end with very little sleep during the Cuba missile crisis. Is there any doubt in your mind that you would be able to function in such circumstances?"

Finally someone had asked him the question. It was on everyone's mind—and being discussed all over the media—but nobody had asked it directly of Reagan himself. At age seventy-three, was he indeed too old, or becoming too unfocused, to effectively lead the nation for a second term?

For a split second it seemed the whole country held its breath, waiting to see how President Reagan would respond. "Not at all," Reagan began. "And I want you to know that also I will not make age an issue of this campaign. *I am not going to exploit, for political purposes, my opponent's youth and inexperience!*"[1] (emphasis mine).

The eruption of laughter and applause—as well as the look on Walter Mondale's face—said it all. With this single response, President Reagan had moved from defense to offense, turning his greatest perceived weakness into a real asset, and it became clear that in that moment he had won the debate. In fact, Mondale commented years later in an interview: "If TV can tell the truth . . . you'll see that I was smiling. But I think if you come in close you'll see some tears coming down, because I knew he had gotten me there. That was really the end of my campaign."[2]

Reagan went on to win the election with one of the biggest landslides in U.S. history, taking forty-nine of the fifty states, and nearly winning the fiftieth—Mondale's home state of Minnesota—as well.

FROM DEFENSE TO OFFENSE

Reagan's approach in answering that question demonstrated the wisdom behind the saying, "The best defense is a good offense." Throughout these chapters, we've been addressing questions that many of the people we hope to reach—and perhaps some of us as followers of Christ—view as weak points in the Christian faith. Our answers have largely fallen within the framework of how to give a good *defense* for what we believe. The Bible tells us to do this when it says we should be ready to give a good answer to anyone who asks for the reason for the hope we have in Christ (see 1 Pet. 3:15).

But we've also seen that the New Testament challenges us to get on the *offense* in order to, as Paul put it, "knock down the strongholds of human reasoning and to destroy false arguments" (2 Cor. 10:4). He goes on to explain how he did this: "We destroy every proud obstacle that keeps people from knowing God. We capture their rebellious thoughts and teach them to obey Christ" (v. 5). This shows that for Paul, too, the best defense was a good offense.

But the world does not want us to go on the offense. It wants to keep the burden of proof on us—to keep us on the defense, rocked back on our heels trying to answer its first question while it loads the firing chamber with the second and third rounds, shooting objections at us faster than we can possibly respond to them.

For example, atheist Richard Dawkins, author of *The God Delusion*, likes to tell Christians that "the onus is on *you* to say why you believe in something"[3] (emphasis mine). His rationale is that since we're the ones making a claim, it is therefore our job to show why that claim is true.

It would be easy to get fretful about this and say, "Oh no, the onus is on me. What am I going to do? The onus is on—wait a minute, what's an *onus*? Anyway, whatever it is, it's on *me*!"

Now that's partly true—as we discussed, we *do* need to give a good defense. But we need to get on the offense, too. For example, you could reply, "You say the onus is on me because I believe in something? Well, what about you—do you believe in the Holocaust? So do I. But who is the onus on regarding *that*—the people who believe it or the people who deny it?"

Obviously, it's on those who deny it. When it comes to well-known facts of history such as the Holocaust, it is the small minority denying common knowledge who bear the burden of proof. Similarly, in a world where the vast majority of people believe in God, and in which many strong arguments have been made for his existence and his activity in people's lives (including the "Twenty Arrows of Truth" I present in my book *Choosing Your Faith*[4]), it's the people who *deny* this common knowledge who should bear the burden of proof.

Honestly, I'd be willing to split the onus right down the middle, because—and this is important—nobody is neutral; everybody is making a claim to something. The atheist is making the claim that there is no God, those in other religions are making their particular claims about God's existence and nature, and we Christians are doing this as well. So all of us should be willing to give a defense for what we believe.

But in this final chapter I want to show how the defense can and should naturally flow into an appropriate and effective offense (without being *offensive*). Or, to put it another way, how we can stop merely answering our friends' questions and start asking them a few key questions of our own. This is critical, since our goal is to help them examine and reassess their own beliefs. Let's look at a few ideas for how we can do this out of the topics raised in the questions we've been discussing.

THE QUESTIONS REVISITED

Question 1: *"What makes you so sure that God exists at all—especially when you can't see, hear, or touch him?"*

In the first chapter, we showed there are many things that are real but can't be seen or sensed in normal ways. We also saw that the existence of the universe as a whole, the fine-tuning of that universe, and the reality of objective moral standards among people around the world all point powerfully to the existence of a God who is outside the universe but who caused it, shaped it in an amazingly precise fashion so it could support life, and built morality into the fabric of what it means to be human. And our individual experience of God supports all this evidence. I'm convinced that the deeper one studies the evidence behind these arguments (with an open mind), the stronger his or her faith will become.

But if our friends want to deny that God exists, then how do they account for the existence of the universe? Is it eternal? Science and philosophy—not to mention the Bible—say it is not. Did it pop into existence out of nothing, by nothing, and for nothing? That would take more faith than believing God made it!

And how did it become so precisely fine-tuned, down to the most infinitesimal detail, in order to sustain life? If there is no God, then our friends need a completely natural explanation for this—one that can account for such amazing design without any kind of an intelligent designer. The more we understand the complexity and precision of the "just so" nature of the universe we live in, however, the more outlandish the naturalistic explanations begin to appear.

And without a transcendent moral lawgiver to ground

moral laws, what is the basis upon which to say anything is ultimately right or wrong? Isn't it all just preferences, tastes, and arbitrary rules? People can *say* they believe that, but then they shouldn't complain when someone steals their stuff or their spouse. Apart from the existence of God, taking those things just happens to be the thief's (or adulterer's) preference; we can't really say that what that person did was *wrong*.

Question 2: *"Didn't evolution put God out of a job? Why rely on religion in an age of science and knowledge?"*
On the contrary, we showed that evolution couldn't even have gotten off the ground without the environment of the universe and the "ingredients" of matter (both of which need an outside cause), the formation of the first life (for which scientists have no natural explanation), and the elaborate instructions for life—the "recipes"—encoded in DNA.

This pushes us back to some of the issues raised under question 1, as well as the puzzle of how life got here in the first place (in which both the fossil record and the biblical record seem to point to a deliberate designer who placed new life forms here fully formed).

So if our friends want to maintain the naturalistic view that evolution "put God out of a job," then how do they explain the "stuff" being here in the first place, the first life arising without explanation, the fossil record (especially the Cambrian Explosion) that shows the rapid appearance of numerous species without any clear-cut transitional ones between species or, again, the amazing information encoded in the strands of DNA?

On the other hand, if they maintain that evolution and

God's existence are compatible with each other, then the real question becomes where they stand with the *God behind that miracle.* Have they put effort into discovering as much as they can about him and his will for the world and for their lives? If evolution is not a barrier to belief in God for our friends, then we should focus on the question of *God.*

Question 3: *"Why trust the Bible, a book based on myths and full of contradictions and mistakes?"*
Often the best thing to ask our friends about this question is simply, "What do you mean? What specific myths are you referring to? Which contradictions bother you the most?"

Usually you'll find that they are simply repeating a rumor they've heard about the Bible, with little or no substance behind it. Or if they do offer an example, it will often be the kind of easily answered "contradiction" that we discussed in the third chapter (and for challenges that are more difficult, we listed books there that can be helpful).

Also, more often than not people are expressing (actually, *repeating*) opinions about a book they've barely read. When that's the case, we're wise to challenge them to invest some time in getting to know the Bible before they criticize it too much. It's also important to make sure they have an up-to-date translation that uses language they'll understand and relate to—such as the New Living Translation of the Bible.

I'm sure you've experienced, as I have, how the Bible speaks with supernatural insight and authority into our human condition. It enlightens our understanding, awakens our hearts, and convicts our consciences—all of which make it "ring true" as God's revelation and, if we have a repentant attitude, draw us to him as the source behind its words and wisdom.

Question 4: *"Everyone knows that Jesus was a good man and a wise teacher—but why try to make him into the Son of God, too?"*

This objection seems pretty powerful at first glance—until one actually reads what Jesus said about himself and his own identity, finds out about his sinless life and miraculous works, and assesses the overwhelming historical case for his resurrection from the dead.

C. S. Lewis powerfully sums up the information about Jesus: "Either this man was, and is, the Son of God: or else a madman or something worse. You can shut Him up for a fool; you can spit on Him and kill Him as a demon; or you can fall at His feet and call Him Lord and God. But let us not come with any patronizing nonsense about His being a good human teacher. He has not left that open to us. He did not intend to."[5]

You can ask your friends, "Have you ever read the Gospels for yourself? If not—or if it's been a long time since you have—then why don't we both read and discuss them? Let's see what Jesus actually said and did, and then we can draw our conclusions." Or if they lack the confidence that they can trust the Bible, ask them to dig into the questions deeper—to study the evidence for and against it—and find out what's really true.

Along the way, we need to constantly demonstrate that we are genuine lovers of truth, unafraid to look at the real evidence and to follow the facts where they lead. At first this can seem quite challenging to our faith, but the deeper we look, the more we'll gain confidence as a Christian, because *truth is on our side*. If they'll follow our example and seek the real truth about Jesus, he promises a good outcome:

> Keep on asking, and you will receive what you ask for. Keep on seeking, and you will find. Keep on knocking, and the door will be opened to you. For everyone who asks, receives. Everyone who seeks, finds. And to everyone who knocks, the door will be opened. (Matt. 7:7-8)

Question 5: *"How could a good God allow so much evil, pain, and suffering—or does he simply not care?"*
As explained in that chapter, there's a time for talking about this issue and a time for *not* talking about it; when your friends are in the midst of pain, it's probably better to focus on loving and serving them than trying to explain the possible reasons behind what they are going through.

That said, there are some important points to make when the time comes to discuss it. First, if your friends "can't believe in a loving God" because of pain and suffering in the world, ask them what their alternative is. No God? In that case, what meaning do pain and suffering have? Because without God, there is no purpose for life, no better destiny, no higher ideal—we're just accidental creatures in a world where only the fittest will survive.

Under that point of view, we as humans have no more

intrinsic value than any other animal. Also, if what we're suffering is related to the crimes or inhumanity of some other person, then that, too, is meaningless because in an atheistic world there is no universal right or wrong. Given that scenario, we might not like it, but we can't blame our circumstances on anything but fate, can we? There's certainly no divine help available anywhere. (Now, our friends' hearts, of course, tell them otherwise—thus pointing them to the reality of right and wrong, good and bad, justice and injustice, and therefore to God, without whom those concepts don't ultimately make any sense.)

And if that last perspective doesn't sit well with our friends, we can ask if they realize that the other alternative is an Eastern pantheistic view that says everything is just an aspect of god—we're all part of an all-inclusive "one." The problems with that, however, are probably even worse than the atheistic alternative, because now any evil that was done and the evil person who did it are all *part of god*! Furthermore, that god is an impersonal force, so we wouldn't have a heavenly Father who cares, nor a "friend in Jesus"—just a force that somehow mystically sustains us and draws us to eventually merge . . . with everything, including evil.

Given the alternatives—not to mention the evidence—our friends will hopefully understand that it's better to grapple with the problem of evil than to deny it through atheism or deify it through Eastern pantheistic philosophies.

On a more personal level, we can remind them that nobody has suffered more than Jesus, who went through unthinkable physical, mental, psychological, and spiritual trauma—all on our behalf (see Phil. 2:5-11). It's because of him that the Bible encourages us.

> Since we have a great High Priest who has entered heaven, Jesus the Son of God, let us hold firmly to what we believe. This High Priest of ours understands our weaknesses, for he faced all of the same testings we do, yet he did not sin. So let us come boldly to the throne of our gracious God. There we will receive his mercy, and we will find grace to help us when we need it most. (Heb. 4:14-16)

Question 6: *"Why is abortion such a line in the sand for Christians? Why can't I be left alone to make my own choices for my own body?"*

You can tell your friends the story about Arnie, Jean, and the box in the middle of the road. Ask them what they would do if they had that experience and thought there was even *a fraction of a percent chance* that a child could be playing inside that box. Any decent human being would do exactly what Arnie and Jean did—they'd pull over to check it out and be on the safe side, and upon discovering the situation, they'd immediately rescue the child.

Then apply the lesson to the situation with abortion. Are they *100 percent* certain that it's not a living human child inside the womb? In light of all the evidence, it's hard to imagine that anyone could be even close to that level of confidence (or delusion). But if they have any doubt whatsoever, shouldn't they do what they just said they'd do upon seeing the box on the highway—and give the child (or possible child) the benefit of the doubt? The right answer should be obvious.

Also, we've shown that these are not choices about a "woman's own body" but about the body of someone else who has been entrusted to her care—someone with a unique genetic makeup; independent brain waves; his or her own heartbeat, blood type, fingerprints, and facial expressions. *This is a full-fledged human life.* If your friends disagree, ask them what exactly they think it is!

Also, given the high regard most people have for Jesus, you can show them his words in Matthew 25:45 (emphasis mine), "I tell you the truth, when you refused to help the least of these my brothers and sisters, you were refusing to help me" and ask them why Jesus words wouldn't apply to *the least of the least* in our society—the unborn?

Question 7: *"Why do you condemn homosexuality when it's clear that God made gays and that he loves all people the same?"*
Jesus was known for two strong traits: he was "full of *grace* and *truth*" (John 1:14, NIV, emphasis mine). We need to reflect both of those characteristics when we talk to people, especially when discussing this volatile topic. With the animosity people feel on both sides, we need especially to lean toward the *grace* side of the equation—yet without denying *truth*.

In chapter 7 we saw the gracious ways in which Jesus interacted with the spiritually wayward Samaritan woman. He focused on her as a person, he interacted with her in a respectful way, and he was gracious toward her, but he didn't neglect the sin in her life or her need for a Savior. We need to show the same kind of respect and clarity that he did.

Here is a question we can ask our friends: "After seeing Jesus' gentle but clear way of pointing to this woman's sexual sin, how do you think he would approach people about homosexual behavior?"

Also, Jesus echoed the words of Genesis 2:24 in the Old Testament when he said, in Matthew 19:4-6, "Haven't you read the Scriptures? . . . They record that from the beginning 'God made them male and female.' And he said, 'This explains why a man leaves his father and mother and is joined to his wife, and the two are united into one.' Since they are no longer two but one, let no one split apart what God has joined together."

So in light of this, we can ask people: "Given Jesus' strong and positive explanation of God's plan for marriage, what do you think he would say about gay sexual relationships?" Also, "Do you see anywhere in Jesus' words—or in the teachings of the Bible as a whole—where the Bible actually *condones* homosexual behavior?"

But, again, don't wield biblical truth as a weapon or as a way to put up a wall. The goal is to win people—to bring them to the loving and forgiving Savior, who delights in turning all kinds of sinners into his own beloved sons and daughters.

Questions 8 and 9: *"How can I trust in Christianity when so many Christians are hypocrites?" "And why are they so judgmental toward everyone who doesn't agree with them?"*
Here's a place where we can agree with the general premise.

Hypocrisy and judgmentalism *are* problems for some Christians—the problem is not so much that they fail, but that they pretend to be better than they are (and better than others). But here's a good question to ask: "What person in the Bible do you think most agreed with your concern and spoke out most strongly against these things?" That's right, it's Jesus. So a follow up question could be, "Since you are already on Jesus' side on this matter, why not learn more about him and how you can become a genuine follower of his—setting a great example for others?"

Another more personal response to the charge of hypocrisy might be, "You know, honestly, I want to be a good Christian—but sometimes I've struggled to live up to the high ideals of Christ. Worse yet, sometimes I've pretended to be doing better at it than I really am. So as much as I hate to admit it, a certain amount of hypocrisy runs through my veins, which is why I'm glad he's a forgiving God! How about you: do you ever struggle living up to your own ideals—or God's?"

On the subject of judgmentalism, we need to dig deeper to find out what problem our friends are seeing. If it's really arrogance and pride, then once again they're on the side of the Bible (and ought to consider following it in other ways as well). But if they're taking offense simply because Christians think they're right and others are wrong, you can gently ask, "But how is that different from what you're doing right now, making the assumption that you're right and they are wrong?"

We need to help our friends understand that *all people* think they're right at any given moment—and as soon as they quit thinking that their current opinion is correct, they immediately change it to something else that they then think *is* right! There's nothing inherently wrong with this tendency—it's only natural, and both you and they are doing it even at the very moment you're discussing this topic—but the real question is: "How do we know who *really* is right about the matter?" That question brings us to the logic and evidence that show the truthfulness of the Christian faith.

Question 10: *"Why should I think that heaven really exists— and that God sends people to hell?"*
Some questions have answers that are hard or even impossible to access in a direct and personal way. If I want to know what it's like to walk on the moon, then I'm going to try to talk to one of the few human beings on the planet who have ever done so—or read what they've written about it. Similarly, we can't directly access heaven right now (*or hell*—who would want to try?), but we can listen to the One who said, "You are from below; I am from above. You belong to this world; I do not" (John 8:23). He, Jesus, was the One who died on the cross but rose from the dead three days later and who explained to his friends, "I am the resurrection and the life. Anyone who believes in me will live, even after dying" (John 11:25).

Jesus also had the credentials of a sinless life, the fulfillment of ancient biblical prophecies, and the many miracles he did—including in the presence of hostile witnesses who never denied the miracles—then it all culminated in his resurrection. These things—and many others—showed him to be a unique person and provided great evidence that he is, as he claimed to be, the Son of God.

A couple of key questions to ask our friends, therefore, include, "In light of Jesus' divine credentials, why *wouldn't* you believe what Jesus taught about heaven and hell? If you're not going to believe Jesus, who *are* you going to believe—and why?"

BACK TO WHERE WE STARTED

I hope you are seeing that truth really is on our side. As Christians, we need not be afraid of the questions people ask, the objections they raise, or the challenges they may throw at us. We believe in Christianity because it is true, we trust in the Bible because it has proven itself to be trust-worthy time and again, and we're followers of Jesus because he is who he claimed to be—and being in a relationship with him genuinely is the best way to live (and the *only* way to die).

In the introduction to this book, I said we need three things in order to appropriately put the information we'd be discussing into action: *preparation, prayer,* and *proximity.*

Congratulations on the first one: *preparation.* Just by reading this book (and hopefully making a few notes in it), you've come a long way in terms of getting ready to talk to people about their spiritual questions. I hope that it also whets your appetite for more and that you'll read some of the other books I've mentioned, knowing that preparation is an ongoing process. (I also hope you'll tell others in your church who would benefit from this information and con-sider going through this book and the discussion questions in each chapter with your church class or small group, passing on some of what you've learned to others in your circle.)

Concerning the second element, *prayer*, I trust you've been prompted along the way to pray for your friends, family members, coworkers, and neighbors who have questions about these issues and who need to know Christ. Let me encourage you to keep on praying for them, and to do so in increasing measure. Also, pray for yourself, that your depth of knowledge and readiness will continue to grow and that God will open more and more doors of opportunity to share his truth with others.

The third element is *proximity*. Perhaps in the past you've avoided contact with people who might challenge your faith or ask you hard spiritual questions. As the title of the book indicates, we've been dealing with the questions that many of us "hope no one will ask." But in keeping with the message of this last chapter, I hope you've sensed a shift in your own basic disposition—from defense to offense— and that you'll therefore no longer *avoid* opportunities for spiritual influence and instead *go looking for them!*

As you do, remember the other things we said at the beginning of this book: that our *purpose* is not to just answer people's questions but to lead them to the Savior. We want to help them find not only answers and truth but also the One who said, "I *am* the way, the truth, and the life. No one can come to the Father except through me" (John 14:6, emphasis mine). And as we communicate his truth, we should always be motivated by *love* for him and for the friends we're talking to.

Now go with confidence—as well as urgency—knowing

that the time is short and the information you have to share is life giving. Focus on answering the questions as quickly as possible in order to get back to the central message of the gospel, which is where the real potency for life change will be found.

> *I am not ashamed of this Good News about Christ.*
> *It is the power of God at work, saving everyone who*
> *believes.*
>
> —ROMANS 1:16

RECOMMENDED RESOURCES

CHAPTER 1: "What makes you so sure that God exists at all—especially when you can't see, hear, or touch him?"

Reasonable Faith: Christian Truth and Apologetics, by William Lane Craig (Crossway, 2008).

I Don't Have Enough Faith to Be an Atheist, by Norman Geisler and Frank Turek (Crossway, 2004).

The Twilight of Atheism: The Rise and Fall of Disbelief in the Modern World, by Alister McGrath (Galilee Trade, 2006).

There Is a God: How the World's Most Notorious Atheist Changed His Mind, by Antony Flew with Roy Abraham Varghese (HarperOne, 2008).

God Is Great, God Is Good: Why Believing in God Is Reasonable and Responsible, by William Lane Craig and Chad Meister, eds. (InterVarsity, 2009).

CHAPTER 2: "Didn't evolution put God out of a job? Why rely on religion in an age of science and knowledge?"

The Case for a Creator: A Journalist Investigates Scientific Evidence That Points toward God, by Lee Strobel (Zondervan, 2005).

Understanding Intelligent Design: Everything You Need to Know in Plain Language, by William Dembski and Sean McDowell (Harvest House, 2008).

Darwin on Trial, by Phillip E. Johnson (InterVarsity, 1993).

Signature in the Cell: DNA and the Evidence for Intelligent Design, by Stephen C. Meyer (HarperOne, 2010).

Three Views on Creation and Evolution, J. P. Moreland and John Mark Reynolds, eds. (Zondervan, 1999).

A Fine-Tuned Universe: The Quest for God in Science and Theology, by Alister McGrath (Westminster, John Knox, 2009).

The Cell's Design: How Chemistry Reveals the Creator's Artistry, by Fazale Rana (Baker, 2008).

CHAPTER 3: "Why trust the Bible, a book based on myths and full of contradictions and mistakes?"

The Case for Christ: A Journalist's Personal Investigation of the Evidence for Jesus, by Lee Strobel (Zondervan, 1998).

The Case for the Real Jesus: A Journalist Investigates Current Attacks on the Identity of Christ, by Lee Strobel (Zondervan, 2009).

Seven Reasons Why You Can Trust the Bible, by Erwin W. Lutzer (Moody, 2008).

Knowing Scripture, by R. C. Sproul (InterVarsity, 2009, rev. ed.).

From God to Us: How We Got Our Bible, by Norman L. Geisler and William Nix (Moody, 1980).

The Big Book of Bible Difficulties: Clear and Concise Answers from Genesis to Revelation, by Thomas Howe and Norman L. Geisler (Baker, 2008).

The Many Gospels of Jesus: Sorting Out the Story of the Life of Jesus, by Philip W. Comfort and Jason Driesbach (Tyndale, 2008).

CHAPTER 4: "Everyone knows that Jesus was a good man and a wise teacher—but why try to make him into the Son of God, too?"

More Than a Carpenter, by Josh McDowell and Sean McDowell (Tyndale, 2009).

Putting Jesus in His Place: The Case for the Deity of Christ, by Robert M. Bowman Jr. and J. Ed Komoszewski (Kregel, 2007).

Fabricating Jesus: How Modern Scholars Distort the Gospels, by Craig A. Evans (InterVarsity, 2008).

Jesus under Fire: Modern Scholarship Reinvents the Historical Jesus, Michael J. Wilkins and J. P. Moreland eds. (Zondervan, 1996).

Reinventing Jesus, by J. Ed Komoszewski, M. James Sawyer, and Daniel B. Wallace (Kregel, 2006).

Jesus among Other Gods: The Absolute Claims of the Christian Message, by Ravi Zacharias (W Publishing Group, 2002).

What Have They Done with Jesus? Beyond Strange Theories and Bad History—Why We Can Trust the Bible, by Ben Witherington III (HarperOne, 2007).

CHAPTER 5: "How could a good God allow so much evil, pain, and suffering—or does he simply not care?"

The Case for Faith, by Lee Strobel (Zondervan, 2000).

Where Is God When It Hurts? by Philip Yancey (Zondervan, 2002, anniv. ed.).

Making Sense Out of Suffering, by Peter Kreeft (Servant Ministries, 1986).

When God Weeps, by Joni Eareckson Tada and Steven Estes (Zondervan, 2000).

A Grace Disguised: How the Soul Grows through Loss, by Gerald L. Sittser (Zondervan, 2004, expanded ed.).

Where Was God? by Erwin W. Lutzer (Tyndale, 2006).

CHAPTER 6: "Why is abortion such a line in the sand for Christians? Why can't I be left alone to make my own choices for my own body?"

Who Broke the Baby? What the Abortion Slogans Really Mean, by Jean Staker Garton (Bethany House, 1998).

Defending Life: A Moral and Legal Case against Abortion Choice, by Francis Beckwith (Cambridge University Press, 2007).

Embryo: A Defense of Human Life, by Robert P. George and Christopher Tollefsen (Doubleday, 2008).

Pro-Life Answers to Pro-Choice Arguments, by Randy Alcorn (Multnomah, 2000, expanded and updated ed.).

CHAPTER 7: "Why do you condemn homosexuality when it's clear that God made gays and that he loves all people the same?"

unChristian, by David Kinnaman and Gabe Lyons (Baker, 2007).

No Perfect People Allowed: Creating a Come-as-You-Are Culture in the Church, by John Burke (Zondervan, 2007).

The Same Sex Controversy: Defending and Clarifying the Bible's Message about Homosexuality, by Jeff Niell and James White (Bethany House, 2002).

Straight and Narrow? Compassion and Clarity in the Homosexuality Debate, by Thomas E. Schmidt (IVP Academic, 1995).

Hard Questions, Real Answers, by William Lane Craig (Crossway, 2003).

CHAPTER 8: "How can I trust in Christianity when so many Christians are hypocrites?"

"And why are Christians so judgmental toward everyone who doesn't agree with them?"

Who You Are When No One's Looking: Choosing Consistency, Resisting Compromise, by Bill Hybels (InterVarsity, 2010, rev. ed.).

Integrity: The Courage to Meet the Demands of Reality, by Henry Cloud (Harper, 2009).

Who Are You to Judge? by Erwin W. Lutzer (Moody, 2003).

Give Me an Answer That Satisfies My Heart and My Mind, by Cliffe Knechtle (InterVarsity, 1986).

CHAPTER 9: "Why should I think that heaven really exists—and that God sends people to hell?"

Life after Death: The Evidence, by Dinesh D'Souza (Regnery, 2009).

Heaven, by Randy Alcorn (Tyndale, 2004).

Heaven: Your Real Home, by Joni Eareckson Tada (Zondervan, 1997).

Hell: The Logic of Damnation, by Jerry L. Walls (University of Notre Dame Press, 1992).

Beyond Death: Exploring the Evidence for Immortality, by Gary Habermas and J. P. Moreland (Wipf and Stock Publishers, 2004).

CHAPTER 10: The questions our friends need *us* to ask *them*

Choosing Your Faith . . . In a World of Spiritual Options, by Mark Mittelberg (Tyndale, 2008).

Faith Path: Helping Friends Find Their Way to Christ, by Mark Mittelberg (David C. Cook, 2009).

Tactics: A Game Plan for Discussing Your Christian Convictions, by Gregory Koukl (Zondervan, 2009).

Becoming a Contagious Christian, by Bill Hybels and Mark Mittelberg (Zondervan, 1995).

Tough Questions series, by Garry Poole and Judson Poling (Zondervan, 2003, rev. ed.).

On Guard: Defending Your Faith with Reason and Precision, by William Lane Craig (David C. Cook, 2010).

NOTES

INTRODUCTION:

1. Billy Kim made this observation at the Baptist World Congress in the year 2000 in Melbourne, Australia.

CHAPTER 1:

1. Mark Mittelberg, *Choosing Your Faith . . . In a World of Spiritual Options* (Carol Stream, IL: Tyndale, 2008), especially chapters 9–11.
2. Or as my mentor, Dr. Stuart Hackett, used to winsomely put it, "and by 'universe' I mean '*the works!*'"
3. The Hubble telescope continues to offer amazing pictures of and information about the universe. You can see many of these pictures online at http://hubblesite.org. This site also offers other fascinating features, such as tracking Hubble's exact current location in space and previews of an even more powerful telescope that is now under construction, which will be sent into orbit in 2014.
4. Albert Einstein, *Ideas and Opinions*, 1994 Modern Library Edition, copyright 1954 by Crown Publishers, Inc. (New York: Random House, 1994), 43.
5. Debate between Richard Dawkins and Francis Collins, as cited on the Richard Dawkins Foundation Web page, http://richarddawkins .net/articles/4047-god-vs-science-a-debate-between-richard-dawkins-and-francis-collins?page=22&scope=latest&type=articles.
6. For more on this cosmological argument and many other evidences for God, see William Lane Craig and Chad Meister, eds., *God Is Great, God Is Good: Why Believing in God Is Reasonable and Responsible* (Downers Grove, IL: InterVarsity Press, 2009).

7. From an interview with Dr. Robin Collins in Lee Strobel, *The Case for a Creator* (Grand Rapids, MI: Zondervan, 2004), 132.

8. For some of the most recent findings regarding this kind of evidence, see Paul Davies, *The Goldilocks Enigma: Why Is the Universe Just Right for Life?* (New York: First Mariner Books, 2008).

9. Paul Davies, *The Mind of God* (New York: Simon & Schuster, 1992), 242.

10. For a fascinating book that sketches out these factors, see Guillermo Gonzalez and Jay W. Richards, *The Privileged Planet: How Our Place in the Cosmos Is Designed for Discovery* (Washington, DC: Regnery, 2004).

11. These two examples are based on related illustrations from Robin Collins's essay, "A Scientific Argument for God's Existence: The Fine-Tuning Design Argument," in Michael Murray, ed., *Reason for the Hope Within* (Grand Rapids, MI: Eerdmans, 1999), 47–75.

12. John D. Steinrucken, "Secularism's Ongoing Debt to Christianity," *American Thinker*, March 25, 2010. To read the article, go to www.americanthinker.com/2010/03/secularisms_ongoing_debt_to_ch.html.

CHAPTER 2:

1. Lee Strobel, *The Case for a Creator* (Grand Rapids, MI: Zondervan, 2004). Brad Dennison's influence is mentioned in the acknowledgments on page 329.

2. Richard Dawkins, *The Selfish Gene*, 30th Anniversary Edition (New York: Oxford University Press, 1976, 2006), 1.

3. Richard Dawkins, "Ignorance Is No Crime," *Free Inquiry* magazine, 21, no. 3 (2001); see article at secularhumanism.org/library/fi/dawkins_21_3.html. Dawkins first said this in a book review he did for the *New York Times* on April 9, 1989.

4. Carl Sagan, *Cosmos* (New York: A Ballantine Book, Random House, 1980), 179.

5. For more on this, see my discussion of philosophical naturalism, or as it is sometimes called, *scientism*, in my earlier book *Choosing Your Faith . . . In a World of Spiritual Options* (Carol Stream, IL: Tyndale, 2008), 136–143.

6. Elaine Howard Ecklund, *Science vs. Religion: What Scientists Really Think* (New York: Oxford University Press, 2010). The summary quoted can be viewed at www.christianbook.com/science-religion-what-scientists-really-believe/elaine-ecklund/ 9780195392982/ pd/392982?item_code=WW&netp_id=799891&event= ESRCN&view=details.

7. Chris Mooney, "Are Top Scientists Really So Atheistic? Look at the Data," *Discover* magazine blog article (April 13, 2010), http://blogs.discovermagazine.com/intersection/tag/elaine-howard-ecklund/.

8. John Polkinghorne, *Quarks, Chaos, and Christianity* (New York: Crossroad, 1994), xii.

9. See www.dissentfromdarwin.org.

10. The entire document, including the list of scientists' names and their credentials, can be downloaded online at discovery.org/scripts/viewDB/filesDB-download.php?command=download&id=660.

11. In my book *Choosing Your Faith* (Carol Stream, IL: Tyndale, 2008), as well as the complementary group study course, *Faith Path* (Colorado Springs, CO: David C. Cook, 2009), I discuss in depth the various ways we can learn and test truth claims in order to end up with a wisely chosen set of cohesive beliefs.

12. This is from Sandage's spoken message as summarized in Lee Strobel, *The Case for a Creator*, 69–70.

13. Patrick Glynn, *GOD: The Evidence* (Rocklin, CA: Prima Publishing, 1997), 26.

14. This was mentioned as a possibility by prominent Darwinist Michael Ruse in an interview with Ben Stein in the movie *Expelled: No Intelligence Allowed*.

15. Ibid.

16. Michael Denton, *Evolution: A Theory in Crisis* (Bethesda, MD: Adler & Adler Publishers, 1986), 271.

17. Klaus Dose, "The Origin of Life: More Questions Than Answers," *Interdisciplinary Science Review* 13 (1998), 348, as cited in Lee Strobel, *The Case for Faith* (Grand Rapids, MI: Zondervan, 2000), 107.

18. William A. Dembski and Sean McDowell, *Understanding Intelligent Design* (Eugene, OR: Harvest House Publishers, 2008), 130,

emphasis mine. Also note that the authors state their case "according to standard dating"; you may or may not agree with that dating—but you can still make this kind of point using the premises that your friends accept. In other words, you can make your point while operating on their playing field.

19. Denton, *Evolution: A Theory in Crisis*, 342, emphasis mine.
20. An interview with Stephen Meyer in Strobel, *The Case for a Creator*, 229, emphasis mine.
21. Dembski and McDowell, *Understanding Intelligent Design*, 131, emphasis mine.
22. Francis S. Collins, *The Language of God: A Scientist Presents Evidence for Belief* (New York: Free Press, 2006), 1–2.
23. Ibid., 2, emphasis mine.
24. Ibid., 1, 3.
25. Strobel, *The Case for a Creator*, 71.
26. Some of the information and quotes on DNA were drawn from my book *Choosing Your Faith*, 171–173.
27. This debate, including the part quoted, can be viewed online at www.youtube.com/watch?v=Q7U_kcRCx88&feature=related. Again, I want to emphasize that you don't have to accept all the possible interpretations that Dr. Craig refers to in order to see and communicate the point that Christians have a variety of views on *how* God created—but our first focus should be on *who* God is and what he wants to do in our lives.
28. J. P. Moreland and John Mark Reynolds, eds., *Three Views on Creation and Evolution* (Grand Rapids, MI: Zondervan, 1999).
29. Ibid., as expressed by Paul Nelson and John Mark Reynolds, 42.
30. Ibid., as expressed by Robert C. Newman, 105–106, emphasis his.
31. Ibid., as expressed by Howard Van Till, 170–171.
32. Timothy Keller, *The Reason for God: Belief in an Age of Skepticism* (New York: Dutton, published by Penguin Group, 2008), 94, emphasis mine.

CHAPTER 3:

1. Kenneth Kantzer was a theology professor at Trinity Evangelical Divinity School during the years I attended there. This is a story he often recounted, specifically as cited in Lynn Gardner, *Christianity*

Stands True (Joplin, MO: College Press, 1994), 39. Also, Dr. Kantzer wrote the foreword for the book.

2. Ibid.

3. Ibid.

4. Given the magnitude of this question about the Bible and the space limitations of one chapter, we'll focus most of our comments on the reliability of the New Testament.

5. Dr. Michael Licona, as quoted in an interview in Lee Strobel, *The Case for the Real Jesus* (Grand Rapids, MI: Zondervan, 2007), 115.

6. James D. G. Dunn, *Jesus Remembered* (Grand Rapids, MI: Eerdmans, 2003), 855, emphasis in original.

7. John's Gospel is almost universally considered the latest of the four, but he was also among the youngest of the disciples; he probably wrote it near the end of his life.

8. Gary Habermas, *The Historical Jesus* (Joplin, MO: College Press, 1996), chapters 9–11.

9. William F. Albright, "Retrospect and Prospect in New Testament Archaeology," in *The Teacher's Yoke*, ed. E. Jerry Vardaman (Waco, TX: Baylor University Press, 1964), 189, as cited in ed. Norman Geisler and Ronald Brooks, *When Skeptics Ask: A Handbook on Christian Evidences* (Grand Rapids, MI: Baker, 1996), 202.

10. The two versions I find most helpful, due to their mix of clarity and accuracy, are the *New Living Translation* (NLT) and the *New International Version* (NIV). To see a variety of high quality Bible translations online—and to contrast and compare them (and to see how studying several of them will enrich your understanding of Scripture) see www.biblegateway.com.

11. Similar things can be said of the Old Testament, especially based on the findings of the Dead Sea Scrolls in the mid-twentieth century. Old Testament manuscripts were discovered that predated what were at the time the oldest manuscripts in our possession by as many as a thousand years—yet the wording was virtually the same. For more information, see Norman Geisler and Ronald Brooks, *When Skeptics Ask: A Handbook on Christian Evidences* (Grand Rapids, MI: Baker Books, 1990), especially chapter 7, "Questions about the Bible."

12. *Parade* magazine (February 4, 1996), 7.

13. Robert Jastrow, *God and the Astronomers*, 2nd ed. (New York: W.W. Norton, 1992), 103.

14. Dan Brown, *The Da Vinci Code* (New York: Doubleday, a division of Random House, 2003), 303–304, emphasis his.

15. Cited by Strobel, *The Case for the Real Jesus*, 27, quoting from Willis Barnstone and Marvin Meyer, *The Gnostic Bible* (Boston: New Seeds Books, 2003), 48, 69, 46. For insightful information on the Gnostic gospels, read Challenge #1 in *The Case for the Real Jesus*, which deals with the claim that "scholars are uncovering a radically different Jesus in ancient documents just as credible as the four gospels."

16. These examples were drawn from my earlier book, *Choosing Your Faith . . . In a World of Spiritual Options* (Carol Stream, IL: Tyndale, 2008), 196–199. More details about prophecy and more evidence for the supernatural origins of the Bible can be found there.

17. Brown, *The Da Vinci Code*, 232.

18. Ibid.

19. Ronald H. Nash, *The Gospel and the Greeks: Did the New Testament Borrow from Pagan Thought?* 2nd ed. (Phillipsburg, NJ: P & R Publishing, 2003), 161–162.

20. Richard Gordon, *Image and Value in the Greco-Roman World* (Aldershot, Eng.: Variorum, 1996), 96, quoted in J. P. Holding, "Did the Figure of Mithras Influence Christianity?" www.tektonics.org (January 23, 2007).

21. Strobel, *The Case for the Real Jesus*, 169–172.

22. Sir William Ramsay, *The Bearing of Recent Discovery on the Trustworthiness of the New Testament* (London: Hodder and Stoughton, 1915), 222, as cited in Josh McDowell, *More Than a Carpenter* (Carol Stream, IL: Tyndale, 1977), 39.

23. Gary Habermas, *The Historical Jesus* (Joplin, MO: College Press, 1996), chapters 9–11.

24. Strobel, *The Case for the Real Jesus*, 58. Evans is respected by conservatives and liberals alike; has written or edited fifty books; and has lectured at Cambridge, Oxford, Yale, and other universities.

CHAPTER 4:

1. Jefferson to Adams, October 12, 1813, quoted in Cyrus Adler, *The Life and Morals of Jesus of Nazareth* (Washington, DC: Government Printing Office, 1904), 5.

2. Tutu lends his endorsement to the jacket of Meyers's book *Saving Jesus from the Church: How to Stop Worshiping Christ and Start Following Jesus* (New York: HarperOne, 2009).

3. Dan Brown, *The Da Vinci Code* (New York: Doubleday, a division of Random House, 2003), 233, emphasis his.

4. Larry W. Hurtado, *Lord Jesus Christ: Devotion to Jesus in Earliest Christianity* (Grand Rapids, MI: Eerdmans, 2003), 135.

5. It should not be unexpected that scholars have debated the significance of all these texts. For an incisive yet readable discussion of these and similar passages that draws on current biblical scholarship, see Robert M. Bowman Jr. and J. Ed Komoszewski's foundational book, *Putting Jesus in His Place: The Case for the Deity of Christ* (Grand Rapids, MI: Kregel, 2007), 135–170.

6. All emphases in these Scriptures are mine. These passages are some of the clearest in showing the deity of Christ, but many skeptics view the Gospel of John, the last of the four Gospels, as less reliable than the others. I don't share their skepticism, but nevertheless I have focused most of the information in this chapter on information and biblical texts that are more widely accepted in the non-Christian world. An excellent resource in this connection is Craig L. Blomberg, *The Historical Reliability of John's Gospel: Issues and Commentary* (Downers Grove, IL: InterVarsity Press, 2002).

7. C. S. Lewis, *Mere Christianity* (New York: Macmillan, 1960), 55–56.

8. John Dominic Crossan, *Who Killed Jesus?* (San Francisco: Harper, 1995), 5.

9. E. P. Sanders, *The Historical Figure of Jesus* (London: Penguin, 1993), 280.

10. On the evidence for Jesus' resurrection, I highly recommend Gary R. Habermas and Michael R. Licona, *The Case for the Resurrection of Jesus* (Grand Rapids, MI: Kregel, 2004), as well as Lee Strobel's *The Case for Christ* (Grand Rapids, MI: Zondervan, 1998).

CHAPTER 5:

1. See Lee Strobel, *The Case for Faith* (Grand Rapids, MI: 2000), 29, for details on the study he commissioned through The Barna Group. They asked people, "If you could ask God only one question and you knew he would give you an answer, what would

you ask?" The number one response was, "Why is there pain and suffering in the world?"

2. Cited by Chad Meister, "Atheists and the Quest for Objective Morality," *Christian Research Journal*, 33, no. 02 (Charlotte, NC: Christian Research Institute, 2010), 32. He is citing a statement by Ted Bundy, paraphrased and rewritten by Harry V. Jaffa, *Homosexuality and the National Law* (Claremont Institute for the Study of Statesmanship and Political Philosophy, 1990), 3–4.

3. Meister, *Christian Research Journal*, 33, no. 02, 2010, 32. Note that Dr. Meister is not saying—nor am I saying—that atheists can't live moral lives, just that their worldview lacks a basis by which to declare what actually *is* moral or not moral.

4. John D. Steinrucken, "Secularism's Ongoing Debt to Christianity," *American Thinker*, March 25, 2010. The article can be viewed at www.americanthinker.com/2010/03/secularisms_ongoing_debt_to_ch.html.

5. C. S. Lewis, *Mere Christianity* (New York: Macmillan, 1960), 45.

6. Ibid., 45–46. Emphases his.

7. Harold Kushner, *When Bad Things Happen to Good People* (New York: Anchor Books, a division of Random House: first Anchor Books edition, 2004; originally published by Schocken Books, Inc., New York, 1981), 49.

8. Ibid., 125.

9. I recommend a book that tackles these issues at a deeper level (and to which I contributed a chapter). It is called *God Is Great, God Is Good: Why Believing in God Is Reasonable and Responsible,* eds. William Lane Craig and Chad Meister (Downers Grove, IL: InterVarsity Press, 2009).

10. Lee Strobel told this story in a sermon he presented at Willow Creek Community Church in South Barrington, Illinois, on July 11, 1999. The sermon was titled, "Why Is There Suffering?" The sermon transcript is available for download at www.willowcreek.com/wca_prodsb.asp?invtid=PR03358.

11. Mary Baker Eddy, *Science and Health, With Key to the Scriptures* (Charleston, SC: Forgotten Books, 2007), 193, 195.

12. Deb Bostwick tells her story on the DVD of my curriculum, *Faith*

Path: Helping Friends Find Their Way to Christ (Colorado Springs, CO: David C. Cook, 2009).

13. Norman Geisler, *Baker Encyclopedia of Christian Apologetics* (Grand Rapids, MI: Baker Books, 1999), 224.

14. Dinesh D'Souza, *What's So Great about Christianity* (Carol Stream, IL: Tyndale, 2008), 214.

15. Galatians 3:13 (NIV) says, "Christ redeemed us from the curse of the law by becoming a curse for us, for it is written: 'Cursed is everyone who is hung on a tree.'"

16. Philip Yancey, *Where Is God When It Hurts?* (Grand Rapids, MI: Zondervan, 1990, 1977), 17–18.

17. C. S. Lewis, *The Problem of Pain* (San Francisco: HarperCollins, 1940, 1996, HarperCollins ed. 2001), 91.

18. Judson Poling said this during a message he gave in the mid-1990s at Willow Creek Community Church in South Barrington, Illinois, during a "New Community Crossfire" service on the question of "Why Does God Allow Us to Suffer?"

CHAPTER 6:

1. Based on statistics cited by the National Right to Life. See Web site, www.nrlc.org/abortion/facts/abortionstats.html.

2. Francis J. Beckwith, *Defending Life: A Moral and Legal Case against Abortion Choice* (New York: Cambridge University Press, 2007), 88.

3. Ibid.

4. The information listed by date, January 1 through late April, has been adapted from the chart at www.cirtl.org/pdfs/NRTL_basic_abortion_facts.pdf.

5. Jean Staker Garton, *Who Broke the Baby?* (Minneapolis: Bethany, 1998), 17.

6. Lejeune said this before the United States congressional hearings on April 23, 1981. Quoted in J. P. Moreland and Norman Geisler, *The Life and Death Debate* (Westport, CT: Praeger, 1990), 34.

7. *Lovejoy Surgicenter v. Advocates for Life Ministries, et al.*, 1989, testimony of Aileen Klass as cited in Randy Alcorn, *Why Pro-Life?* (Sisters, OR: Multnomah, 2004), 27.

8. www.lifenews.com/nat2151.html.

9. As reported by ABC News at abcnews.go.com/Health/ MindMoodNews/planned-parenthood-clinic-director-joins-anti-abortion-group/story?id=8999720.

10. For a more in-depth discussion about this passage by Greg Koukl see www.str.org/site/News2?page=NewsArticle&id=5700.

11. Garton, *Who Broke the Baby?* 48.

12. Ibid.

13. Ibid., 49.

14. This story was told by its narrator to Gretchen Passantino, who passed it on to me.

15. This letter, from which I've removed specific names and dates, was received by our church when I was on the pastoral staff at Willow Creek Community Church in South Barrington, Illinois. It was originally published in Lee Strobel, *God's Outrageous Claims* (Grand Rapids, MI: Zondervan, 2005), 180–181.

CHAPTER 7:

1. Excerpted from John 4:1-6 (emphasis mine). Throughout this chapter I'll draw from the account of Jesus and the Samaritan woman in John 4:1-42.

2. It is true that Jesus prioritized reaching the "lost sheep of Israel"—but clearly that was only the initial part of his ultimate goal, which was to spread his love and truth to the entire world (see Matt. 28:18-20). As he said in John 12:32, "When I am lifted up from the earth, I will draw everyone to myself." This account in John 4 is an early illustration of that broader divine mission.

3. "LGBTQ community" is an abbreviation frequently used for those who are *Lesbian, Gay, Bisexual, Transgender*, as well as those who are *Questioning* their "sexual identity."

4. This is something I've heard Lee Strobel say frequently in question-and-answer sessions we've done together in churches, as well as in conversations with individuals who ask him about God's view of homosexuality.

5. The obvious exception would be if there were undue levels of personal risk in doing so—because of either the aggressive nature of the person or the temptation that this kind of proximity might

put you under. In those cases both wisdom and Scripture would tell you to avoid the situation. In some cases a ministry opportunity is right for one Christian but not for another (see Rom. 14). We must follow God's leadings in these matters and respect what we know to be true about our own areas of weakness or vulnerability.

6. New Testament scholar Merrill Tenney writes, for example, "It was an unusual time for women to come to a village well for water . . . perhaps she did not care to meet the other women of the community. In consideration of her general character, the other women may have shunned her." *The Expositor's Bible Commentary, Volume 9,* ed. Frank E. Gaebelein (Grand Rapids, MI: Zondervan, 1981), 54.

7. David Kinnaman and Gabe Lyons report in their book *unChristian,* for example, "Out of twenty attributes we assessed, both positive and negative, as they related to Christianity, the perception of being antihomosexual was at the top of the list." That perception is so strong, they explain, that "when you introduce yourself as a Christian to a friend, neighbor, or business associate who is an outsider, you might as well have it tattooed on your arm: antihomosexual, gay-hater, homophobic. I doubt you think of yourself in these terms, but that's what outsiders think of you." David Kinnaman and Gabe Lyons, *unChristian: What a New Generation Really Thinks about Christianity* (Grand Rapids, MI: Baker Books, 2007), 92–93.

8. For more information on Lee Strobel's ministry, as well as free teaching videos from Lee, myself, and numerous other friends and colleagues on a variety of topics related to the truth of Christianity, see www.leestrobel.com.

9. That's a term Lee Strobel and I use to describe the ways God wants to use all of us as Christians. We've written about this in a story-driven, six-week devotional called *The Unexpected Adventure* (Grand Rapids, MI: Zondervan, 2009). For information and free videos see www.theunexpectedadventure.com.

CHAPTER 8:

1. Garry Poole, who sent me this story, is the author of an important book that I highly recommend: *Seeker Small Groups: Engaging*

Spiritual Seekers in Life-Changing Discussions (Grand Rapids, MI: Zondervan, 2003).

2. *New Oxford American Dictionary*, 2nd ed. (New York: Oxford University Press, 2005), s.v. "hypocrisy."

3. David Kinnaman and Gabe Lyons, *unChristian: What a New Generation Really Thinks about Christianity* (Grand Rapids, MI: Baker, 2007), 46–47.

4. Lee Strobel, *God's Outrageous Claims: Discover What They Mean for You* (Grand Rapids, MI: Zondervan, 2005), condensed and adapted from pages 72–75, emphases his.

5. *Decision* magazine (October, 2000), 39.

6. Kinnaman and Lyons, *unChristian*, 55.

7. Pastor Jim Dixon, during a weekend service on May 2, 2010, at Cherry Hills Community Church in Highlands Ranch, Colorado. To listen, go to www.chcc.org/sunday_service_love.aspx.

8. Paul Copan said this in an interview with Lee Strobel in *The Case for the Real Jesus* (Grand Rapids, MI: Zondervan, 2007), 246.

9. Ibid., p. 247.

10. Erwin Lutzer, *Who Are You to Judge?* (Chicago: Moody Press, 2002), 42.

CHAPTER 9:

1. Marie Little's memorial service was held on August 15, 2009, at Willow Creek Community Church, in South Barrington, Illinois (where I served for many years as the director of evangelism). Marie's husband, Paul Little, was killed in an automobile accident in 1975. He was the author of the classics *Know What You Believe*, *Know Why You Believe*, and *How to Give Away Your Faith*—all published by InterVarsity Press.

2. Dallas Willard's story and comments are told by Philip Yancey in his book *Reaching for the Invisible God* (Grand Rapids, MI: Zondervan), 79.

3. C. S. Lewis, *The Weight of Glory: And Other Addresses* (San Francisco: HarperCollins, 1949, 1976, rev. 1980, first HarperCollins ed. 2001), 26.

4. Gary R. Habermas and J. P. Moreland, *Immortality: The Other Side of Death* (Nashville, TN: Thomas Nelson, 1992), 81.

5. These quotes from C. S. Lewis are drawn from several sources, all listed at the Web site of the C. S. Lewis Society of California. See www.lewissociety.org/quotes.php.

6. Dinesh D'Souza, *Life after Death: The Evidence* (Washington, DC: Regnery, 2009), 216. Also, D'Souza summarizes from Harold Koenig, *Medicine, Religion and Health* (West Conshohocken, PA: Templeton Foundation Press, 2008).

7. Ibid., 216.

8. C. S. Lewis, *The Great Divorce* (San Francisco: HarperCollins, 1946, 1973, HarperCollins ed. 2001), 75, emphasis his.

9. Ralph D. Winter and Bruce A. Koch, "Finishing the Task: The Unreached Peoples Challenge," www.joshuaproject.net/assets/FinishingTheTask.pdf.

10. Mahendra Singhal spent the rest of his life working tirelessly to share the love and truth of Christ with Hindu people around the world. You can watch a video of him sharing his testimony at http://vimeo.com/5964358.

11. K. Connie Kang, "Next Stop, the Pearly Gates: Nearly two-thirds think they're going to heaven, while few believe they're hell-bound, poll finds," *Los Angeles Times*, 24 October 2003. Emphases mine.

12. Randy Alcorn, *Heaven: Biblical Answers to Common Questions* (Carol Stream, IL: Tyndale, 2004), 54.

13. This is a condensed version of a story Bill Hybels told about his own experience, in his Easter service message at Willow Creek Community Church, South Barrington, Illinois, on April 4, 2010.

14. C. S. Lewis, *The Problem of Pain* (San Francisco: HarperCollins, 1940, 1996, HarperCollins ed. 2001), 8–9.

CHAPTER 10:

1. This was from the October 21, 1984, presidential debate between Ronald Reagan and Walter Mondale. The complete transcript of the debate can be seen at www.lexis.com/research/retrieve?_m=e00e057ab270fb8171fccce7f3909b6f&_fmtstr=FULL&docnum=1&_startdoc=1&wchp=dGLbVtz-zSkAb&_md5=fa1744326e444f9b7f4619724472c1e4, and a video clip of this particular exchange can be viewed at www.youtube.com/watch?v=LoPu1UIBkBc.

2. Mondale made this comment in a May 25, 1990, PBS interview

with Jim Lehrer, which can be read at www.pbs.org/newshour/
debatingourdestiny/interviews/mondale.html.

3. Those were Dawkins's words when he appeared on *The O'Reilly Factor* television program on Fox News, April 23, 2007. He made a similar statement in an interview with Don Cray for the article "God vs. Science," *Time* (Nov. 05, 2006)—see www.time.com/time/magazine/article/0,9171,1555132,00.html.

4. Mark Mittelberg, *Choosing Your Faith . . . In a World of Spiritual Options* (Carol Stream, IL: Tyndale, 2008), chapters 9–11, starting on page 159.

5. C. S. Lewis, *Mere Christianity* (San Francisco: HarperCollins Edition, 2001), 52.

ABOUT THE AUTHOR

MARK MITTELBERG is a best-selling author, a sought-after speaker, and a leading strategist in evangelism and apologetics-oriented outreach. He is the primary author of the Becoming a Contagious Christian training course, through which more than one million people around the world have learned to effectively and naturally communicate their faith to others.

Mark's most recent book, *The Unexpected Adventure* (written with Lee Strobel), is a six-week devotional designed to inspire Christians and entire congregations to enter into the excitement of sharing Christ. His previous book, *Choosing Your Faith . . . In a World of Spiritual Options*, strengthens the faith of believers and is a great resource to give to friends who are figuring out what to believe. Mark also developed a DVD study course—Faith Path: Helping Friends Find Their Way to Christ—based on that book and wrote the articles for the *Choosing Your Faith New Testament*. His other books include the updated *Becoming a Contagious Church*, which sets forth an innovative blueprint for mobilizing churches for evangelism, and the classic best seller *Becoming a Contagious Christian*, which he coauthored with Bill Hybels. Mark was contributing editor for *The Journey: A Bible for the Spiritually Curious*. He was also a contributor to *Reasons for Faith: Making a Case for the Christian Faith* (edited by Norman Geisler and Chad Meister) and *God Is Great, God Is Good: Why Believing in God Is Reasonable and Responsible* (edited by William Lane Craig and Chad Meister), which won the 2010 *Christianity Today* award for best book in the area of apologetics.

Mark was the evangelism director at Willow Creek Community Church for many years and is a frequent contributor to *Outreach* magazine. He was also an editorial consultant for Lee Strobel's *Faith under Fire* television show, on which he was a periodic guest. He and Strobel have been ministry partners for more than twenty years.

After receiving an undergraduate degree in business, Mark earned a master's degree in philosophy of religion from Trinity Evangelical Divinity School in Deerfield, Illinois. In recognition of his achievements in the areas of evangelism and apologetics, he was recently honored by the conferring of a doctor of divinity degree from Southern Evangelical Seminary in Charlotte, North Carolina. Mark and his wife, Heidi, have two teenage children; they live near Denver, Colorado.

Your Beliefs Determine How You Live.

Are You Choosing Wisely?

Do You Know Why You Believe What You Do?

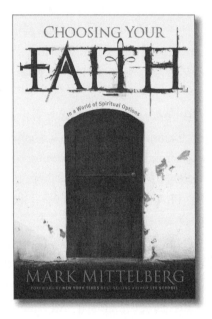

"*Choosing Your Faith* raises the critical questions that every human being needs to ask and guides us into understanding the importance of knowing why we believe what we do."

—Dan Kimball, author of *They Like Jesus but Not the Church*

"A lot of books tell you what to believe. But *Choosing Your Faith* shows you how to *decide* what to believe. Read it. You are sure to be challenged and encouraged."

—Luis Palau, international speaker and author

WILLOW CREEK ASSOCIATION

T he Willow Creek Association was founded in 1992, to serve a widespread movement of God that had begun stirring in the hearts of church leaders. Fearing that church was too often designed for the already convinced, they strived to create environments where those still outside the family of God were welcomed—and could more easily consider God's loving offer of salvation through faith.

These innovative churches and leaders—from many different regions and backgrounds—were connected at the deepest level by their all-out dedication to Christ and His Kingdom. Willing to do whatever it required to build churches that help people move along the path toward Christ-centered devotion; these are the leaders and churches WCA was designed to serve.

Today, more than 10,000 churches from 80 denominations worldwide are formally connected to the WCA and each other through WCA Membership. Many thousands more come to the WCA for networking, training, and resources. They now are connected, not just by their desire to create safe places where men and women can encounter Jesus Christ for the first time, but also to encourage all believers at every step of their faith journey, to continue moving toward a fully transformed, Christ-centered life.

For more information about the ministry of the
Willow Creek Association, visit: **willowcreek.com**

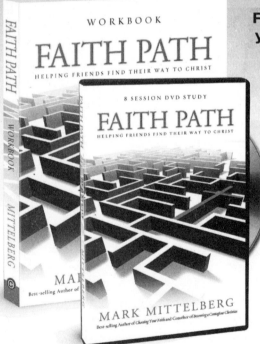